Accounting for Mother Nature

CHANGING DEMANDS FOR HER BOUNTY

Accounting for Mother Nature

CHANGING DEMANDS
FOR HER BOUNTY

Edited by Terry L. Anderson,

Laura E. Huggins, and Thomas Michael Power

STANFORD ECONOMICS AND FINANCE
An Imprint of Stanford University Press
Stanford, California

Stanford University Press
Stanford, California

Printed in the United States of America on acid-free, archival-quality paper

Library of Congress Cataloging-in-Publication Data

Accounting for mother nature : changing demands for her bounty / edited by Terry L.
Anderson, Laura E. Huggins, and Thomas Michael Power.
    p. cm.
  Includes bibliographical references and index.
  ISBN 978-0-8047-5698-3 (cloth : alk. paper)
  1. West (U.S.)--Economic policy. 2. Conservation of natural resources--Economic
aspects--West (U.S.) 3. Right of property--West (U.S.) 4. Public lands--West (U.S.)
5. Natural areas--Management. I. Anderson, Terry Lee, 1946- II. Huggins, Laura E., 1976-
III. Power, Thomas M.
  HC107.A17A23 2008
  330.978--dc22

                        2007033821

Typeset by Bruce Lundquist in 10.5/14 Adobe Garamond

Contents

Illustrations

Map

Accounting for Mother Nature

CHANGING DEMANDS FOR HER BOUNTY

Introduction

The American West has always been the source of romantic visions: the carefree cowboy riding the open range, the prospector panning for gold and instant riches, or the homesteader "making the desert bloom like a rose" in return for title to the land. It is easy to immerse oneself in Charles Russell and Frederic Remington paintings of bucking broncos, cattle drives, or endless herds of buffalo. The thought of leading a pack of mules into the mountains where few others have trodden makes us all yearn for those good old days of yesteryear.

In contrast to visions of the Old West, visions of the New West conjure up grand mountain vistas, wild rivers, and free-roaming wildlife. There is no better presentation of our romance with the West than the story (1976) and the movie (1992) *A River Runs Through It*. Set in rural Montana in the early 1900s, this is the coming-of-age story of the author (Norman Maclean) and his brother realizing the divine beauty of their land and their interaction with it, symbolized by and culminating in a fly fisherman's casting skill. In the movie, Robert Redford narrates, "When I am alone in the half-light of the canyon, all existence seems to fade to a being with my soul and memories.

And the sounds of the big Blackfoot River and a four-count rhythm and the hope that a fish will rise. Eventually, all things merge into one, and a river runs through it."

The problem is that now, at the beginning of the twenty-first century, we are seldom "alone" on the river, any river. Maclean's elegant text combined with the beautiful images in Redford's movie helped popularize fly-fishing in the West. The rich and famous such as Ted Turner, Peter Fonda, and Tom Brokaw attracted more attention to the West when they decided to buy a chunk of it. At the same time, far less affluent people were buying second homes and condominiums at ski resorts and housing developments along the rivers that run through it. As a result, many of the famous western trout streams (including Maclean's beloved Blackfoot River) have become crowded with anglers practicing the "four-count rhythm." In fact, people are moving to the West in such numbers that the region is sometimes called the "Third Coast."

While we can each dream our romantic visions of the Old West and the New West without interfering with one another, acting out our dreams brings competition and conflict over how Mother Nature's bounty will be used. The debate over commodity use versus amenity use centers on these two different views of the "wealth of nature." The *commodity view* holds that wealth from nature results from tangible commercially valuable outputs that can be produced from nature. These are usually minerals, cattle, and wood. The *amenity view* holds that wealth from nature is derived directly from nature itself without it being transformed into other outputs and without necessarily being sold in commercial markets. Examples of amenity goods are scenic vistas, wildlife habitat, and wilderness areas. As long as resources were abundant relative to the population and its demand for amenities, there was little conflict over defining the wealth of nature.

In a few cases, commodity demands and amenity demands are complementary, as with reservoirs that produce flood control, irrigation, and electricity while providing recreation opportunities; but for the most part amenity demands conflict with commodity production. Pursuing one type of wealth precludes enjoying the other. More commodity production reduces the potential for amenity production, and vice versa. Conflicting demands between water for irrigation and in-stream flows in the Klamath Basin are an example discussed by Anderson and Huggins (Chapter 5), and the conflict between mining and recreation is addressed by Meiners and Morriss (Chapter 7). Competition and conflict between commodity users and amenity users are obvious, but conflicts also arise within those groups. For example, backpackers oppose snowmobiling, mountain bikers oppose horseback riders, and on and on.

This volume focuses on why these conflicts occur and how they might be eliminated or at least minimized. The simple answer to both questions is that the institutions that govern who controls how resources are used and the people in control must have incentives to find "win-win" solutions to competing uses.

In Part One, the institutions that govern western resource allocation are explored. Power (Chapter 1) elaborates on the distinction between local economic impacts and on how changing demands on the wealth of nature are articulated. Because much of the institutional structure in the West evolved when commodity demands dominated, Power argues that institutional evolution and redesign are necessary if newer amenity demands are to be reconciled with commodity demands in a less acrimonious way. Anderson (Chapter 2) makes the case for relying more on markets to allocate resources between competing demands and emphasizes that this requires property rights that are clearly defined, enforced, and transferable.

Many environmentalists argue that nature is the kind of thing that money cannot buy. "Exchanging, selling, calculating tradeoffs, or otherwise commoditizing biodiversity in the global sanctuary of creation simply to maximize immediate human gain represents the primordial blasphemy of confusing sacred space with the market place," fumes Timothy Weiskel, an environmental ethicist at the Harvard Divinity School (quoted in Harris 2003). Others argue that the only real way to protect nature is to calculate its worth: "Follow the money, and you end up in a very green place. This is the new story of the West. Conservation is now as much about economics as it is about less tangible aspects like the solace of open space" (Barcott 2005).

Power and Anderson recognize that amenity demands have both market and nonmarket characteristics. Marketable amenities are those for which private property rights are or can be defined and enforced and for which only those willing to pay are allowed access. Fee fishing is one example, and housing development that incorporates local amenities is another (see Anderson and Leal 1997). Nonmarketable amenities, on the other hand, are those for which it is difficult to establish property rights and therefore to exclude nonpayers. A pristine view is an example. Economists contend that such "public goods" will be underproduced, but David Haddock

(Chapter 2) challenges this conclusion, arguing that, in many cases, private individuals capture sufficient private value to produce efficient amounts of public goods despite free-riders.

One of the biggest stumbling blocks to market allocation of the wealth of nature is the complex set of weak and rather undefined claims to environmental entitlements. Environmental and public process laws have given entitlements to broad groups of citizens (e.g., Montana citizens have a constitutional right to a "clean and healthful environment"). But those entitlements are neither clearly defined nor transferable, which changes the incentive system. Actors can stay focused on the values that they think they have a right to without taking seriously the cost in terms of valuable opportunities to others that may be lost. In that situation, finding a win-win outcome (e.g., "willing buyer, willing seller") may be impossible.

Other reasons why property rights and markets are not used more to allocate the wealth of nature include:

· Some amenities are "produced" as unintentional byproducts of private activities to which consumers have free access. Ted Turner's 358,643-acre ranch in New Mexico, for example, not only provides a home to a reintroduced population of desert bighorn sheep, which are managed by the Turner Endangered Species Fund, but also protects a beautiful viewshed for the public. Similarly, almost all forestlands, grasslands, and wetlands, whether private or public, produce a broad range of valuable environmental services without any human action.

· Some amenities are the complex result of natural processes that rely on both public and private lands and resources. In the case of water, for example, moisture often comes in the form of snow influenced by natural weather patterns; snow may fall at high elevations on federal lands managed for timber; it then melts into public rivers, and rivers are diverted for private agricultural and municipal uses. Balancing and contracting among uses where there are so many interconnections is difficult, to say the least.

· Public lands, meaning lands owned by different levels of government, are involved in the production of ecosystem services, and the management of those lands is subject to the conflicting demands of various groups of citizens who believe that they have legitimate claims on the wealth of nature.

· The costs of organizing diffused groups of amenity demanders and amenity suppliers so that they can negotiate a better level of amenity production may be so high that those transaction costs outweigh the potential improvement in amenity values. As a result, productive agreements are never reached, and the wealth from nature is dissipated.

· Managing congestion and use costs as the number of beneficiaries or the level of use increases may also be difficult. For example, with millions of visitors to Yosemite Valley each year, development and traffic congestion pressures continue to be a problem—one for which it is difficult to create an "equitable" solution.

For these reasons, neither Power nor Anderson sees a panacea in particular institutional changes. Vested private interests benefit from current institutional mechanisms. For example, the Mining Law of 1872 gives mining interests more ability to patent federal lands. And bureaucratic interests, especially at the federal level, do not want to give up their grip on western resource allocation. To be sure, current institutions are antiquated and a more decentralized locus of control would be better equipped to take advantage of time- and place-specific information and to balance competing demands. Getting from here to there, however, will not be easy.

Part Two offers some ways of making this transition within the context of current bureaucratic institutions. Daniel Kemmis (Chapter 3) calls for experimentation within the structure of the U.S. Forest Service. Following the lead of John Wesley Powell, the famous explorer of western waterways, he calls for creating clear national guidelines for specific outputs (commodity, amenity, or some combination) and then devolving more authority to local collaborative groups or trustees to determine how best to meet those guidelines. Holly Fretwell (Chapter 4) compares and contrasts state park and national park management and suggests that states have found more innovative ways of linking consumers (visitors) with producers (park managers), improving both the fiscal and environmental performance.

Part Three explores the property rights approaches for maximizing the wealth of nature. Conflict over water use in the Klamath River Basin is a quintessential example of conflicts between old and new western demands. Terry Anderson and Laura Huggins (Chapter 5) draw upon the Klamath experience to show how stipulating property rights at the local level and removing hurdles to trading between off-stream and in-stream demands could replace acrimony with cooperation. Donald Leal (Chapter 6) draws on his policy analysis of individual fishing quotas to suggest that such property rights can efficiently and equitably promote more sustainable fisheries management. Roger Meiners and Andrew Morriss (Chapter 7) call for expanding the Mining Law of 1872 to allow patenting of claims to federal lands for other uses such as recreation and ecosystem service production. And Dominic Parker (Chapter 8), based on his extensive survey of land trusts, argues that these voluntary organizations could be made even more effective if we moved away from tax deductions for easement contributions and toward direct tax funding for private groups producing amenity values.

Finally, Part Four examines various problems in measuring the wealth of nature. With his review of the wealth of nature literature, Andrew Hanssen (Chapter 9) explores the evolution of the wealth of nature paradigm, and Timothy Fitzgerald and Myrick Freeman (Chapter 10) evaluate various ways of measuring wealth from nature and discuss the potential for market measures to do this. Both of these chapters provide a critique of a growing body of literature trying to quantify the value of nature and ecosystem services, especially that of Robert Costanza, director of the Gund Institute for Ecological Economics. In 1997, Costanza estimated the value of the services performed by the environment at $33 trillion and argued that investments in ecosystem preservation can yield returns of 100 to 1. Fitzgerald and Freeman dispute the methodology and magnitude of Costanza's findings.

There is no doubt that wealth from nature is positive and growing, and of particular importance to many parts of the United States. But, Ronald Johnson (Chapter 11) challenges the notion that protection of natural landscapes and the environment will, in general, offset declines in natural resource-based extractive industries. The evidence presented in his chapter reveals that declines in natural resource extraction sectors were not quickly followed by expansion in other sectors of natural resource–oriented states. It was not specialization in natural resource extraction that caused poor economic performances in natural resource–dependent states but rather their relative low density, isolation, and difficulty in holding and attracting better-educated workers.

The focus on how the use of Mother Nature's bounty affects local economic well-being mixes two issues together. The first is the assertion that some set of site-specific qualities that have come to be called *amenities* contributes significantly to resident well-being, but "consumers" must be present in the region to appreciate the benefit of directly enjoying the amenities. The second is how the presence of those local amenities affects the location of economic activity. Much of the economic literature on the wealth of nature, including Chapter 9 and Chapter 11, focuses on the latter—the impact of natural amenities on local economic vitality.

In summary, this volume explores the potential for markets, as one of the institutions for balancing the demands on nature's bounty, to improve the environment and the economy at the same time. The authors examine how institutions thwart market solutions to natural resource allocation that conserve the wealth of nature and how those institutions could be changed to promote market solutions. Furthermore, when those institutions won't necessarily maximize the wealth of nature, the authors ask whether there are ways to mimic markets. If market-mimicking institutions cannot be made to work for certain amenities or ecosystem services, what are the appropriate loci of scale and level of public accountability for collective solutions to problems?

Bob Dylan was right when he wrote, "For the times they are a-changin'." In the distant past, the West's natural resources were widely abundant and the economies of the West depended on converting those resources into lumber, metals, and hydroelectricity. More recently, however, the relationship between the economy and the environment has moved away from resource extraction toward resource protection that supports a healthy economy. Finding a new balance between commodity and amenity production from the wealth of nature that better matches contemporary economic values and opportunity costs will benefit everybody.

References

Anderson, Terry L., and Donald R. Leal. 1997. *Enviro-Capitalists: Doing Good While Doing Well*. Lanham, MD: Rowman & Littlefield Publishers.

Barcott, Bruce. 2005. "As a Matter of Fact, Money Does Grow on Trees." *Outside*, March.

Columbia Pictures. 1992. *A River Runs Through It*. Directed by Robert Redford.

Harris, Lissa. 2003. "At What Cost?" *Grist*. April 8. Available online: http://www .grist.org/news/maindish/2003/04/08/what/ (cited June 26, 2006).

Maclean, Norman. 2001 [1976]. *A River Runs Through It and Other Stories*. Twenty-fifth Anniversary Edition. Chicago: University of Chicago Press.

PART ONE

Perspectives on the Wealth of Nature

CHAPTER ONE

Natural Amenities and Ecosystem Services

The Need for Additional Institutional Innovation

THOMAS MICHAEL POWER

The term *wealth of nature* covers the natural sources of an enormous range of potential goods and services flowing from the earth itself and from the natural systems the planet supports.[1] In the broadest sense, our economic activities depend on inputs from only two sources: the wealth of nature and human ingenuity and effort. Of course, that human component relies on the wealth of nature for survival.

In the past, much of the wealth of nature has been productively developed in a context of private property rights, markets, and commercial exchange: for example, farmland, mineral deposits, timberlands, and forage for livestock. It is also clear that marketlike incentives and mechanisms can contribute significantly to the solution of environmental problems that threaten the wealth of nature. Transferable entitlements are increasingly used to allocate scarce environmental resources such as fishing, water, grazing, and recreational rights; as well as to facilitate the disposal of air and water effluents and waste.

The question explored in this volume is whether there is a subset of the wealth of nature for which individual actions, property rights, and market exchanges are not well suited to promote efficient and equitable production and distribution of the gifts of nature. Where this is the case, the following chapters explore alternative institutional arrangements that facilitate collective action to protect access to that wealth of nature while avoiding its inefficient dissipation. The focus is on the appropriate locus and scale of control of that collective action.

The Breadth of the Wealth of Nature: Ecosystem Services

Human well-being relies critically on the gifts of nature, which are the only source for our material means of survival and many of the qualities that make our lives rich, interesting, and satisfying. Economics and economies, at their most general level, wrestle with the issue of how scarce resources are protected or developed so that they can be effectively transformed into the goods and services that satisfy people's needs and desires. Goods and services flowing from the earth and its natural systems often fit into this economic category: scarcity and the capacity to contribute to human well-being.

The conventional economic categories of production and consumption can help clarify the ways in which the gifts of nature contribute to human well-being. The consumption of ecosystem services refers to goods and services that flow from the natural environment and that people directly use, such as clean natural water, the scenic beauty of natural landscapes, outdoor recreational opportunities, fisheries, and other wildlife. People are capable of valuing these ecosystem services directly because they directly contribute to human well-being in the same way that human-produced goods and services do.

On the production side, these ecosystem services are the outcomes of complex biophysical processes that have many natural inputs and many interrelated ecosystem functions. The economic value of these inputs and ecosystem functions are indirect, tied as they are to human valuing of the outcomes of human significance, the ecosystem services we humans recognize as directly affecting our well-being (Boyd and Banzhaf 2005). This is similar to the determination of the economic value of inputs to human production processes where the value of the inputs is tied to the value of the consumer goods and services they are capable of helping produce.

Natural Resource Settings Where Marketlike Institutions Are Effective

Market or marketlike institutions or public policies that incorporate marketlike incentives and tradeoffs have been productively used to guide both the production of natural resource commodities and solutions to environmental problems. An analysis of those contexts in which marketlike institutions have proved effective in helping to manage the wealth of nature may provide useful information about the potential range of the effective use of such economic instruments in managing natural and environmental resources.

NATURAL RESOURCE COMMODITY PRODUCTION

In the modern version of land-based economic activities such as agriculture, mineral extraction, forest products, and fishing, considerable human labor is combined with large quantities of capital and equipment to coax from the earth various valuable products that are then largely sold in national and international markets. The facts that production requires extensive human effort and capital investment and the outputs are normal goods that can be privately possessed and controlled allow normal market institutions to operate even when the land or resources may be government owned. The commitment of labor and capital supports a private claim to at least some share of the gift of nature that is harvested. In this setting transferable entitlements can be specified based on investment and labor effort, and commercial investment and market exchange can operate relatively easily.

ENVIRONMENTAL DAMAGE ASSOCIATED WITH ECONOMIC ACTIVITY: AIR AND WATER EFFLUENTS AND DAMAGE TO LAND RESOURCES

When air and water quality diminish or natural landscapes are damaged as the result of economic activity, there is often a direct causal connection between the organized use of labor, equipment, and land resources in the production of particular products and the environmental damage that occurs. This relationship allows both the establishment of responsibility for the damage and an evaluation of the private benefits derived as a result of the environmental damage. It also suggests the logical recipients of any initial allocation of effluent entitlements. The human agency involved and the connection between the market-oriented activities and the environmental damage increase the likelihood that similar marketlike responsibilities and incentives can be developed to limit and manage the environmental damage in an efficient manner. The more the polluting economic activities are dispersed (e.g., non–point-source pollution) and the less they are tied to commercial activities (e.g., normal day-to-day living activities by thousands or millions of people), the less successful the use of such economic instruments has been.

The Realm of Natural Production

Some of the goods and services on which our well-being depends are not produced primarily through human agency;[2] instead, they are truly gifts of nature, with human effort playing no role or only a minor one. Examples include climate, natural water flows, natural waste assimilation, wildlife and wild fish, and complex biophysical systems that contribute to biodiversity.

Many of these gifts of nature also have significant public good character-istics, in that they are nonexcludable and nonrival; that is, it is difficult to exclude people from enjoying them once they are available (nonexcludable), and up to some point, where congestion or overuse occurs, one person's enjoyment of them does not reduce the enjoyment of others (nonrival). In addition, if the number of people who enjoy these goods and services is very large and highly dispersed, it is difficult and costly for beneficiaries of these gifts of nature to organize themselves to protect these types of natural resources.

Property rights or entitlements are also often only vaguely defined for many environmental services. Beneficiaries may feel strongly that they have the right to continue to enjoy particular gifts of nature, but other citizens who use those gifts of nature for commodity production also believe they have the right to their use. Conflicting claims result, which marketlike insti-tutions by themselves cannot easily resolve.

Many of these environmental services have an additional problematic characteristic: they are the product of complex and not-well-understood bio-physical processes. Although beneficiaries of the environmental service may understand and value it highly, they may not understand or recognize the nat-ural processes that lead to its production. Even specialized scientists may have only a partial grasp of the production function. Changes in the global climate, the survival of endangered species, the assimilation of natural waste, and the production of naturally clean water are some examples. If these ecosystem services are largely gifts of nature, rather than the product of human agency, and their beneficiaries do not understand how the services are produced, it is not clear how the beneficiaries could act to protect access to the services even if they could overcome the transaction cost and the difficulty of making ben-eficiaries of those ecosystem services pay for them (the free-rider problem).

In the past most of these dispersed gifts of nature did not have much of an economic aspect because they were abundantly available relative to human demand. This lack of scarcity meant that difficult choices and tradeoffs did not have to be made. As the number of humans has expanded and the intensity and extent of human economic activity have increased, more and more of the gifts of nature are becoming relatively scarce and threatened with overuse, damage, or loss. Hence their protection and management are becoming more relevant to our well-being.

The characteristics of this particular set of the gifts of nature appear to contrast significantly with the characteristics of the wealth of nature to which markets and market-mimicking mechanisms have been thus far applied. For that reason, additional institutional innovation is needed to find decentralized policies and mechanisms for dealing with this more problematic set of the gifts of nature.

The Social Nature of Some Natural Wealth

The use of markets and market-mimicking mechanisms to manage and control some types of natural wealth assumes that markets, monetary incentives, and individual or private action are culturally acceptable tools for managing natural wealth. However, it is at least possible that certain prevalent cultural and social values may conflict with the use of such economic instruments in managing some types of natural wealth. In this case, those economic instruments may simply not be acceptable or, if used, might not work very well.

Two social values may restrict the realms to which a market or commercial mentality can be applied: hostility to the extension of a commercial mentality to certain realms, and the desire to protect the rights and privileges associated with membership in noncommercial social organizations. Most cultures have put in place fairly clear boundaries on the operation of purely commercial values. Even in the most pro-business, free-market countries, there are broad social realms in which financial incentives and the pursuit of self-interest are not considered appropriate. For instance, family members rarely would expect or appreciate monetary compensation for services provided to other family members. Furthermore, family members are not only or primarily appreciated for their economic contribution to the household. Families, in a very important sense, serve as a buffer for individual members against the values and demands of the commercial world. The same can be said of religious, civic, social, and cultural organizations. This is one of the reasons we have such large and burgeoning private nonprofit and public sectors in our society.

One explanation for this social and cultural retreat from the world of commerce is the belief that commercial attitudes and values threaten to degrade other important social and cultural values.[3] It matters to us what motivates the behavior of those with whom we interact. The more personal or intimate the interaction, the more that motivation matters. Narrow pursuit of self-interest alone is not considered a reliable basis for most social and personal relationships (Anderson 1990). In fact, it may not be a sufficient basis for efficient commercial relationships either (Arrow 1972). Trust, honesty, and empathy are important elements of all productive human relationships, both inside and outside of the commercial realm. Encouraging an expansion of narrow self-interested behavior may be seen as a threat to the larger set of social and cultural values that define various versions of the "good life" and a good society.

To develop the relationships that allow people to interact productively, some buffer is often necessary to the "nicely-calculated less or more" benefits and costs (Wordsworth 1888). This is one of the reasons all societies have developed noncommercial institutions and social realms. Once such a social realm has been put, at least partially, off-limits to a purely commercial mentality, people react with suspicion or hostility to proposals to expand markets or marketlike mechanisms into it. This may be one reason that substantial parts of the population will resist market-mimicking mechanisms as solutions to environmental problems.

The second potential social aspect of the wealth of nature is associated with humanity's ongoing desires to belong to collective organizations: families, tribes, churches, communities, and nations. Belonging to such collective groups brings with it certain rights of membership that partially define our social identity and status.[4] These rights include the right to participate in choosing leaders, the right to seek redress of grievances, the right to be judged by an assembly of citizens, the right to use the commons or other shared space and resources in traditional ways, the right to security in time of need or threat (as opposed to abandonment), and the right to participate in group rituals and celebrations, some secular, but many steeped in traditional religion.

As a people, we are not through specifying citizens' rights of membership. For example, the state of Montana adopted a constitution in the mid-1970s that declared that citizens of the state had a right to a clean and healthful environment. State courts have interpreted this to impose a positive obligation on the state to protect the environment from degradation. Broad environmental laws at the federal and state levels have also sought to assure citizen access to an impressive range of environmental amenities: the availability of clean air and water; the protection of natural landscapes; the survival of plant and animal species; opportunities for outdoor recreation, and so on.[5] The result is that citizens believe they have certain entitlements when it comes to natural amenities, and they act legally and extralegally to defend those perceived environmental entitlements as part of their rights of citizenship.

Whether one believes in the legitimacy of these common property claims or doubts the efficacy of common property regimes, this popular opposition to changing the public status of much of the wealth of nature cannot be ignored. It is real, powerful, and often effective. Proposed public policy has to at least take it into account.

Problematic Contemporary Gifts of Nature: Natural Landscape Amenities

One way to test the applicability of the conventional free-market environmental tool kit is to consider some of the most important contemporary gift-of-nature problems. In the United States (and other developed nations), natural amenities appear to have become increasingly important to people, and because of this, they have come to influence people's decisions about where to live and therefore where economic activity is located.

Modern communication and transportation technologies have dramatically reduced the sense of isolation, and its cost, that is associated with what had previously been considered remote locations. In addition, changes in the worldwide distribution of economic activity and changes in what we ask the economy to produce have led to a relative decline in the importance of extractive natural resource activities and heavy industry. The relative shift to light manufacturing and services has increased the value-to-weight ratio of the goods our businesses produce and reduced the relative importance of transportation costs in determining the location of economic activity. Furthermore, rising incomes have made it easier for people to act on their preferences for what they perceive to be high-quality living environments. Higher levels of education and cultural change may also have modified people's judgment as to what defines that environment. The combination of these changes has made the population, and therefore economic activity, relatively more willing and able to move to locations that appear to offer higher-quality living environments.

In the conventional economic base view of the economy, such residential choice is only possible for exceptional individuals who do not have to work for a living or who are willing to eke out subsistence living. All others are assumed to have to move to where employment opportunities are available. This economic base way of thinking is entirely driven by labor demand.

In general, however, economic results are rarely driven only by demand; the forces of supply also play a role. In the setting we have been discussing, the shift of population to preferred locations represents a shift both in labor supply and in the location of markets for goods and services. One would expect such changes in labor supply to have economic consequences. Places where people are accumulating would have a surplus labor force and wages would be relatively depressed; at least some firms would be expected to take advantage of such lower wages. The increased population and expanding local markets are also likely to increase the viability of a broader range of commercial businesses, leading to the development of a more sophisticated commercial infrastructure. This, in turn, will help capture and hold dollars within the local economy, triggering a larger multiplier impact.[6]

Economists since Charles Tiebout have emphasized the role of site-specific qualities in influencing decisions about residential location (Tiebout 1956). In addition to employment and income opportunities, potential residents are likely to look at the quality of public services such as schools that are provided to residents and the cost they have to pay for them in the form of local taxes. But local public services are just one set of site-specific qualities that affect the well-being of residents. A complex bundle of local characteristics associated with each potential residential site—such as local climate, the risk of crime, time lost to traffic congestion and commuting, air pollution, outdoor recreation and indoor cultural opportunities, and scenic beauty—will be evaluated. This bundle of site-specific qualities has come to be labeled amenities.

The point is, in an important range of circumstances, people's pursuit of attractive living environments can trigger local economic changes that support ongoing local economic development. Such amenity-supported local economic development may lie behind some of the most important changes in the economic geography of the United States over the past half-century: the shift of people and economic activity from center cities to the suburbs, the migrations from the Frost Belt to the Sunbelt, and the resettlement of the mountain West. The ongoing loss of population from most of the rural Great Plains counties may be a negative example of the "amenity phenomenon."

It is important to note that this sorting of the population among various locations at least partly on the basis of local amenities and the changes in the regional economy that result are the result of classic market choices except that most of the amenities driving people's decisions to move have strong public good characteristics and, in general, are not produced or priced by the commercial sector of the economy.

It is possible that amenity-supported economic development is ultimately a self-defeating process. It may continue to attract people and economic activity until the growing population and economy use up open space, pollute air and water, create congestion within both developed areas and recreational areas, consume wildlife habitat, and generally convert natural landscapes into urban landscapes and suburban and exurban sprawl. As that degradation proceeds, the expansion may slow, stop, or even reverse itself. But by then, many of the amenities may have been destroyed. The area will have been loved to death.

This can be seen as a traditional public good / externality problem and/or a problem tied to the use of common resources. Large numbers of people value a complex set of environmental services associated with publicly and privately owned open space and natural areas. The open spaces may be owned by a large number of individuals, and the publicly owned lands may be encumbered by a broad set of regulations seeking to serve the interests of a variety of stakeholders. Many of the amenities have public good characteristics, including visual enjoyment of open space and scenic vistas, reduced density tied to the existence of those open spaces and undeveloped public lands, and the existence of migratory wildlife and high-quality water and air. There may also be open-access resource problems associated with hunting, fishing, and dispersed outdoor recreation on both private and public lands. With the large number of both consumers and producers of these amenities, transaction and enforcement costs may be high and free-rider problems serious.

It is unclear whether market forces or marketlike institutions and incentive systems can help rationalize the protection and use of these natural landscape amenities in this complicated economic setting. The characteristics of the ecosystem services being sought, the nature-based production process that is the source of these services, and the sociocultural context within which any solution must operate will make it difficult to simply apply the more familiar tools in the free-market environmental tool kit.

It is, of course, possible that private action will lead to some level of protection for these natural landscape amenities. Wealthy individuals with a strong preference for them could represent a significant market demand. For example, billionaire cable television network innovator Ted Turner has bought large parcels of private land with unique landscape values across the western United States, and other wealthy individuals have similarly bought large pieces of rainforest, mountain wilderness, and other endangered areas around the world. As argued in Chapter 12, it is conceptually possible that a small number of wealthy individuals with high effective demands for local natural landscape amenities could arrange for the optimal provision of such amenities.

Whether this possibility is likely to be realized is an empirical question tied to the actual distribution of individuals' demands and the distribution of transaction costs. Residents whose well-being relies on certain local amenities may doubt the wisdom of depending on a few wealthy people taking an interest in the amenities and successfully negotiating for their protection and provision at appropriate levels.[7]

But private action in a market setting is not the only possible decentralist solution to the problem of natural landscape amenities or, more broadly, ecosystem services. Our social imagination must range more broadly than that.

Problematic Collective Solutions: The Problem of Our Public Lands

Public ownership of natural landscapes in the form of national and state parks, forests, wildlife refuges, and wilderness areas has not been without its own set of problems. These publicly owned lands, as discussed in Chapter 4, often are overused, the maintenance and protection of the lands and facilities are underfunded, and support for visitors is sparse or nonexistent.

Given the politically influenced bureaucratic control of these lands from distant capital cities, many do not find this deterioration of public lands surprising. A variety of reforms in funding and management control of public lands have been proposed and will be discussed in Chapter 4. One proposal that has been at least partially adopted at the state and federal levels is to fund more of the management of these public lands through visitor and user fees that are retained by local managers. This gives managers an incentive to pay attention to what visitors want and to try to protect or improve the lands and facilities so that people will continue to visit them. The locally retained fees also provide a funding source for such improvements.

Congress and various state legislatures have authorized the use of visitor fees to fund public land management and facility maintenance. The public, however, has not always responded favorably to these marketlike arrangements for access to public lands.

Beginning in 1996 Congress authorized managers of various units of federal lands to charge access and use fees on a demonstration basis. The bulk of the revenues raised were to be used on-site to maintain or improve land and facilities rather than being sent off to the federal treasury. Many public land agencies enthusiastically embraced this new source of revenue. A last-minute rider on the federal 2004 omnibus spending bill provided permanent authorization to charge a wide variety of fees for recreational access and use of federal lands, including river corridors, trailheads, and wilderness areas. The new law, following the recent trend to market legislation, was called the Federal Lands Recreation Enhancement Act.

The negative political response was quick, with Montana leading the attack. With the governor's support, that state's legislature voted almost unanimously to urge the repeal of this expanded authorization for recreational fees. The Oregon legislature followed suit, unanimously passing a similar resolution, as did the Colorado and Alaska legislatures. Strange bedfellows made common cause in their opposition: wilderness advocates joined motorized recreationists, wood products and logging associations joined parks associations, wise-use folks joined up with preservationists.

The typical political rhetoric denouncing this expanded fee program ran something like this: these lands are our heritage as American citizens, and if the "feds" think they can charge us to use something we already own, these near unanimous votes across all ideological lines should inform them that they are terribly mistaken. Note the claim that access to these public lands is a right of citizenship. Violation of such perceived rights has triggered political outrage and worse for millennia. Advocates of such fees need to pay attention to the source of this opposition.

In some ways this opposition to access fees is puzzling. Skiers have always purchased lift tickets or season passes to ski at resorts located on public lands. The national parks have been charging entrance fees for a long time.

Hunters and anglers buy licenses. Most developed campgrounds on public lands have charged fees for many decades. All of these fees are now paid without significant protest. So why do people object to extending and making permanent the fee demonstration programs?

Actually, the new law recognizes the primary sources of opposition to fees: charging for mere access to public lands, and the use of fees primarily as an additional source of federal revenue by charging whatever the market will bear. When a fee is obviously tied to the costs of facilities and services provided, few oppose it. Almost no one expects to get a free meal or free accommodations in a national park. When the link between a fee and the goods and services the government has provided is clear, the fee tends to be accepted. But when a fee is charged for the right to gain access to the gifts of nature and the fee is set to collect revenues unrelated to costs, there is considerable hostility. In this setting, the fee is seen as the equivalent of a tax—hence the assertion of double taxation when citizens are asked to pay it.

Calling this a tax is probably not correct, but in the economist's vernacular, it is an effort to capture the rental value of nature. Citizens appear to recognize the difference between paying to help cover the actual costs associated with their activities and paying for something that did not cost the fee collector anything. Economists, of course, can explain why, when there are competing uses among which choices have to be made, such charges play a useful economic role. But this message is unlikely to be convincing when rights of citizenship are believed to be at stake and/or when conflicting uses are not perceived to be a problem.

The drafters of the Federal Lands Recreation Enhancement Act were aware of these problems with public acceptance, so the new law actually limits fees to locations where the government provides amenities and services. Where the values are purely gifts of nature, with little or no human-produced investment or effort, fees are not allowed. In fact, the U.S. Forest Service eliminated many of the fees it had been charging for things like stopping at scenic overviews and camping at undeveloped sites. It also limited the federal land managers from charging fees to cover the costs of protecting endangered species. The latter limitation was tied to another distinction: the difference between individual, on-site benefits and broader public benefits not necessarily associated with individual on-site use. Visitor fees could not be used to recover the latter under the new law.

In some circumstances state legislatures have acted to keep state recreation land managers from charging fees. In Montana, for instance, a Republican legislature designated all of the state's largest state parks as "primitive" and forbade both the levying of fees for access and the construction of amenities that would justify such fees. The motivation behind this was not a desire to create wilderness parks but simply the desire to keep fees from being charged for mere access to public lands.

City parks, greenways, and trails are almost always available for use without charge even though they are largely human-created, manicured landscapes that are costly to build and maintain. Most citizens take pride in these public amenities that are open to everyone, partly because they see them as a right of citizenship. Most American towns originally had a centrally located town square or commons. A public space for civic gatherings was provided just as it had been since at least the days of classical Greece and Rome.

In the late nineteenth century, increases in urban densities and human congestion made public health a new justification for scattered natural areas within cities. Reformers believed that it was unhealthy for the new concentrations of working-class people to have no access to open space, sunlight, fresh air, outdoor recreation, and other environmental services. Public health, a public good, was the justification. This justification has long since disappeared, and these parks have simply become one of the expected amenities of urban life—one of the rights of citizenship.

Another reason people resist paying fees for use is the feeling that paying a fee for services in some situations degrades the value of the service being sought. This certainly is often the case within families, friendships, and spiritual communities: charging your spouse for intimacy, a friend for a kind word, or a dying person for last rites would strike most people as offensive. Financial payments can also threaten the value of judicial, legislative, and electoral decisions. Objective evaluations in education, science, safety, and sports are other examples where financial payments that seek to influence those evaluations can undermine the value of the judgments. This is the basis of the assertion by some of those engaged in backcountry recreation that paying an admission fee undermines the meaning and value of interacting with nature, eliminating the "wild" from nature and giving those natural areas elements of a commercial amusement park.

People often arrange to obtain services in a manner that eliminates the need for payments for every service received. For instance, many social and recreation clubs provide a broad range of services to members at zero cost. Members pay a fixed membership fee, and payment of that fixed charge gives members the right to use certain facilities and receive certain services. Country clubs and fraternal organizations have operated this way for a century or more. This could be cynically described as people seeking to pretend that they are aristocrats who can command privilege, even though they have simply prepurchased costly services. But it is likely that people are actually seeking to create extended rights to a social environment in which commercial exchange is held at bay. Given this, it should not be surprising to find that residents of a community prefer paying for parks, greenways, and public space through their taxes rather than through individual payments for use.

Access fees are not just controversial to users who are asked to pay them. The likely effect of these new revenue streams on the land management agencies is also worrisome to some for exactly the reason that they are attractive to others. When public land managers have to rely for revenues on those who use public lands, we can expect the managers to pay closer attention to the interests and desires of their clients. As a result, it is argued, facilities and the land will be managed in a way that serves visitors rather than on the basis of bureaucratic inertia and pork-barrel politics.

There is no doubt that revenue streams associated with user groups have significantly affected how land managers view their jobs. A familiar example with a very long history is state fish and game agencies, which are heavily funded through the sale of hunting and fishing licenses. As a result, agencies have traditionally focused their efforts not on *all* wildlife and *all* fish but on those that hunters and anglers favor. Rather than seeking to maintain healthy ecosystems that support natural biodiversity, the fish and game agencies have sought to maximize the pounds of huntable wildlife and catchable game fish. This often has led to the reduction or removal of wildlife that prey on big game and the introduction of exotic fish. In Montana, for instance, the Fish and Game Commission has opposed both the return of the wolf to its historic habitat and the listing of the grizzly bear as an endangered species. The agency's revenues flow from only certain wildlife, and its wildlife management strategy reflects this fact.

The powerful effect that revenue streams can have on management decisions worries many who would like to see public lands better managed to reflect a broader range of concerns about biodiversity and ecosystem services. If agency decisions primarily seek to serve the interests of those users of public lands who are responsible for the largest flow of revenues, land managers may be hesitant, for instance, to control or regulate motorized recreation, including off-road vehicles, or mineral extraction activities that are seriously damaging the land and wildlife. The problem is created by the fact that it is easy to associate revenues with certain on-site activities but difficult to associate revenues with a much broader range of ecosystem services because of their public good characteristics and the complex and not fully understood natural processes that produce them. In this setting, an increasing reliance on locally generated fees from users of public lands to fund public land management may lead to destructive results.

None of this tells us exactly what funding structure may be most effective and acceptable for different public spaces and natural areas. Clearly, regular usage charges are both efficient and acceptable in some settings, and open access supported by tax revenues or private contributions may be the only workable and acceptable arrangement in other settings. Of course, there are a broad range of alternative funding possibilities that mix public and private funds, donations and fees, and fixed and variable charges. The point is that when designing such funding arrangements, decision makers must take into account deeply held cultural values about the appropriateness of fee-for-service arrangements in different settings and the rights of citizenship.

Market Solutions, Privatization, and Collective Action

Many of the gifts of nature or ecosystem services that have been the topic of public policy debates have characteristics that render them unlikely candidates for commercial provision:

· Natural production with minimal human agency
· Significant public good characteristics
· Overlapping entitlements that are not very well defined
· Traditionally not provided through commercial exchange

The first three of these characteristics may explain why such ecosystem services have not been provided by commercial businesses in the past. This historical noncommercial status of these gifts of nature may also lead to cultural objections to the extension of marketlike arrangements for their provision.

In some ways, government has been the default solution for the protection and management of the wealth of nature. Government has come to own and manage large parts of the natural landscape, especially in the western states. As discussed in Chapters 3 and 4, this has not always led to

good outcomes. In contrast, Chapter 8 underlines the role that private organizations (with federal tax code support) have been playing in protecting
natural and agrarian landscapes.

The language with which we usually discuss how to assure the ongoing
provision of these valuable ecosystem services at appropriate levels often is
heavily ideological. Those who are skeptical of the efficacy or appropriateness
of an expanded governmental role tend to talk about "central government,"
"central planning," and "command and control"—with the implication that
government action will be like the bureaucratic totalitarianism of the Soviet
Union. On the other side, those who are skeptical of private solutions and
the use of marketlike incentives envision "commercialization" and large bureaucratic transnational corporations taking control of more and more of
nature and the public realm.

Such language, while ideologically useful to some, is not very helpful
in developing effective public policy. Polarizing language tends to strangle
our social imaginations. Because of the characteristics of the gifts of nature,
it is highly unlikely that they will ever become the realm of commercial
business. Therefore, commercialization is largely off the table. This does
not mean that the federal government must be in charge or that private
noncommercial organizations have no role to play. It also does not mean
that marketlike incentives might not improve the provision and use of these
ecosystem services.

Collective action, in the sense of people coming together to provide goods
and services for themselves and for others for whom commercial businesses
have not adequately provided, need not be governmental action. When it
is governmental action, it can be very localized, down to the neighborhood
level, and it can also be more or less insulated from politics. The range of
social choice is broad.

This collective action can take the form of nonprofit private organizations. Early in the nineteenth century, Alexis de Tocqueville described how
Americans spontaneously formed multiple organizations to achieve their
collective objectives. The size and growth of the nonprofit sector of the U.S.
economy documents the continuation of this organizational creativity into
the twenty-first century. Nonprofits have been active in protecting and enhancing various gifts of nature by acting directly to protect wildlife habitat
through purchases, both fee simple ownership and easements. They have
also entered into partnerships with government at various levels to manage environmental resources and educate the public about how to protect

natural landscapes while using them. One could imagine an expanded role for such private nonprofit organizations in the future as contract managers of public lands subject to a variety of public guidelines and mixed public-private boards.

Americans have also been creative in designing governmental and quasi-governmental organizations of different scales and loci of control. Citizens have formed special improvement districts and taxed themselves to provide basic infrastructure. They have formed local school districts, large and small. They have formed volunteer fire departments with the power to tax. Rural areas have formed irrigation and grazing districts. Cities have empowered neighborhood councils to guide some public service and land-use decisions. Independent government organizations have been set up with the intent of insulating the organizations' decisions from normal political pressures. The management of some state university systems, for instance, is independent of both executive and legislative branches of government. Some publicly owned utilities and regulatory institutions are insulated through appointed boards serving long, overlapping terms. Government action need not involve distant and unresponsive command and control or wasteful pork-barrel politics.

What is important is not just whether the institutional framework is private or governmental; what is important is whether the locus of control and the scale of the organization are appropriate to the character of the problem. Local issues rarely need national solutions. The locus of control and the scale of the organization are important in determining the effectiveness of the action taken as well as the accuracy and adequacy of the information necessary for good decisions. Flexibility and adaptability also often depend on decision makers being close to the problem and operating on a small enough scale to be able to both act quickly and change course quickly as appropriate. Daniel Kemmis discusses some of these institutional innovations in Chapter 3.

The appropriate scale and locus of control can be problematic, however. For instance, having a national effluent trading program for pollutants that have significant local impacts can shift and concentrate environmental damage within certain areas, with the result that such areas see pollution levels rise even while overall national effluent releases are declining. Whatever the efficiency of this outcome, equity objections are certain to be raised. Although economists usually seek to avoid dealing with equity issues, citizens, governments, and courts do not. Efficient solutions that shift burdens heavily to certain groups of people while shifting benefits to others are likely to generate strong opposition.

Public control can be combined with the use of market exchanges to efficiently attain social ends. This is the logic of tradable emission quotas, entitlements to shares of fishing quotas, and water and grazing rights. Through a political, legal, or negotiation process, society sets the total allowed impact and allocates the initial tradable rights, and market exchanges do the rest. The donation of conservation easements to private nonprofit trusts in exchange for reduced tax liabilities also represents a combination of private, at least partially self-interested, behavior, government support, and active promotion and enforcement by private nonprofit organizations. Chapter 8 explores the strengths and weaknesses of the land trust movement.

It is also at least conceptually possible that the pace and pattern of residential development could be controlled in a similar fashion with local governments auctioning off the rights to certain amounts of different types of development each year. Alternatively, if allowing the government to collect part of the rental value of such developments were objectionable, every property owner in an area open to development could be given a fractional share of the development rights and developers could purchase those rights from the property owners. In either case, collective control would be exercised over the rate and geographic pattern of development, but markets would be used to determine which developments proceeded. The point is that the use of the market mechanism does not necessarily mean that Adam Smith's "invisible hand," the market, necessarily displaces social controls over desired aggregate social outcomes.

Although market mechanisms can reduce divisive and potentially wasteful political wrangling, two important and difficult political decisions—determining allowable impacts and assigning entitlements—have to be made before such mechanisms can be relied on. First, the political process has to be used to determine the total allowable impact, whether it is aggregate pollution levels, total water diverted from rivers or pumped from the ground, levels of catch for various species of fish, or intensity of grazing. Since the intent often is to reduce the overall impact and, possibly, to continue to reduce it over time, this will be a difficult and contentious process. Second, assigning entitlements will be controversial especially if the total existing claims exceed the total impact society intends to allow. In some important ways, all of the important political decisions have to be made before market mechanisms can be deployed to guide the efficient use of the entitlements that are assigned.

This is not to suggest that resolution of these problems is impossible or that it has to take on the character of a conflict-ridden zero-sum game. Extralegal negotiations and mediation and other innovative conflict resolution processes may in some circumstances lead to mutually agreeable resolutions that are superior to both court decisions and legislative edict. However, both legislative action and legal strategies will still be the fallback solutions that may motivate the efforts to seek negotiated settlements among the conflicting interests.

Conclusions

The wealth of nature provides a flow of scarce and valuable goods and services that are important to our well-being. Unconstrained competing demands for these can lead to damage, waste, and divisive conflict. To avoid these negative outcomes, new institutional arrangements and related incentive systems need to be created to manage access to and use of this natural wealth. The range of institutional possibilities is much broader than the polarizing alternatives—unregulated open access, commercialization, and central government control—that often dominate the public dialogue about the management of the wealth of nature.

It is important to realize that collective arrangements, meaning citizens acting together, need not involve government ownership or control. Similarly, private arrangements need not mean commercialization. Nor does the deployment of marketlike instruments imply an acceptance of market outcomes no matter what they might be. Only our social imaginations limit the innovative institutional arrangements we can craft. We need creative entrepreneurs not only in the commercial sector but also in the private nonprofit and government sectors.

Actual practice has shown that markets and marketlike instruments can help in managing environmental resources effectively and equitably in many important settings. We need continued innovation to explore both the new opportunities for and limits of such tools. However, the character of some important environmental services as well as cultural and political constraints may limit the acceptability of marketlike instruments in some important settings. Where this is the case, we also need innovation within the private nonprofit sector, at the local grassroots level as well as the national and international levels. Furthermore, we need to continue to explore the decentralization or devolution of control and management of federal lands and resources. We have only recently begun to explore innovative combinations of private and public, local and national interests guided by contractual or trust arrangements. In the face of growing pressure on our natural landscapes and increasingly bitter conflict over their management and use, simply defending the status quo or the institutional arrangements of the past does not appear to be a productive response. Institutional innovation is.

Notes

1. Economists have always distinguished between capital stocks and the regular flows of valuable goods and services they provide. The value of the capital stock is usually calculated in terms of the present (or capitalized or amortized) value of those future flows of benefits. Wealth is a stock; the flows of benefits are income based on the stock of wealth. In the context of this book, the "gifts of nature" or "ecosystem services" we discuss are the regular flows, the present value of which could be expressed in terms of a stock wealth (the "wealth of nature") or natural capital. Since in most of the following discussions the distinction between wealth and annual flows of benefits will not be central, we will use the phrases *wealth of nature, gifts of nature,* and *ecosystem services* somewhat interchangeably.

2. Of course, many "natural systems" are actually the result of the interaction of nature and human activities over millennia. Human hunting, use of fire, agriculture, diversion of water, etc., have all had profound effects on natural systems long before urbanization and industrialization. "Natural" is not used here in the naive romantic sense of "unaffected by human activity." Instead, it refers to systems that are not now primarily managed by human agency.

3. See, for instance, Steven Kelman (1982), *What Price Incentives?: Economists and the Environment* (Boston: Auburn House).

4. Interestingly, although we now tend to use the words *freedom* and *liberty* interchangeably to refer to autonomy and independence, *free* is derived from northern European tribal languages and referred to someone who was joined to a tribe of free people by ties of kinship and rights of belonging. The tribe was an autonomous group with its own separate identity and social rules, but being free referred to an affiliation with that group and its customs, rules, and privileges. Being free was not a matter of individual autonomy and independence but of being connected to a unique social group. David Hackett Fischer (2005), *Liberty and Freedom* (New York: Oxford University Press), 4–6.

5. This proliferation of environmental laws may have been tied to the failure of courts to enforce traditional common law rights against environmental nuisance. During the Industrial Revolution, as economic activity became more intensive in its use of natural systems, U.S. courts largely shifted from protecting property owners who were harmed by environmental damage to protecting industrial activities be-

cause of their perceived centrality to regional and national economic development. The right to use one's property for its highest and best use was deemed to trump any right to the quiet enjoyment of one's property undamaged by environmental spillovers. By the middle of the twentieth century, new laws began to put limits on those environmental spillovers. See Eric T. Freyfogle (2003), *The Land We Share: Private Property and the Common Good* (Washington, DC: Island Press), chapter 4.

6. For a critique of the conventional economic-based view of the local economy, see Thomas Michael Power (1996), *Environmental Protection and Economic Well-Being* (Armonk, NY: M. E. Sharpe), chapter 7. For a further discussion of amenity-supported local economic development, see Thomas Michael Power (1996), *Lost Landscapes and Failed Economies* (Washington, DC: Island Press), chapter 2.

7. If there are significant transaction costs associated with the wealthy apprecia-tors of the amenity who are negotiating protection with the developers whose activi-ties might degrade the amenity, it can be shown that the demands of the many indi-viduals who also appreciate the amenity but at much lower individual levels are not irrelevant to defining the optimal outcome and that optimal outcome may well not be the one associated with the individual action of the few wealthy appreciators.

References

Anderson, Elizabeth. 1990. The Ethical Limits of the Market. *Economics and Philosophy* 6: 179–205.

Arrow, Kenneth J. 1972. Gifts and Exchange. *Philosophy and Public Affairs* 1: 343–362.

Boyd, James W., and H. Spencer Banzhaf. 2005. Ecosystem Services and Govern-ment Accountability: The Need for a New Way of Judging Nature's Value. *Resources* 158: 16–19. Washington, DC: Resources for the Future.

Tiebout, Charles. 1956. A Pure Theory of Local Expenditures. *Journal of Political Economy* 64(4): 416–424.

Wordsworth, William. 1888. *The Complete Poetical Works*. London: Macmillan; available at http://bartleby.com.

CHAPTER TWO

Maximizing the Wealth of Nature

A Property Rights Approach

TERRY L. ANDERSON

The "New West" means many things to different people, but for the economist and policy maker it is best thought of in terms of increased amenity demands on the region's natural resource base. In recent years the demand for amenities, or what Thomas à Kempis called the "gifts of nature" as early as 1380, such as clean air, clean water, and open space, has increased relative to the demand for commodities produced from those same resources but requiring human inputs either in the form of labor or capital. Many residents in the New West, for example, are less willing to trade off wilderness and roadless areas for lumber production.

In contrast to the New West, the "Old West" was an era when commodity demands dominated. The Old West is alleged to have been a rapacious frontier where cowboys, miners, loggers, farmers, and railroad tycoons ran roughshod over people and natural resources with little concern for resource stewardship. In that world, rich people got richer at the expense of the environment. State nicknames capture the essence of the old. Montana was called the Treasure State, Idaho the Gem State, Wyoming the Cowboy State, Washington the Evergreen State, and California the Golden State.

The shift from old to new has brought with it new competition for resources. In some cases amenity demands and commodity demands can be
complementary, while other cases necessarily require a substitution of resources between uses. The difference between complementarity and substitution is captured in a bumper sticker of the Montana Land Reliance,
which reads "Cows Not Condos." In other words, keeping land in agricultural production is complementary with the amenity value the Montana
Land Reliance wishes to maintain, namely, open space and an agricultural
tradition, while converting agricultural land into housing developments is
not. On the other hand, environmental demands for old-growth forests are
seldom compatible with timber harvests. Where there is a complementary
use of resources, different demands can be met without sacrifice, but where
substitution is required, competition for resources requires sacrifices or, in
the vernacular of economists, opportunity costs.

This raises two basic questions: How will the competing demands for
resources be resolved? and will the institutions that resolve them promote
cooperation or conflict? To understand how different institutions affect how
the wealth of nature is used, this chapter first develops a "property rights
tool kit." The second section then uses this toolbox to analyze the Old West,
where competition for resources resulted in the evolution of private property rights and laid the basis for resource markets and gains from trade. The
third section describes a transition from the Old West to the New West in
which institutions, driven mainly by a political process from Washington,
D.C., generate conflict rather than cooperation. The final section argues
that a return to the "good old days of yesteryear" could displace some of the
conflict that permeates resource use in the West and replace it with more
cooperation, whether through markets or more community-based local
institutions.

A Property Rights Toolbox

Property rights are best thought of as the "rules of the game," which determine who has the right to use, access, and derive value from valuable assets.
As such, property rights might be as formal as the title to your house or car
or as informal as your right to hike in a forest. They might be very carefully
delineated by survey lines, deeds, covenants, or easements; they might be restricted by explicit rules such as regulations that say when, where, and what
you can do on public lands; or they might be defined by social norms and

customs where you can know the extent and limits of your rights only by being a member of the community (see Anderson and Huggins 2003).

Crucial to all forms of property rights is the extent to which they limit access and thereby prevent the tragedy of the commons (Hardin 1968). The *tragedy of the commons* refers to overuse of a resource resulting from unrestricted access where additional users realize that if they do not use the common resource and capture its value, someone else will. Hence, unrestricted rights to hunt or fish for wildlife, to observe the eruption of Old Faithful, or to burn garbage, result in the diminution of the resource's net value.

Given the diminution of value caused by the tragedy of the commons, there are few resources for which property rights of some type to do not evolve once the diminution of value is recognized. Whether and when property rights evolve depends on the benefits and costs of defining and enforcing the property rights (see Demsetz 1967; Anderson and Hill 1975). On the benefit side is the obvious gain to be had from better resource stewardship. If a fishery is overfished, reduced fishing can increase the net value from the resource (see Chapter 6); if a national park is overcrowded, its net value can be increased by restricting access; if a groundwater basis is overpumped, its net value can be increased by reducing pumping.

The cost side of defining and enforcing property rights is more complicated. First, costs will vary with the mobility of the resource. Defining and enforcing property rights to visible immobile resources (e.g., land) is less costly than doing so for highly mobile, difficult-to-observe resources (e.g., fish in the open ocean). Second, the cost of defining and enforcing property rights will vary with technology (see Anderson and Hill 1990). Surveying instruments, fencing, and satellites are all examples of such technologies. A third cost is the cost of agreeing who has what property rights. These costs will increase with variables such as the value of the property right in question and decrease with more precedent for property rights and with homogeneity of the people in the group competing for property rights.[1] Fourth, the cost of defining and enforcing property rights will depend on the cost of taking collective action to exclude non–rights holders. Here, the nature of government makes a crucial difference. Especially if there are economies of scale in policing, it will be more costly for decentralized governments to enforce property rights. Finally, there are the costs of preventing the government, which is the collective enforcer of property rights, from redistributing those rights. As discussed in Chapter 5, disputes over water in the Klamath Basin are complicated by a redefinition of rights brought on by the Endangered Species Act. The takings clause of the U.S. Constitution lowers the cost of enforcing property rights against political takings, but reliance on majority rule votes or bureaucratic regulations raise this cost. Chapter 7 examines how legislative and bureaucratic decisions regarding mining property redistribute the wealth of nature, weaken property rights, and discourage stewardship.

Assuming that property rights can be defined and enforced, a crucial question in a dynamic economy is how resources get reallocated when values change. If property rights are transferable on a willing buyer–willing seller basis, exchanges will occur as long as there are gains from trade. For example, when a housing developer sees more value in land than the existing farm owner, the developer can buy the land and transfer it to the higher-valued use. Similarly, when the Nature Conservancy works with a landowner to get a conservation easement that preserves endangered species habitat, gains from trade result. If property rights are not transferable on a willing buyer–willing seller basis, people who believe there is a higher-valued use of the resource have little choice but to turn to collective (political) action to effect the change. A prime example is grazing permits for federal lands. Because the permits are not transferable to nongrazers, those who believe that nongrazing promotes a higher-valued use of the land can only lobby politicians to remove cattle from public lands. Similarly, mining patents can be obtained only by mineral exploration and development and not by "environmental exploration and preservation" (see Chapter 7).

Contrasting exchange with political reallocation, the former requires gains from trade and promotes cooperation while the latter is a zero-sum game in which one party's loss is another's gain and in which conflict dominates. To make matters worse, political reallocation uses time and money (lobbying, campaign contributions, political campaigns, etc.) that can turn the reallocation into a negative-sum game.

Economists refer to the political process for reallocating property rights as *rent seeking*. *Rent* is an economic term used to describe the value of natural resources in situ. In other words, it is the value after other labor and capital resources are combined with the natural resources in activities such as cultivation, harvesting, or marketing. If this residual natural value is positive, and the value is being allocated or reallocated to new owners by political activities, rational competitors will expend effort seeking the rents. Ultimately, the rents will be allocated to someone, and in the process, time and effort will be spent. Because the rents existed before the allocation or reallocation began, the net value after rent seeking can be negative, depending on how much competition there is in the political process. Even if the outcome is not a negative-sum game, political reallocation at least dissipates some of the natural resource's value.

The extent to which property institutions encourage gains from trade and cooperation or rent seeking and conflict depends largely on whether the institutions evolve from the bottom up or top down. More decentralized evolution of property rights means that the people developing those property rights have more of a stake in whether they encourage gains from trade or rent seeking. On the American frontier, for example, people developing property rights in advance of formal government bore the costs of unnecessary definition and enforcement costs. Hence, cattlemen's associations used the communal roundup, a necessary activity for branding and marketing cattle, as a means of excluding new entrants to the open range (see Anderson and Hill 2004). In contrast, when politicians in Washington, D.C., established the homesteading system, they encouraged a "race for property rights" that caused much hardship (see Libecap and Hansen 2004). The case will be made below that as the frontier has moved from local jurisdictions to state and national ones, the tendency has been for negative-sum rent seeking and conflict to supplant positive-sum exchange and cooperation.

The Not So Wild, Wild West

Dime novels and western movies give us images of the frontier West as a "wild and woolly" domain where cowboys killed Indians, gunslingers routinely shot one another and innocent bystanders, big cattle ranchers fought sheepherders, and, to use words attributed to Mark Twain, "whiskey is for drinkin' and water is for fightin'." Such depictions are not all wrong. The Indian Wars were a shameful part of western history that resulted when the standing army, created during the Civil War, found itself looking for skirmishes to fight (see Anderson and McChesney 1994). Fistfights did occur and people did get shot in barroom brawls (McGrath 1984). Cattle ranchers did fight with sheepherders when the latter brought sheep into areas where cattle ranchers had customary grazing rights (see Anderson and Hill 2004; Libecap 1981). Furthermore, because water was the lifeblood of agriculture in the arid West, farmers and ranchers battled to establish prior appropriation claims (see Anderson and Snyder 1997).

Such romantic and exciting stories, however, miss the important ways in which people on the frontier created the institutions necessary for peaceful and productive settlement. The property rights toolbox developed above helps explain the evolution of property rights on the frontier. The theory suggests that because resource endowments in the West were so different from those in the East, necessity became the mother of institutional invention and innovation.

A few examples capture why the Old West was not so wild and how local institutional innovations provided incentives for resource stewardship. At the heart of most property rights was the notion that "first possession" was a cost-effective mechanism for establishing ownership.[2] From California to Montana, miners established claims rather peacefully through the rules of the mining camps (see Umbeck 1977). Because the six-shooter made nearly everyone equal in the use of force, and because each claim had about the same productivity, miners honored first-possession claims that were approximately of equal size. Similarly, the prior appropriation doctrine for water rights was hammered out in the mining camps and agricultural valleys and remains the basis for water law throughout the American West.

On the grazing frontier, efforts to define and enforce property rights increased as hundreds of miles of barbed wire fences were built, but initially, property rights to land were much less formal. As pressure on grazing resources increased with the arrival of cattle herds from Texas, grazers established property rights to land by simply posting notice on signs or in local newspapers that a grazer had claimed land. For example, on April 12, 1884, Charles S. Johnston posted a claim in the *Glendive* (Montana) *Times* that he did "hereby notify the public that I claim the valley, branching off the Glendive Creek, four miles East of Allard, and extending to its source on the South side of the Northern Pacific Railroad as a stock range."[3]

Though customary range rights were informal, they were sufficiently well enforced that they were valuable and traded in the marketplace. Enforcement came mainly from the cattlemen's associations, which functioned as a local government. Historian Ernest Staples Osgood (1929, 115) summarized the three aims of the associations: "first, to preserve the individual's ownership in his herd and his increase; second, to afford protection to the individual's herd; and third, to control the grazing of the public domain or to prevent over-crowding." These aims, which might have been achieved by an individual in the earlier days of comparative isolation, could now be realized only through group effort. Biannual roundups provided a way of excluding grazers who were not members of the associations and hence were not allowed to graze in the region. The roundups entailed scale economies that could be achieved by working together. If grazers could not participate in the roundup, they could not efficiently enforce their rights to their cattle.

The prior appropriation doctrine is an especially good example of a property rights system that has survived the test of time and promoted water transfers from one diversion use to another. The recent work by Gary Libecap (2005) debunking myths about the Owens Valley water transfers to Los Angeles provides even more evidence of how the property rights to water and land, devised in many cases before the arrival of formal government, remain effective today in encouraging efficiency and cooperation. The problem is that restrictions on transferability coupled with political allocations have replaced positive-sum games, where the gains from trade encourage cooperation, with zero-sum games, where transfers from one party to another result in conflict.

This brief summary of "the not so wild, wild West" suggests that local people are capable of creating property institutions that can allocate resources among competing demands. At the time property rights were evolving on the western frontier, the resource demands were mainly for commodities such as cattle, logs, crops, and minerals. The system of secure private property institutions provided security of ownership that got the incentives right for encouraging production of these goods. When public lands were established early in the twentieth century, rights to use those lands also focused on commodity production. The difference between the two sets of property rights was that the former generally (though not always, as with water rights) allowed exchange that could move resources to higher-valued uses whereas the latter did not.

The Frontier Moves to Washington

On the frontier before the arrival of formal governmental institutions, the actors had a direct stake in whether resources were wasted in the process of defining and enforcing property rights. Because their time and money were at stake in developing institutions, they had an incentive to conserve on how many resources were used in establishing property rights. As Lueck (2003) points out, the rule of first possession, as in the case of water rights, was one way of reducing the cost of defining and enforcing property rights. Though first possession can create a race to be the first possessor, as it did in the case of the homestead acts, local institutional development discouraged racing and minimized the effort that had to be put into retaining property rights.[4]

The arrival of formal government, however, removed this constraint by removing those establishing the rules of the game from the stakes in the game. As argued above, the farther governmental decisions are removed from local constituencies, the more likely it is that interest groups will shift the costs to others while capturing the benefits for themselves. These benefits are referred to as rents by economists because they are returns above and beyond the opportunity costs of obtaining them. Thus the act of manipulating the political system to acquire these benefits is called rent seeking. In essence, rent seeking is the act of redistributing valuable assets from one party to another using the coercive power of government to effect the transfer.

Of course, not all governmental activities involve rent seeking. Government can play a positive role in institutional development by reducing the costs of defining, enforcing, and trading property rights. It can also lower the cost of using collective action to overcome the free-rider problem inherent in the production of public goods (see Chapter 12).

Examples of lowering the cost of establishing property rights abound. Once cattle ranchers on the frontier had established branding as a way of identifying their cattle, they turned to territorial and state governments to register and enforce their brands. This lowered the transaction costs for the cattle market. The rectangular survey more clearly specified boundaries of land rights, and courthouses provided the locus of registering the deeds associated with those boundaries. Today, state governments are adjudicating water rights that evolved before formal governments existed. In Montana, for example, a water court has been working for nearly two decades to determine priority dates and quantities for all the basins in the state. Once this costly process is completed, it will be much easier for market trades to occur.

The homestead acts provide an example of a property institution that defined and enforced private ownership of land, but at significant costs caused by the race to claim those rights that the acts encouraged. By requiring settlement to secure title to land, homesteaders had to be "sooners," to take a term from Oklahoma's land rush history. In many cases this meant "premature" settlement and failure to "prove up" on the homestead (see Anderson and Hill 1990). Though private ownership did result, it was fragmented into parcels that were too small for economic viability and came at significant costs in terms of premature settlement and expenditures on unnecessary improvements (see Libecap and Hansen 2004).

The allotment of Indian lands is another example of how the federal government's attempt to establish private property rights opened the door for rent seeking. With the Dawes Act of 1887, Congress authorized allotment of small parcels of reservation land to individual Indians to be held in trust by the Department of the Interior until the Indians were deemed "competent" to hold clear title. Not only were these parcels too small for economic viability, the trust status made them unusable as collateral for loans and placed bureaucratic impediments in the way of owner management. The rent-seeking aspect of allotment came in the fact that once reservation lands were allotted, the remainder of reservations were declared "surplus" and opened for non-Indian homesteading. In the end, non-Indians ended up with significant portions of some reservations, and the trust lands were not put to very productive uses.[5]

In setting aside millions of acres as public lands, the federal government opened another door for rent seeking through bureaucracies such as the National Forest Service, the National Park Service, and the Bureau of Land Management (BLM). Today, these agencies control nearly one-third of the land in the United States, with 83 percent of Nevada under federal management and 68 percent of Alaska. Though referred to as *public lands*, they are better thought of as *political lands*, the rents from which are allocated through political and bureaucratic processes. Scientific and multiple-use management may play a role in the allocation of these resources, but ultimately, politics carries the day (see Chapter 3).

When the political lands were first restricted from privatization, management was much less centralized and even bordered on privatization in the sense that specific individuals or groups captured the values generated from the land. Indeed, in the case of national parks, there was de facto ownership during the early years when nearly every one of the large western parks was controlled by railroads in one way or another.

Yellowstone National Park offers a perfect example.[6] The Northern Pacific Railroad recognized the value of the park's amenities to its passenger traffic. With homesteaders trying to establish claims to the most unique places, such as Mammoth Hot Springs and Old Faithful, the railroad realized that some of the potential rents would go to these homesteaders if they were successful. With a virtual monopoly on transportation to Yellowstone but with no way to establish private ownership for itself, the Northern Pacific lobbied Congress to set aside the area as a national park and therefore not open to homesteading. Once privatization was stopped, the railroad proceeded to obtain monopoly control of internal services such as stagecoach transportation, lodging, and meals. These monopolies, combined with its route from Chicago, gave the railroad virtual ownership and provided the incentive to preserve the amenities. As one official put it: "We do not want to see the Falls of the Yellowstone driving the looms of a cotton factory, or the great geysers boiling pork for some gigantic packinghouse, but in all the native majesty and grandeur in which they appear today, without, as yet, a single trace of adornment which is desecration, that improvement which is equivalent to ruin, or that utilization which means utter destruction" (Runte 1990, 23). The arrival of other railroads to Yellowstone coupled with the allowance of automobiles into the park in 1916 broke the Northern Pacific's virtual monopoly, and the management vacuum was filled by the National Park Service. During its early years, the National Park Service took in enough revenue to fully cover their costs and then some. Parks were seen more as playgrounds where people could camp, sightsee, fish, and generally recreate, and these uses did not compete with one another. Politics entered the picture mainly through concession contracts.

In more recent years, however, the National Park Service has become more of a political football as different demands have interpreted the service's charge of maintaining parks "unimpaired for the enjoyment of future generations" (see Chapter 4). Does this mean more wilderness areas? Does it mean fewer campgrounds? allowing snowmobiles? reintroducing species such as wolves? And the list goes on. Each of these questions represents a competing demand and requires the National Park Service to reallocate the resources under its charge. Not surprisingly, nearly all of its decisions are challenged in court.

The Forest Service and the BLM provide similar stories. Gifford Pinchot, who is credited with the formation of the Forest Service, envisioned an agency that would scientifically manage the public lands to maximize timber production and water quality according to the German model in which he was trained. With this single purpose, the agency essentially had only one constituency, loggers, to which it had to respond, and the agency's mission was consistent with its constituency's interest. When grazing was added as a commodity to be produced on Forest Service lands, there was no conflict between logging and grazing constituencies because the two outputs complemented one another; more clear-cuts meant more grass.[7]

As incomes have increased since World War II, Forest Service lands have become a recreational playground and a bureaucratic battleground. Even within the recreational community, there are conflicts over use. For all-terrain-vehicle users or snowmobilers, old logging roads provide excellent trails. Hence logging and off-roading or snowmobiling can complement one another. On the other hand, logging and vehicular traffic usually are not viewed as compatible land uses for hikers, skiers, and general wilderness aficionados. To charge the Forest Service with balancing these demands, Congress passed the Multiple Use Act of 1964, and to constrain land management agencies in the way they carried out their management, it passed the Federal Land Policy and Management Act and the National Forest Management Act in 1976. None of these acts, however, provided a blueprint for trading off one use against another in any positive-sum way. Rather, they legislated bureaucratic processes that pit one user group against another in zero-sum games. This rent-seeking boxing ring produces "multiple conflicts over multiple uses" (see Anderson 1994).

The BLM has a similar history. Originally, the agency managed grazing lands that were not productive enough to warrant homesteading. Local grazing districts run by committees of local grazers acted as owners. With good local knowledge of forage, rainfall, and other variables that affected grazing, these local districts effectively maximized the value of the grazing output. Because these lands were less attractive for recreation than the national forests, there were few conflicting demands for them, making the goals of the BLM and its constituents congruent.

In recent years, pressures on the BLM have followed the path of the Forest Service. Amenity demanders have battled to reduce grazing in the interest of increasing wilderness, wildlife, and recreation. Economist Gary Libecap (1981, 93) concludes that between 1960 and 1980, "ranchers lost much of the security of tenure and decision-making power . . . The beneficiaries of the shift have been the Bureau of Land Management and its conservationist supporters." And again the result has been "multiple conflicts over multiple uses."

Perhaps the best (or perhaps more appropriately, the worst) example of rent seeking comes with western water. The Reclamation Act of 1902 was aimed at "making the desert bloom like a rose." By building dams and delivery systems, the federal government supplanted private irrigation development (see Anderson and Hill 2004) with massive subsidies to farmers (see Rucker and Fishback 1983). As long as the reclamation projects were primarily for irrigation and secondarily for hydroelectric production, conflicts over water management were few. The Bureau of Reclamation had contracts to deliver water to farmers with little concern for in-stream consequences. The Klamath Basin debacle in Oregon epitomizes the changes that have resulted from conflicting demands for water (see Chapter 5).

Back to the Future

In contrast to the property-based institutions that evolved on the western frontier, many of the political institutions that evolved during the twentieth century were not designed to accommodate changing values. With private property rights to land, water, and minerals, people can exchange their property rights to accommodate different values and promote efficiency. To be sure, the primary values for which market transactions accounted were commodity values, though the history of Yellowstone, of dude ranching, and more recently of recreational properties suggests that amenities are not totally ignored.[8] In contrast, political institutions for managing land, water, and wildlife generally can reallocate resources only by taking rights from one individual or group and redistributing them to another. As a result, federal agencies and even some state agencies find themselves locked in political or court battles over virtually every decision they make. The question is: Can we learn from our past to improve the future of the West?

One way to encourage institutional reform that promotes cooperation is to devolve decision making to levels where the actors have a greater stake in the outcome. On the frontier, the people creating property institutions had a clear stake in the process and the end result. Fighting is a negative-sum game because resources are expended in redistributing valuable assets. Not only do people at the local level have a greater stake in positive-sum outcomes, they often have better knowledge about the values of the resources in question. Without going to the extreme of full privatization of all resources, consider some devolution possibilities for land, water, and wildlife that could encourage positive-sum games.

LAND

As economist Robert Nelson (1996) has noted, political land management has created private rights to public lands. For example, grazers on federal lands have had relatively secure property rights to their grazing permits, and these secure rights have given them an incentive to be good stewards. Environmentalists who would prefer not getting cow manure in their Vibram soles tried to get the Clinton administration to remove grazing from the federal estate using slogans such as "No Moo in '92" and "Cattle Free in '93."[9]

One simple solution to this problem is to make existing permits transferable to nongrazers on a willing buyer–willing seller basis. This approach is exemplified by the efforts of the Grand Canyon Trust and the Conservation Fund to purchase the Kane and Two Mile ranches in Utah between the Grand Canyon and the Grand Staircase–Escalante National Monument. These two groups have raised $4.5 million with which they have acquired 1,000 acres of private land and the associated grazing permits for 900,000 acres of public land. According to Bill Hedden, executive director of the Grand Canyon Trust:

> We don't pretend that we can just march in and manage the land better than anyone else. But our goals are different than traditional ranchers. We can manage to improve the habitat for antelope fawn survival or to ensure that there is an adequate small mammal prey base for goshawks and spotted owls. . . . We need new ways to do things, and this private partnership represents one of the new ways. We're seeing this attitude of "let's work this damn thing out," in a lot of places around the West. (Quoted in Larmer 2004, 6)

Timber management provides another example of how devolution and accountability can improve efficiency, fiscal responsibility, and environmental stewardship. Donald Leal (1995) made side-by-side comparisons of federal and state forest management in Montana. He found that, while federal forests on average lost fifty cents on every dollar they spent, state forests made two dollars for every dollar they spent. Moreover, state forests produced more environmental amenities such as clean water and wildlife habitat.

The difference between the two was the management incentives. Federal forest managers must grovel at the feet of congressional committees for their budgets and, for the most part, send their revenues to the black hole of the federal treasury. State forests, in contrast, are part of the state school trust lands and are charged with earning a profit for the school trust, not just today, but into the future. In so doing they are willing to make tradeoffs between which uses will generate more profits. Hence, recreation, viewsheds, and other amenity values will be traded off against timber production if they can generate more revenue. This happens because there is a bottom line against which managers can be held accountable and because there are "shareholders" such as students, teachers, administrators, and parents, all of whom have a stake in efficiency. Goals and accountability are the basis for the proposal to reform management of national forests put forth in Chapter 3. This proposal follows the approach used for the Valles Caldera National Preserve in which Congress created a nine-member board of trustees appointed by the president. The law requires trustees to have expertise in areas important to the trust's mission, such as livestock, forest, and wildlife and fish management. In balancing the various land uses, the trustees are also charged with making the preserve financially self-sustaining.[10]

WATER

Given that western water law is firmly rooted in the prior appropriation doctrine, water markets provide even more potential for devolution. If states would accelerate the adjudication of water rights, actors would know with whom they could bargain to reallocate water to new uses. In particular, allowing environmental interests to lease or purchase water rights and leave the water in-stream for aquatic values is an important step toward resolving disputes between irrigators and environmentalists.[11] Though a state agency can often hold water rights for in-stream purposes, most western states restrict private groups from transferring rights from off-stream to in-stream uses. In Montana, for example, the legislature had to change the law in 1995 to allow private groups to lease water and leave it in-stream. Between 1990 and 1997, purchases, leases, and donations were reported in nine of eleven western states, totaling more than 2.3 million acre-feet of water (see Landry 1998). Groups such as the Oregon Water Trust, Washington Water Trust, and Montana Water Trust are filling a niche for voluntary, nonconfrontational water trades to keep water in-stream.

WILDLIFE

Finally, the management of wildlife and wildlife habitat could benefit greatly from making the demanders and suppliers more squarely face the costs and benefits. The Defenders of Wildlife program to compensate livestock owners for losses caused by wolves reintroduced into Yellowstone National Park is an example. By raising private funds and structuring an evidentiary system for proving whether losses are caused by wolves, Defenders of Wildlife has accepted a share of the cost of what it wants. Leasing or purchasing land for wildlife habitat is another example of how markets can shift production from traditional commodities to higher-valued amenities. And this need not be the domain of government. Nonprofit groups, clubs, and associations and for-profit firms can and do broker such transactions.

To further encourage such markets, agencies, especially at the state level, can do much more to make wildlife and its habitat an asset rather than a liability. Under state wildlife law, the wildlife belongs to and is managed by state agencies. Private landowners may be compensated for crop losses and other damages, but generally they have little say in management and almost no incentive to improve habitat. A "ranching for wildlife program" such as the one in Colorado offers one way of making wildlife an asset. Such programs allocate a certain number of hunting permits to landowners, who can then sell them to hunters at the market price. To get these permits, the landowner must develop a habitat management plan and have it approved by the state agency. As one Montana rancher described the tradeoffs between traditional land uses and wildlife habitat, "If it pays, it stays." Markets for hunting and other recreation on private land provide a way of making amenity values pay.[12]

Conclusion

We can learn a good deal from the Old West, which was an institutional crucible. There, people bore the costs and reaped the benefits of developing institutions that encouraged good stewardship and discouraged negative-sum battles. They developed customary grazing rights, mining laws, and the prior appropriation water doctrine. These institutions served well for allocating natural resources among alternative uses, especially for the production of commodities.

In the New West, demands for natural resources to produce amenities have risen relative to demands for commodity production. Reallocating resources between these two uses has been a challenge for two reasons. First, some laws restrict transferring property from one use to another. This is the case with the prior appropriation doctrine, which restricts transfers to in-stream use (see Chapter 5), and grazing permits on federal lands, which cannot be transferred to nongrazing interests. Second, political institutions control the allocation of many resources, especially public lands and wildlife. Reallocation in the political process generally pits amenity demanders against commodity demanders in a game in which one side's loss is the other side's gain. Conflict rather than cooperation is inevitable.

Recognizing existing property rights, whether they be private, as with land, or political, as with grazing permits, and encouraging the exchange of these rights can link the New West with its Old West heritage. This will require devolution from centralized governmental control to lower levels of decision makers. The lowest denominator for devolution is to individuals or groups who can voluntarily exchange property rights in the marketplace. Markets for conservation easements (see Chapter 8), grazing permits, water rights, and hunting habitat provide examples of how devolution to this denominator can supplant conflict driven by rent seeking with cooperation driven by gains from trade. Short of private property and markets, devolution to lower levels of collective action can also help. State school trust land and state park management is less contentious and more economically and environmentally sound. Local open-space bonds provide benefits to local citizens without forcing a small subset of landowners to bear the cost of development restrictions. Private ownership and devolution of governmental control offer the best hope of taking us back to a future where free and responsible individuals cooperate with one another as stewards of the West's heritage and natural bounty.

Notes

1. For a detailed discussion of these variables, see Libecap (1981).

2. See Lueck (2003) for a discussion of why first possession is often used to establish ownership.

3. Quoted in Osgood (1929), 183.

4. For example, frontier land claims clubs had fewer requirements for retaining a claim than did the homestead acts. Moreover, the requirements that did exist were more productive than many of those under the homestead acts, such as the requirement that trees be planted on the arid plains where they would not grow. See Anderson and Hill (1983).

5. For details of this story, see Anderson and McChesney (1994) and Anderson and Lueck (1992). The latter show that trust lands are 40 to 90 percent less productive than fee simple lands on reservations when measured in terms of the value of agricultural output per acre.

6. For a complete discussion of the role of the Northern Pacific Railroad in the establishment and early management of Yellowstone, see Anderson and Hill (1996).

7. For a discussion of how public lands generate private rights and hence an incentive for the bureaucracy to manage for those private rights holders, see Nelson (1996).

8. For an account of early amenity entrepreneurs, see Anderson and Leal (1997).

9. Though their efforts have been largely unsuccessful, they have reduced the security of some grazing permits. With security of tenure reduced, there is less incentive for long-term stewardship, as Watts and LaFrance (2001) have shown.

10. For a complete discussion, see Yablonski (2004).

11. For a complete discussion, see Anderson and Snyder (1997) and Landry (1998).

12. The success of such programs is described by Leal and Grewell (2001).

References

Anderson, Terry L., ed. 1994. *Multiple Conflicts over Multiple Uses*. Bozeman, MT: PERC.

Anderson, Terry L., and P. J. Hill. 1975. The Evolution of Property Rights: A Study of the American West. *Journal of Law and Economics* 18: 163–179.

———. 1983. Privatizing the Commons: An Improvement? *Southern Economic Journal* 50(2): 438–450.

———. 1990. The Race for Property Rights. *Journal of Law and Economics* 18: 163–179.

———. 1996. Appropriable Rents from Yellowstone: A Case of Incomplete Contracting. *Economic Inquiry* 34 (July): 506–518.

———. 2004. *The Not So Wild, Wild West: Property Rights on the Frontier*. Stanford, CA: Stanford University Press.

Anderson, Terry L., and Laura E. Huggins. 2003. *Property Rights: A Practical Guide to Freedom and Prosperity*. Stanford, CA: Hoover Press.

Anderson, Terry L., and Donald R. Leal. 1997. *Enviro-Capitalists: Doing Good While Doing Well*. Lanham, MD: Rowman & Littlefield.

Anderson, Terry L., and Dean Lueck. 1992. Land Tenure and Agricultural Productivity on Indian Reservations. *Journal of Law and Economics* 35 (October): 427–454.

Anderson, Terry L., and Fred McChesney. 1994. Raid or Trade? An Economic Model of Indian-White Relations. *Journal of Law and Economics* 37 (April): 39–74.

Anderson, Terry L., and Pamela A. Snyder. 1997. *Water Markets: Priming the Invisible Pump*. Washington, DC: Cato Institute.

Demsetz, Harold. 1967. Toward a Theory of Property Rights. *American Economic Review* 57(2): 347–359.

Hardin, Garrett. 1968. *The Tragedy of the Commons*. Science 162 (December): 1243–1248.

Landry, Clay J. 1998. *Saving Our Streams Through Water Markets: A Practical Guide*. Bozeman, MT: PERC.

Larmer, Paul. 2004. Buying Ecological Leverage. *High Country News*, August 2.

Leal, Donald R. 1995. *Turning a Profit on Public Forests*. PERC Policy Series No. PS-4. Bozeman, MT: PERC.

Leal, Donald R., and J. Bishop Grewell. 2001. *Hunting for Habitat: A Practical Guide to State-Landowner Wildlife Partnerships*. Bozeman, MT: PERC.

Libecap, Gary D. 1981. *Locking Up the Range: Federal Land Controls and Grazing*. San Francisco: Pacific Institute for Public Policy Research; Cambridge, MA: Ballinger.

————. 2005. *Rescuing Water Markets: Lessons from Owens Valley*. PERC Policy Series No. PS-33. Bozeman, MT: PERC.

Libecap, Gary D., and Zeynep Hansen. 2004. Small Farms, Externalities, and the Dust Bowl of the 1930s. *Journal of Political Economy* 122(3): 665–694.

Lueck, Dean. 2003. First Possession as the Basis of Property. In *Property Rights: Cooperation, Conflict and Law*, ed. Terry L. Anderson and Fred McChesney. Princeton, NJ: Princeton University Press.

McGrath, Roger D. 1984. *Gunfighters, Highwaymen, and Vigilantes: Violence on the Frontier*. Berkeley: University of California Press.

Nelson, Robert H. 1996. *Public Lands and Private Rights: The Failure of Scientific Management*. Lanham, MD: Rowman & Littlefield.

Osgood, Ernest Staples. 1929. *The Day of the Cattleman*. Chicago: University of Chicago Press.

Rucker, Randall R., and Price V. Fishback. 1983. The Federal Reclamation Program: An Analysis of Rent-Seeking Behavior. In *Water Rights: Scarce Resource Allocation, Bureaucracy, and the Environment*, ed. Terry L. Anderson. San Francisco: Pacific Institute for Public Policy Research.

Runte, Alfred. 1990. *Trains of Discovery*. Niwot, CO: Robert Rinehart.

Umbeck, John R. 1977. A Theory of Contract Choice and the California Gold Rush. *Journal of Law and Economics* 20(2): 421–437.

Watts, Myles J., and Jeffery T. LaFrance. 2001. Grazing Rights. In *Conservative Conservation: Policy Proposals for the New Century*, ed. Donald R. Leal. Bozeman, MT: PERC, 15–18.

Yablonski, Brian. 2004. Valles Caldera National Preserve: A New Paradigm for Federal Lands? In *PERC Reports* 22(4). Bozeman, MT: PERC, 3.

PART TWO

Devolution to Facilitate Change

CHAPTER THREE

Institutional Reform for Public Lands?

DANIEL KEMMIS

System Dysfunction

The public lands system in the United States must overcome its own version of a "perfect storm" if it is to serve the nation effectively under twenty-first-century circumstances. Our public lands, the vast majority of which lies in the eleven western-most states and Alaska, are burdened by a steadily more outdated regulatory and governing framework. To compound this, much of the West has been and for the foreseeable future will be facing a rapid population increase, which puts even more pressure, both physical and political, on the public lands.

For the past few years, the need to examine new approaches to public land management has been gaining broader recognition from both sides of the political aisle. Not long ago, former Democratic Secretary of the Interior Cecil Andrus called the public land governance system "the tangled web of overlapping and often contradictory laws and regulations under which our federal public lands are managed" (Andrus et al. 2000). Republican Congressman Scott McInnis, former chairman of the Subcommittee on Forests and Forest Health, referred to "a decision-making apparatus that is on the verge of collapsing under its own weight" (Conflicting Laws 2001). Forest Service Chief Dale Bosworth regarded this phenomenon as "analysis paralysis" (Conflicting Laws 2001), and former Forest Service Chief Jack Ward Thomas simply called it "the blob" (Snow et al. 1998).

The Forest Service itself recognizes the nearly impossible circumstances under which it operates. A 2002 report detailing the agency's inability to fulfill primary management duties, appropriately titled "The Process Predicament," stated that "large portions of the National Forest System are in poor or declining health" and concluded "the Forest Service operates within a statutory, regulatory, and administrative framework that has kept the agency from effectively addressing declines in forest health" (USDA Forest Service 2002, 42). Throughout the report, the Forest Service maintained that one result of its "process predicament" is the declining health of forests in the West. That linkage may be debatable, but it is harder to argue with the fact that the health of civic culture and public discourse is seriously undermined by the time-consuming and often frustrating procedures that are now so typical of daily life in and around the Forest Service.

The effect on morale within the agency is no less pronounced. Hardworking managers cannot be expected to remain enthusiastic about their jobs when the results they strive so hard to achieve often disappear into a procedural or judicial quagmire. Moreover, while several factors—especially the ever-more-ubiquitous global marketplace—have contributed to the decline in the timber economy in many communities surrounded by public land, the frustration of many of those communities' residents over the paralysis they see within the Forest Service is very real.

Before any possible solutions to this "predicament" are discussed, it may be helpful to examine some of the historical forces that have produced this situation. Without any pretense to comprehensiveness, I believe the following factors have each played a significant role: (1) the dynamic relationship between land tenure systems and political economy, and (2) changes in democratic theory and practice.

Two caveats are in order here. First, the boundaries between these phenomena are much more blurred and permeable than the following analysis will sometimes appear to acknowledge. Second, although each of these factors has contributed to the problems now besetting the public lands system, each of them is also producing at least a glimmer of hope for some workable solutions.

Land Tenure and Political Economy

Throughout history, in every society, the form and evolution of land tenure systems have played a substantial and often determinative role in shaping the political and economic systems of a particular place. The seventeenth- and eighteenth-century revolutions in England, America, and France, for example, were intimately bound up with the abolition of feudal tenures, the enclosure of commons, and the abandonment of primogeniture. The point here is not to analyze in any depth this historical nexus between land tenure and political and economic systems, but only to observe that, first, it has always been a crucial nexus, and second, the land tenure system that was created out of whole cloth and imposed across the western United States roughly a century ago could no more remain immune to historical changes than any other tenure system has ever done. Indeed, given the breathtaking speed with which that system was created and the lack of organic, adaptive evolution attending its creation, it would be quite surprising if the march of history had not eventually created some substantial strains within it.

Again, a close analysis of this dynamic is beyond the scope of this chapter. But even a cursory glance at a few high points on the historical landscape will help us understand why the system of public land tenure was almost guaranteed to develop severe malfunctions.

In the first place, the system of public ownership was created alongside another, equally extensive, equally inorganic and untested system of land tenure: that created by the Homestead Act and its various progeny. The homestead system had appeared as a means of settling vast stretches of land that had been wrenched away from their tribal inhabitants, who had developed their own territorial and inhabitory patterns across those landscapes. Both the homestead and the public lands systems, then, may be seen as part of the "legacy of conquest" that Patricia Nelson Limerick described in her seminal book by that title (1987). In both cases, the rapid change from tribal to American jurisdiction required an equally rapid development of legal systems of land tenure. It would be surprising indeed if such hastily enacted systems, applied at such a monumental scale, did not eventually produce internal strains and unintended consequences.

In the case of the homestead system, those strains and consequences have revealed themselves in successive waves over the century and a half since the passage of the first Homestead Act. Today, yet another wave of depopulation of the Great Plains only underscores how prescient John Wesley Powell was in his 1878 "Report on the Lands of the Arid Region of the United States" (1962) when he warned of the fundamental flaws embedded in the homestead legislation. A decade later, when Powell visited several soon-to-be state capitals during the wave of new-state admissions of 1889–1890, he issued similar warnings about the dangers he saw attending the centralized approach being applied to the then-emerging system of public lands. Those warnings received no more response in Washington than the arid lands report had generated.

The legacy of conquest included, then, a patchwork of hastily devised land tenure systems across the West. In fact, there were several other major components of this patchwork "system." One resulted from the fact that the indigenous tribes were not totally eradicated nor wholly dispossessed of their territory. As a consequence, Indian Country, with its own complex blend of tenure systems, remains a significant part of the western scene. Second, alongside the homestead system, Congress created another form of privatization of western lands when it granted thousands of sections of the public domain to private corporations to induce them to build transcontinental railroads. And third, as each new western state entered the Union, another substantial portion of the public domain (generally one section in each township) was granted in trust to the states for the support of public education.

Cutting across many of these tenure systems lay another level of complexity involving mineral rights, often severed from surface ownership. Furthermore, the precious water, so essential to inhabitation of the arid lands, generated its own unique and convoluted tenure patterns.

Much of the twentieth-century political and economic history of the West would be determined by the interplay of these different land tenure systems. No comprehensive analysis of these dynamics is possible here, but a few major features will help set the stage for a more detailed discussion of issues now surrounding the public land portion of this picture.

Thoroughly incentivized by public largess, the transcontinental railroads were indeed constructed. In the process, they further fragmented tribal homelands and contributed substantially to the decimation of the bison herds so indispensable to the Plains Indians. The railroads also fed the ill-fated homesteading boom of the northern plains in the early twentieth century, and they were largely responsible for the creation of towns all along the line, many of which are now on the verge of extinction as the failures of the homestead system continue to unfold. The railroad lands themselves have played various economic roles, often being leased by neighboring farmers and ranchers, and many being conveyed to timber companies whose logging practices made all but impossible a coordinated or ecologically sustainable relationship with the interspersed public lands. Most recently, many railroad-cum-timber lands have become increasingly valuable for residential development, their value enhanced substantially by the fact that the surrounding public lands cannot be developed.

The public lands themselves were dedicated from the beginning to "multiple use," which was generally interpreted during the first three-quarters of the century to mean that they should buttress the economic activities arising on the privatized portion of the landscape. This was always true of the grasslands, and after the Second World War, it became increasingly true of the timberlands. What would later become known as "timber-dependent communities" almost always depended on federal timber. Not surprisingly, the economic activities on the plains and in the mountains generated their own politics, generally intent on maintaining the subsidies and extraction-friendly policies of the public land system, but always at the same time fiercely resentful of what westerners perceived as the all-too-intrusive federal presence. "Get out and give us more money," was how Bernard De Voto famously characterized the core of this western political ideology (1947).

De Voto's verbal facility describes an important example of the contradictions that have so often characterized western history. But there is a deeper contradiction, embedded in this patchwork of land tenure systems, that is still contributing to the difficulties federal land managers face. This contradiction centers on the uneasy relationship between the public lands and the homestead system.

The homestead acts comprised a major segment of American public policy. Their aim was the white settlement of the vast territory the United States acquired during the period of continental conquest. That settlement was not only meant to create individual homesteads, but to create democratic societies. In other words, the people settling those landscapes were expected to govern them. They were expected to create towns and local economies that could sustain themselves into the future, as the settlers of New England, the South, and the Midwest had done.

But in none of those other sections of the country had the national government suddenly said, "Actually, you only get to settle half the land, and you now need to make your economies work under these new circumstances." It is easy enough to discount the long-standing western resentment of the federal presence in the region, especially given the bizarre and politically immature forms in which that resentment has often been expressed. Yet when the Sagebrush Rebels of the 1980s sought to overturn the federal reservation of more than 80 percent of Nevada's land on the basis that Nevada had not been admitted to the Union on an "equal footing" with eastern states, they were identifying a unique and uniquely challenging feature of the land tenure systems that the West had inherited.

Those strains had intensified as the dynamics between land tenure and economic forces unfolded throughout the twentieth century. The spreading affluence that followed the Second World War, for example, led directly to the increasing demand for timber from the federal lands, as more and more Americans pursued the dream of home ownership. But that same affluence also contributed to more travel; more vacationing; more hiking, camping, and skiing; more fishing and hunting—all of which began to put a broader range of pressures on the public lands, gradually producing the "conspiracy of optimism" that Paul Hirt has so trenchantly described (1994).

This layering of expectations across the public lands has contributed substantially to the current gridlock in the system, and we will return to this theme in the following section. Meanwhile, some new developments in land tenure have begun to produce glimpses of possible solutions to some of the difficulties afflicting the public lands system.

Spreading affluence and technological advances have contributed to a continental migration into the mountains that is now well into its second decade. This in-migration has coincided almost precisely with a sharp decline in timber harvests from the public lands, driven by global market forces and, to a lesser extent, by stricter environmental regulations and more aggressive environmental politics. This combination of declining extractive activity and increasing population has in turn been accompanied by some promising innovations in land tenure.

The most visible and striking of these developments has been the rapid growth and spread of the land trust movement across the West. Land trusts and conservation easements had become popular outside the West long before they attracted much attention in this region, and the reason is not far to seek. With such extensive stretches of landscape already protected from development by the reservation of the public lands, one might have expected that expensive, difficult mechanisms like land trusts would never play a major role in part of the country. Yet by the 1990s the Rocky Mountain West had become not only the region with the nation's fastest population growth but also the one with the fastest growth in land trusts. Clearly, the two phenomena were related.

Such large-scale in-migration to a region where so much land is already off-limits to development has heightened the pressure on the most attractive parcels in private ownership. Not infrequently, those parcels have substantial aesthetic or ecological value, and it is this value that brings land trusts into the picture. This set of mechanisms, which blends elements of private and public land tenure, often operates at the physical interface of public and private ownerships. More than that, land trusts often play a role in influencing the economic uses of both public and private land. For example, a land trust that seeks to protect privately owned ranches from subdivision may well find itself drawn into trying to protect a given ranch's public land grazing allotment, as part of the package required to keep the ranch viable as an economic unit. In a similar vein, land trusts attempting to protect former railroad land grants from subdivision may become engaged in "community forest" discussions aimed at maintaining the private lands as "working landscapes," which, in the West, very often requires coordination with land-use planning on adjacent public parcels.

The purpose here is merely to suggest how the historical changes now occurring in the West have in turn begun to produce innovations and refinements in the land tenure system. These innovations in their turn may provide some solutions to the institutional problems besetting one major component of that land tenure system: the public lands.

The widespread resort to land trust mechanisms to address western land-use challenges should remind us that, in fact, trusts have been part of the picture all along. Almost all of the state lands are held in trust, under the terms of the various statehood enabling acts. With most of the attention focused for so many decades on the more extensive and more controversial federal portion of the public domain, the state trust lands have, with some notable exceptions, escaped close examination (Souder and Fairfax 2000). No such examination is in order here, but the experience of state trust lands may become more relevant, given how often the concept of trust mechanisms now arises in discussions about western land issues.

In addition to the phenomenal spread of private nonprofit land trusts, there has also been increasing interest in and experimentation with public trusts. Two recent examples are the congressionally created Valles Caldera National Preserve in New Mexico and the Presidio trust in California. In the first case, Congress was persuaded to acquire a large working ranch for the national government. Rather than simply add the ranch to the holdings of the Forest Service or the Bureau of Land Management, Congress mandated the creation of a board of trustees, a majority of whom must be from New Mexico, to manage the property. Essentially the same mechanism was created for the Presidio in San Francisco when it was converted from its previous incarnation as a military reservation. The resort to a trust mechanism, rather than relying on the prevailing form of tenure for national public lands, is (like the land trust movement itself) an indication that changing economic and political circumstances are producing changes in the land tenure system of the West. To understand more about what is producing these changes and how they might ease the strains in the public land system, we shift our focus from land tenure to democratic theory and practice.

Democracy and the Public Lands

The relationship between the public lands and American democracy could well be the topic of an entire book. The disposition of public lands in what we now know as the Midwest was a key element in Henry Clay's "American System" in the 1820s and 1830s. Proceeds from the sale of public lands were considered by far the likeliest source of funds sufficient for any voluntary buyout and resettlement of slaves when that option for ending slavery was being seriously considered before the Civil War. The Homestead Act, an intricate system for privatizing the public domain, was an extension of the Jeffersonian belief that small, independent farms were and always would be the backbone of American democracy.

As it happens, the setting aside of the public lands before and after 1900 came hand and glove with a very significant change in American democratic theory and practice. Both Gifford Pinchot and Theodore Roosevelt understood the creation of the national public land system as part of a concerted effort to expand the reach and role of the nation and the national government. By the time of Roosevelt's Bull Moose Party run for reelection in 1912, he was calling this effort the "New Nationalism." The first item on that nationalist agenda was economic. Corporations had outgrown the capacity of individual states to hold them accountable, which meant to Roosevelt and other Progressives that only the federal government could impose democratic accountability on these economic giants. It was this empowering of the national government to do a job that state and local governments could no longer handle on their own that lay at the heart of the New Nationalism.

But that New Nationalism was about more than balancing big business with the countervailing force of big government. It was also about a re-definition of democracy in America. It was about cultivating a deeper sense of national identity, so that people would come increasingly to think of themselves not as Bostonians or Philadelphians, not as Virginians or Californians, but as Americans. In *The Promise of American Life*, published in 1909, Herbert Croly, the philosopher of the New Nationalism, argued that the great American experiment in democracy could now fulfill itself only by developing a widely shared sense of national purpose (1993).

The setting aside of the public lands was one of the most visible ways in which Roosevelt, Pinchot, and others injected into American public life this now pervasive strain of national democracy. With stops and starts, but generally with forward movement, the nationalization of our public life accumulated force throughout most of the twentieth century. The civil rights movement, for example, felt that it had no choice but to turn to the national government to enact its agenda, and within a few years, the environmental movement did the same.

The National Environmental Policy Act (NEPA), adopted in 1969, serves as the capstone to the entire national environmental statutory structure. The language of NEPA describes succinctly and matter-of-factly the nationalist perspective that permeates the structure. The purpose of the act is "to establish a national policy for the environment."[1] In the absence of anyone else claiming stewardship for the environment, it is fortunate that the national government was willing to do so. The good that has been done by such environmental statutes as the Clean Air Act, the Clean Water Act, or the Endangered Species Act has been of genuinely historic proportions. In each case, the action was taken in the name of national democracy. The purpose of the Wilderness Act is "to establish a National Wilderness Preservation System for the permanent good of the whole people,"[2] while the National Forest Management Act is dedicated to "assuring that the Nation maintains a natural resource and conservation posture that will meet the requirements of our people in perpetuity."[3]

The question is whether these noble national objectives can be obtained through the mechanisms of national democracy that we have established to accomplish them. There is strong reason to believe that, in some cases at least, they cannot, and that in any case these national democratic mechanisms have contributed very substantially to the often-observed dysfunctions of the public land system.

There are at least two different problems with this effort to practice national democracy in the management of public lands. One is essentially the problem that Paul Hirt (1994) identifies—the tendency to ask the public lands to supply some of what everyone wants, with no workable mechanism for balancing such demands or curtailing them to fit the actual physical capacity of the lands themselves. Another way to put this is that we have imposed on the public lands a surplus of good intentions. Every single piece of legislation that applies to these lands is not only well intentioned, but I would argue that in every case, the central objective sought by the legislation is a sound and worthy goal. One way of understanding what has created the phenomenon referred to as "analysis paralysis" is that those various pieces of legislation have all been passed in isolation from one another, so that they do not in fact form a public land management "system" at all but something much more like Jack Ward Thomas's "blob."

If this were the whole of the problem, then another good dose of national democracy might supply a cure. As we will discuss briefly below, Congress might convene another version of a public land law review commission, beginning by saying, "Here are all of the overarching national objectives that we want to obtain from the public lands; now devise a coordinated set of governing mechanisms to achieve these objectives, replacing the hodge-podge of separate statutes and regulations now in place."

But there is a deeper problem here, which no amount of national democracy seems likely to be able to resolve. The problem is how anyone can possibly construct a genuinely democratic system of public land governance that gives every citizen of the country an equal and effective voice in what happens on every acre of public land. The simple answer is that it cannot be done. In fact, the only way even to approximate such an objective is to create a highly procedural form of citizen involvement that is all but guaranteed to produce widespread frustration, litigation, and bureaucratic gridlock. Not surprisingly, that "procedural republic" is what we have produced.[4] And not surprisingly, after decades of intense, highly motivated, highly organized involvement with that form of participation, we have begun to evolve another way of engaging concerned citizens in the on-the-ground problems that will never cease to arise on and around the public lands. This other approach is what has come to be known as the *collaboration movement*, or as *community-based conservation*. This is a fundamentally democratic movement, in the basic sense of giving citizens an opportunity to be effectively engaged with shaping the circumstances that most directly affect them. It is a form of democracy that has arisen directly from the unavoidable failures of the national democratic model, as applied to the public lands.

Some Possible Solutions

This very cursory historical review has been intended to provide some understanding of where the strains within the public lands system have come from. In the process, we have encountered some hopeful signs as well. We turn now to a more focused look at a diversified portfolio of solutions.

Diversified portfolios are of course standard practice in the investment world. Brokers often place a portion of their client's money in stocks, another amount in bonds, and some in real estate to maximize the chances of substantial gains and diminish the risk of losses. By a similar logic, a public lands "policy portfolio" should probably now include at least three simultaneous elements: comprehensive review of the entire public lands system, incremental reform of the system, and a deliberate period of experimentation.

The first element of this portfolio involves a twenty-first-century form of a public land law review commission. It has been nearly forty years since Congress commissioned the last comprehensive review of public lands, a longer period than separated any previous commissions. Yet it is within the past thirty years that most of the current problems with the system have surfaced. Beginning a new public land law review raises a number of questions, including how it would be formed, who would be included, and what the political costs would be. Although the prospects of success are tenuous, under the right circumstances, a comprehensive review of laws might have a chance to get to the heart of the problems facing the public land agencies. It could at least attempt to systematically address the basic structural problems that plague those agencies.

The second piece of a possible public lands portfolio involves incremental changes to the operating system, with specific attention focused on opportunities for change on a more immediate scale. An example of this type of incremental reform was the bipartisan congressional effort to address the problems associated with the failing payment-in-lieu-of-taxes program.[5] As poor incentives and dwindling resources combined to eliminate most of the program's intended benefits, both sides of the political fence saw the need to address these problems, which generated the political capacity to successfully adjust the program. The result was the bipartisan Secure Rural Schools and Community Self-Determination Act of 2000. Even that modest amount of bipartisanship began to unravel as the original legislation neared its sunset date and the Bush administration proposed selling public land to finance the program. Nevertheless, Congress, agencies, and other interested parties should continue to look for opportunities to address systemic problems, bringing positive incremental change to the system wherever the opportunity presents itself.

The third element of the proposed portfolio is deliberate experimentation and reflects several recent proposals to experiment with new approaches to managing public lands. Many of these proposals call for legislatively authorized experiments or pilot projects that are to be implemented, monitored, and evaluated through various forms of collaborative governance. One of the more promising examples of this approach has emerged under the title of Region Seven.

In 1998, a group of individuals with a variety of perspectives on the Forest Service met several times at the University of Montana's Lubrecht Experimental Forest to discuss the complex issues facing national forest management and governance. This symposium, now known as the Lubrecht Conversations, addressed the changing management philosophies within the Forest Service, collaborative methods in forest management, shifting public expectations, and the agency's complicated mission. It concluded by proposing that the Forest Service establish a framework for deliberate experimentation in national forest management. The group described a framework that would test innovative approaches to forest management, focusing on collaborative governance structures and other mechanisms to overcome some of the problems that now beset the agency. They suggested that the experiments be implemented under a "virtual region" within the Forest Service, called Region Seven. The significance of the name Region Seven derives from the unusual configuration of Forest Service regions. As a result of a 1965 national review of Forest Service management and organization, Region Seven of the Forest Service was absorbed into Regions Eight and Nine. Region Seven in effect disappeared, and the Region Seven designation has not been used since.

The Lubrecht Conversations proposed that Region Seven be given new life, not as a normal, geographically contiguous region, but as a collection of experimental projects on national forest lands across the country. Such a framework would allow innovative solutions to be tested and evaluated at sites throughout the national forest system, and encourage agency managers and public land stakeholders to develop better options than those that currently exist.

Perhaps the strongest element of Region Seven is its emphasis on incorporation of the most promising adaptive management concepts into the governance of public lands. Adaptive management derives from an acknowledgment that, while ecosystems are appropriate units for public land planning, those ecosystems are too complex and unpredictable to be managed according to traditional planning models. As the scientific community has shown time and time again, ecosystems simply will not conform to five- or ten-year plans. Conceding this, adaptive managers start with the best-informed management plan they can devise, knowing at the outset that applying that plan to a living ecosystem will likely produce unexpected and unintended results. As those results begin to accrue, adaptive managers revisit their plans, adjusting them to the endless complexity of the ecosystem in question.

Region Seven would apply this adaptive approach not simply to public land management, but to public land governance as well. The proposal recognizes the impossibility of providing an immediate and final fix to every problem within this very complex governing system and instead concentrates on building adaptability into the system. The value of such an experimental approach is that it does not attempt to change the entire public lands system at once, but recognizes problems and invites and tests innovative solutions in a few carefully chosen settings.

Although the experimental component of the policy portfolio needs to be aggressively adaptive, and therefore should not be heavily constrained in advance, some overarching principles should guide development and implementation of a framework like Region Seven. To encourage the generation and careful testing of alternative approaches to national forest management, enabling legislation for Region Seven should

- Establish a national forum for selecting promising projects
- Establish a broadly representative advisory committee to guide project selection and monitoring
- Emphasize the experimental, adaptive nature of projects while promoting to the public a need to explore new methods for managing public lands
- Authorize and encourage projects across a range of administrative and geographic scales

· Require monitoring of both process and outcome against firmly established baselines
· Require a cumulative record of project activities and outcomes
· Ensure broad dissemination of lessons learned

The first step would be to conduct a national competition for the selection of experimental projects to test new models of management or governance. A commission made up of respected representatives of all major public land stakeholder constituencies would be organized to solicit proposals for alternative approaches to public land management and governance, select promising projects, and guide the implementation process. The projects selected would make up the new Region Seven.

The Region Seven projects should test a broad range of models. The types of experiments tested would depend largely on what public land stakeholders, both local and national, are currently trying or would like the opportunity to try. Two broad categories of potential experiments seem especially promising, both because of widespread interest in them and because of the particular ways they seek to address some of the deeper dysfunctions within the public lands framework. These two categories are market approaches and place-based collaborative mechanisms.

Each of these approaches offers an alternative decision system, which can arguably transcend some of the most vexing problems manifested by the prevailing decision structure. These approaches are not mutually exclusive, as we will see, but at the outset it may be helpful to focus on how market approaches address the "conspiracy of optimism" problem, while collaborative approaches provide an alternative to the "procedural republic."

If the "conspiracy of optimism" arises from a decision structure that seems incapable of choosing among different potential uses of any particular segment of the public domain, a market approach provides a well-tested way of making those choices. Under such an approach, whichever mix of proposed uses can generate the most income from some portion of the public domain would be given preference. If a conservation group cares enough about protecting a stand of old-growth trees, among other objectives, it will outbid those whose proposed mix of uses includes cutting the old growth.

There is strong disagreement among public land observers about whether such an approach could work, and particularly whether it can protect the public interest. The purpose here is not to resolve that dispute but to acknowledge that it is a matter about which reasonable people can disagree and to suggest that, in addition to trying to resolve the dispute by argumentation, a few on-the-ground, practical tests might usefully inform the debate.

A framework like Region Seven would be very likely to elicit one or more proposed experiments where, perhaps after some initial period of federal budgetary support, the experimental area would be expected to generate most or all of its own operating expenses. Some of these proposals might rely on market mechanisms to determine which land uses would generate those revenues. A variation on this theme might involve experiments with trust mechanisms patterned on state school trusts, where some designated trust beneficiary would hold trustees responsible for generating the highest rate of return from the land in question. The Region Seven selection panel might be expected (or even could be statutorily required) to make sustainability a key objective of any such trust. Again, market mechanisms might be relied on to maximize the return, subject to a requirement for sustainability, or any other enforceable public objective imposed upon the trustees.

In a similar vein, a Region Seven framework would almost certainly generate a number of collaborative proposals, ranging from planning models in which a collaborative body would write a management plan for the area while existing public land managers would be charged with implementing the plan, to collaborative governance models, testing what would happen if a collaborative group were empowered both to write and to oversee implementation of the management plan.

Collaborative approaches to land management or governance are as controversial as market approaches, and again, the purpose here is not to take sides in the debate, but only to suggest that a few carefully chosen and closely monitored experiments could provide information that would make the debate more constructive.

In the case of collaborative mechanisms, one of the chief concerns is how national as opposed to purely local interests can maintain their influence in such a setting. It is fairly easy to imagine a range of experiments that would shed light on the capacity of collaborative mechanisms to address this concern. For example, as with market mechanisms, this collaborative category would very likely include one or more trust models, under which the public land in question would be managed by a board of trustees, pursuant to a binding trust instrument. In effect, this approach would expand the type of initiative Congress authorized with the Valles Caldera

National Preserve from newly acquired to already existing public land. It would still be done on a strictly experimental basis, limited both in time and in geographical scope.

It would be important for a framework like Region Seven to be thoroughly open-ended in terms of the types of experiments that might be proposed and authorized. So, for example, there should be no bias in favor of any particular mechanism such as trusts. Still, for analytical purposes, it is worthwhile to focus on this category of potential experiments.

As noted above, trust mechanisms—particularly land trusts—have now become so prevalent that they must be seen as a major and growing component of the land tenure system in the West. Beyond this, trusts may provide a fairly elegant way of addressing both some of the problems with the existing system of federal land management and some of the concerns with alternatives like market or collaborative approaches.

What trusts seem to offer is a promising blend of accountability and flexibility. One way of understanding the genesis of the "process predicament" or "analysis paralysis" is that, in an effort to make federal land managers accountable to every individual American citizen, we have so severely reduced the flexibility of the decision system that it has, in fact, become paralyzed. While reasonable people can disagree about the extent of this paralysis, only the most ardent ideologues will deny its existence altogether, let alone its debilitating effect on agency morale. An adaptive approach to governance must at least be open to better ways of balancing accountability with flexibility.

Trust mechanisms at least appear to promise that better balance. They combine the pragmatic, problem-solving flexibility of collaboration (among stakeholder trustees) with the strict accountability that is so deeply embedded in the very concept of trusteeship. One very important dimension of this combination is the possibility of safeguarding national interests and priorities while taking full advantage of local knowledge. Thus, in the case of the Valles Caldera National Preserve, Congress has dictated that a majority of the trustees must be New Mexicans and that they must represent a range of stakeholder interests, but Congress has also imposed on those trustees the enforceable obligation of managing the preserve in such a way as to achieve a clearly delineated set of national objectives. In achieving these objectives, the trustees are freed from many of the procedural requirements of the prevailing decision system. What they are not freed from is the requirement to meet national objectives.

One argument in favor of an experimental framework like Region Seven is that it would expand substantially but deliberately the range of experiments with trust mechanisms beyond those currently in place. It is simply not good public policy to rest judgment about something as complex as trusteeship on one or two experiments. There are too many fortuitous or exogenous circumstances that can produce failure (or for that matter success) in any one instance. It would be unfortunate indeed if the future of trust approaches were left to depend on either the success or the failure of the Valles Caldera and the Presidio.

Limiting trust experiments in this way would also preclude testing the use of market approaches in a trust context because neither of the existing national trusts is designed to test such approaches. Market-based trusts would likely be modeled much more closely on the state trust land concept, with a clearly designated beneficiary receiving the financial (and perhaps also nonfinancial) benefits of the trust. Although it is conceivable that the blue ribbon panel selecting Region Seven experiments would approve some trust proposals that only seek to maximize financial return, it seems far more likely (given the mix of interests on the panel) that approved trust proposals would also be required to pursue nonfinancial objectives such as habitat protection and sustainability. Just as collaborative trust mechanisms promise a balancing of local knowledge and national objectives, market-driven trust mechanisms may provide a way of combining the decisional rigor of markets with the pursuit of public interests that pure markets may seem to threaten.

It should be apparent that there are no clear boundaries separating these categories. Market-driven trust models, for example, may well be collaborative, and collaborative models may undertake to generate their own operating revenue. Nor, again, are these various trust models meant to exhaust the list of potentially fruitful categories for experimentation.

What is clear is that, if any of these experiments are to be of consequence, it is imperative that they be carefully monitored and evaluated and that the results be honestly analyzed and discussed. The resulting information must be broadly disseminated so that as many people as possible can learn from the experiments and adapt the lessons to their own settings. The experiments should also be allowed to operate for at least five years, and preferably ten or even fifteen years, so that their long-term viability can be legitimately evaluated.

Conclusion

A number of historical forces have resulted in public land planning and management becoming increasingly embroiled with statutory, regulatory, and judicial imperatives that too often prevent the system from working effectively or adapting to new circumstances. This in turn has left both agency personnel and the affected public deeply dissatisfied with the process and often with the results. This situation especially affects the West, where the majority of public lands are found and where the demands on these lands are sure to grow substantially over the coming years.

No comprehensive solution to this state of affairs is likely to be achieved in the foreseeable future, although the possibility of a comprehensive public land law review should not be ruled out. Meanwhile, sound, broadly supported incremental improvements must continue to be an option. Finally, Congress should seriously consider authorizing a period of deliberate experimentation during which a number of carefully conceived, broadly supported, and closely monitored experiments could test the viability of alternative forms of public land planning and management. The Region Seven concept presents, to the West and the rest of the nation, the opportunity to move beyond adaptive management to adaptive governance for our public lands.

Notes

Portions of this article are adapted from previous articles by the author, particularly "Re-examining the Governing Framework of the Public Lands," *University of Colorado Law Review* 75 (Fall 2004), and "Region 7: An Innovative Approach to Planning On or Near Public Lands," *American Planning Association's Land Use Law and Zoning Digest* (August 2003): 3.

  1. 42 U.S.C. Sec. 4331.
  2. 16 U.S.C. Sec. 1131.
  3. 16 U.S.C. Sec. 1600.
  4. The phrase "procedural republic" is from Michael Sandel (1984), "The Procedural Republic and the Unencumbered Self," *Political Theory* 12 (February): 81–86.
  5. Under the PILT program, the federal government compensates local governments for losses to their tax bases due to the presence of many types of federally owned land. The level of pay is calculated under a complex formula, which includes federal acreage in the county, county population, and previous payments in a county.

References

Andrus, Cecil D., John C. Freemuth, Marc C. Johnson, and Patrick A. Shea. 2000. *Policy After Politics*. Paper presented by the Andrus Center for Public Policy, Boise, ID, June 1. Online at http://www.andruscenter.org/AndrusCenter.data/Components/PDF%20FILES/PAP_whitepaper.pdf.

Conflicting Laws and Regulations—Gridlock on the National Forests: Oversight Hearing Before the Subcommittee on Forests and Forest Health of the House Committee on Resources, 107th Congress. 2001. Statements of Rep. McInnis, Chairman, Subcommittee on Forests and Forest Health, and Dale Bosworth, Chief, U.S. Forest Service. Online at http://www.house.gov/resources/107cong/forests/2001dec04/mcinnis.htm and http://www.house.gov/resources/107cong/forests/2001dec04/bosworth.htm.

Croly, Herbert. 1993 [1909]. *The Promise of American Life*. New Brunswick, NJ: Transaction.

De Voto, Bernard. 1947. The West Against Itself. *Harpers* (January), 245.

Hirt, Paul. 1994. *A Conspiracy of Optimism*. Lincoln: University of Nebraska Press.

Kemmis, Daniel. 2003. Region 7: An Innovative Approach to Planning On or Near Public Lands. *American Planning Association's Land Use Law and Zoning Digest* (August), 3.

———. 2004. Re-examining the Governing Framework of the Public Lands. *University of Colorado Law Review* 75(4), 1127–1132.

Limerick, Patricia Nelson. 1987. *The Legacy of Conquest: The Unbroken Past of the American West*. New York: W. W. Norton.

Powell, John Wesley. 1962 [1878]. *Report on the Lands of the Arid Region of the United States*, ed. Wallace Stegner. Cambridge, MA: Harvard University Press, Belknap Press.

Snow, D., J. Burchfield, O. Daniels, D. Kemmis, T. M. Power, J. W. Thomas, et al. 1998. The Lubrecht Conversations: A Diverse Group Discusses the Future of the Forest Service in a Changing West. *Chronicle of Community* 3(1): 5–16.

Souder, John A., and Sally K. Fairfax. 2000. *State Trust Lands: History, Management and Sustainable Use*. Lawrence: University Press of Kansas.

USDA Forest Service. 2002. *The Process Predicament: How Statutory, Regulatory, and Administrative Factors Affect National Forest Management*. Online at http://www.fs.fed.us/projects/documents/Process-Predicament.pdf.

CHAPTER FOUR

The State of the Parks

Enhancing or Dissipating the Wealth of Nature?

HOLLY LIPPKE FRETWELL

In the minds of many, parks represent the purest "wealth of nature"—nature in its glory, rather than nature as a commodity. Large or small, parks capture the beauty and wildness, or at least the distinctiveness, of the natural world. Yet extensive study suggests that the nation is far from maximizing this wealth. This chapter will explain why and identify some of the steps that can be taken—and in some cases are being taken—to realize the true wealth of nature represented by the vast acreage devoted to parks in the United States.

For reasons historical, political, and ideological, millions of acres throughout the United States have been taken out of the private sector and placed under government control. The federal government manages an estate covering more than 700 million acres (Fretwell 2000, 3), and states own and manage an additional 200 million acres.[1] Of these lands, national parks now cover more than 84 million acres, and state parks include 13.5 million acres. Unlike most of the public lands, which allow commercial uses—including timber extraction, livestock grazing, mining, and recreation—parks focus specifically on recreation and the protection of wildlife and habitat.

Though the great majority of park acreage in the United States is managed by the National Park Service (NPS), it is not clear that this is the most efficient method for management. The popularity of state park systems greatly exceeds that of national parks. The national parks' tally of 277 million visitors in 2002 is dwarfed by the 758 million people who visited state parks that year. Visitation rose at a rate between 1 and 2 percent annually for both federal and state parks, or about 79 and 130 million visits, respectively, each year since 1980 (see Figure 4.1). Given their closer proximity to constituents and the protected landscapes, state governments may be more advantageously located to provide outdoor recreation opportunities than their national counterparts.

Parks Past to Present

The first known American public parks were state parks. The Great Ponds and Province Lands of Massachusetts were set aside in 1641 (Myers and Green 1989, 3). As the nation began to take shape, some federal lands were ceded to the states for their protection. The Mariposa Grove and Yosemite Valley were placed under the jurisdiction of the state of California as parklands in 1864. Federal protection of parklands quickly followed, with Yellowstone designated the first national park in 1872.

Some of the earliest national parks make up what are today considered the crown jewels of the nation's park system. Yellowstone, Sequoia, Mount Rainier, and Glacier national parks, each designated near the beginning of the twentieth century, all provide visions of the natural wonders in America.

The history of these initial national parks reflects a peculiarity of the United States' expansion. Early visitors to the Yellowstone region realized the beauty of the area and the significance of its location, and some were able to capitalize on it through the creation of toll roads (Anderson and Leal 2001, 45). Investors in the Northern Pacific Railroad also perceived its value as a tourist attraction and potential source of passenger traffic. Seeking to build a line across the northern part of the country, the financiers funded an expedition to explore the region and its unique beauty. Indeed, it was just such reports from explorers to Congress that brought about national park consideration (Anderson and Leal 2001, 45).

A key institutional problem facing both railroad and toll road owners was the Homestead Act. Passed in 1862, the law limited the amount of acre-

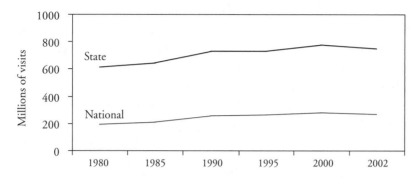

Figure 4.1. Millions of park visits

sources: National—Public Use Statistics Office, 2006, National Park Service, National Park System Visitation Report, online at http://www2.nature.nps.gov/stats, visited February 12, 2007. State—National Association of State Park Directors, various years, *Annual Information Exchange: State Park Statistical Data,* Tallahassee, FL.

age any one person could claim to 160 acres[2]—not much compared with the two million acres that now comprise Yellowstone National Park. At the time, state government was nonexistent in the region, which was still part of the Montana and Wyoming territories. Protecting all the newly found wonders in Yellowstone required an act of Congress.

Congress responded by designating Yellowstone the world's first national park. Precedent was set, and Yellowstone National Park was followed by the creation of five more national parks before the century's end. Whether encouraged by farsighted conservationists or forward-thinking entrepreneurs, the system of national parks grew rapidly to thirty-seven park units before an agency was created to manage them under a single umbrella.[3]

This government agency was designed to oversee the care and protection of the national parks, but many parks were still expected to provide their own operating funds through revenues. A number of the early units were highly unusual places and had reached a point where the tourist dollars generated were sufficient to cover operating expenditures. But political control over potential park revenues was soon imposed. The NPS was created in 1916, and in 1918 Congress mandated revenues from all parks be deposited in the national treasury.

Early on, it was recognized that national parks were meant to be unique, or at least unusual. The first director of the NPS, Stephen Mather, believed that many resources should be protected, but not all had the grandeur to be a national park (Myers and Green 1989, 4). Some areas, he believed, should be captured under state park systems, many of which were coming into fruition during the same era as the first national parks. In the early years, state parks were often near population centers, whereas most national parks were in remote areas of the West. Today, that distinction is blurred. National parks exist throughout the country, often neighboring state parks. Every state in the nation now has a state park system.

The demand for and interest in both state and national parklands has continued to grow. Unquestionably, more people are choosing to spend their recreational time outdoors, in visits to parks, forests, or other outdoor recreational areas. Nonetheless, park management agencies have been slow to respond to these demands. Park managers note that insufficient funds are their number one concern, yet few parks charge fees sufficient to cover park operating costs.[4] At the same time, acreage and management responsibility continue to expand.

The number of visitors to state parks continues to exceed that of their national counterparts, even though national parks cover more than six times the acreage of state parks. With a few exceptional additions (notably parklands in Alaska, such as Denali, Wrangell–St. Elias, and the Gates of the Arctic in 1980), acreage under the NPS has grown at a rate that is typically just less than one-half a percent per year. The national parks have added about 7 million acres since 1980. State park acreage has expanded at a faster rate, just less than 2 percent per year, though slower in absolute numbers, incorporating 4.2 million additional acres since 1980 (see Figure 4.2).

Thus, government agencies manage what will soon be more than 100 million acres of parkland, with little consideration given to reducing the

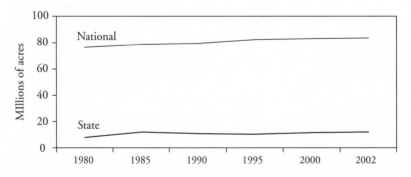

Figure 4.2. Millions of park acres

SOURCES: National—Public Use Statistics Office, 2006, National Park Service, National Park System Visitation Report, online at http://www2.nature.nps.gov/stats, visited February 12, 2007. State—National Association of State Park Directors, various years, *Annual Information Exchange: State Park Statistical Data*, Tallahassee, FL.

acreage under their control. While many industries have seen a move away from public sector control and deregulation (transportation, utilities, and communications, for example), where the environment is concerned, including parklands, government continues to be the major "provider." It is possible that the transfer of parkland management, from public to private control, or at least decentralization from federal to more local control, could improve stewardship and enhance the value in nature.

Should Parks Be Public?

How parks should best be managed in order to maximize the wealth of nature that they offer raises the question of state versus national park management, or some kind of devolution to more local control. At the same time, some may wonder why parks should be public anyway. Indeed, Milton Friedman was explicit about this issue in his famous book *Capitalism and Freedom* (1962). Although he agreed that some "neighborhood effects" justified city parks, he saw no reason for a national park in the West such as Yellowstone to be managed publicly: "Parks are an interesting example because they illustrate the difference between cases that can and cases that cannot be justified by neighborhood effects, and because almost everyone at first sight regards the conduct of National Parks as obviously a valid function of government. In fact, however, neighborhood effects may justify a city park; they do not justify a national park like Yellowstone or the Grand Canyon" (Friedman 1962, 31).

Friedman argued that it is easy to charge fees at destination parks where entry and exit points are limited. As a result, if citizens are interested in destination parks, private enterprise will have the incentive to provide them. In contrast, it is much more difficult to charge the beneficiaries to use a city park because there are almost inevitably many points of entry. Beneficiaries of the more local-type park include the park users, passersby, and nearby homeowners. It is hard to identify each person who gains value and harder yet to exclude any of them from receiving the benefit.

The opposing side of the debate is that even destination parks provide some public good amenities that are difficult to pay for through user fees. Indeed, the justification for public ownership of large-acreage parks stems not so much from the pleasure people get from visiting a park, but rather from the protection of natural wealth in those parks.

Parks, both state and national, are generally aimed at providing recreation for people today and in the future and protecting natural amenities.

The national parks have a well-defined purpose: "to conserve the scenery and the natural and historic objects and the wildlife therein and to provide for the enjoyment of the same in such manner and by such means as will leave them unimpaired for the enjoyment of future generations."[5] Though state parks differ widely in their mission statements, a recent survey indicates that the primary focus of state park systems is either recreation or natural resource protection, or both.[6]

Parklands provide some value to society that is difficult to capture in the marketplace. Even people who do not visit parks may still benefit from knowing that parks are being protected and will exist in the future for either themselves or their kin (see Boudreaux and Meiners 1998; Krutilla 1967). Indeed, most parklands are provided by the public sector, and this may indicate something inherently different about the production of parklands that is not present in the production of more typical goods. On the other hand, because public systems are usually provided to users at a price below cost, it is likely that they have stifled the private provision of parks.

Mammoth Onyx Cave, for example, is a private park that sits directly adjacent to Mammoth Cave National Park in Kentucky. The private owners used to offer cave tours similar to those in the Mammoth Cave before it gained national park status. Once Mammoth Cave was taken under the NPS umbrella, user fees were cut in half. Without similar government support, the neighboring private owners could not compete with the subsidized rate. Mammoth Onyx Cave is now known as Kentucky Down Under. To stay in business, the owners changed their emphasis from cave tours to an animal park with an Australian theme that differentiated them from the neighboring national park (Fretwell 1999b, 7).

Should Parks Be National?

Just as there is debate over the public nature of parks, there is debate as to whether parks should be owned and paid for by the federal government or more locally. Both state and national parks exist in almost every state of the nation (Delaware is the only state with no national park). Although each state has protected its own unique places, some provide benefits of a very local nature, while others are farther reaching. This same idea holds true across the national parks.

It can be argued that some of the crown jewels of the NPS provide some level of national importance. Yellowstone National Park, for example, is world renowned for both its beauty and its significance as the world's first national park. Other examples are the Statue of Liberty, Mount Rushmore, the Grand Canyon, and the Everglades. Each of these parks is generally held in high esteem with the American public, whether they have visited them or not. Take a moment to think of all the national parks you are aware of. How does that number compare with the nearly four hundred park units that exist?

Is there some benefit from the national provision of parklands? The argument is that citizens, nationwide, benefit, and it is difficult for a state or local agency or group to collect fees from all the beneficiaries across the nation.

The economic literature that defines the transaction costs involved with collective action helps address the possible need for public versus private park provision. In the terms of Steven Cheung, a firm may be defined as anything from a contractual relationship between two parties to a contract affecting the whole economy, such as a communist regime (1983, 17). The optimal size of a firm depends on the transaction costs (see also Anderson and Watson, 2008). A similar way of determining optimal size may be appropriate for park management. We now look at the potential benefits to be gained from the collective or government management of parks.

One of the difficult costs to measure with regard to a park or protected area is the actual value it provides to consumers. Because it is difficult to enforce payment from everyone who receives benefits, the private producer is likely to provide a quantity less than that desired by society.

An analogy of snow removal may help explain this. Which party takes responsibility for road clearing after a snowstorm largely depends on ownership, beneficiaries, and transaction costs. An individual who lives on a private drive may clear his or her own road or contract out with a second party to do the clearing. When the number of dwellings on a private drive increases, however, the cost of contracting will also rise. Together, homeowners must determine when and how the roads are going to be plowed and negotiate the terms of payment. If one homeowner decides not to pay and becomes a holdout, the other owners may decide to plow anyway for their own benefit. This would make the holdout a free rider, benefiting from the cleared drive without paying for it. The more homeowners there are, the more difficult it is to complete negotiations without holdouts. The purpose of homeowner associations and covenants is often to lower the cost of this kind of transaction. Hence, some collective action may be beneficial to provide snowplowing services because it can be negotiated at much lower transaction costs. The most effective level of action is the level of governance most closely associated with the beneficiaries.

It can be argued that the level of governance for parks should be managed in a similar fashion. Where exclusion is difficult, some governmental provision may be beneficial. This would be most efficient when the citizens paying the costs are the same as the citizens receiving the benefits. For efficient park management there seems to exist a positive relationship between the size of the region where beneficiaries live and more centralized management.

Think about the Statue of Liberty, a symbol of human liberty, but also of friendship between citizens of France and the United States. The sculpting and assembly costs of the statue were large, more than $500,000 in the mid-1880s (equivalent to about $9.5 million today). The entire tab was paid by the private sector. The statue's reconstruction in the United States nearly failed. While nearly all citizens benefit from its great symbolism and many who actually see it benefit from its beauty, there was no private mechanism to force all beneficiaries to pay. Hence, some beneficiaries donated generously to see the resurrection of the great statue, while others did not pay a dime. Until the final days before reconstruction, only about half of the necessary funds had been raised.[7]

In this situation, where there are many beneficiaries across a large geographical region, it is difficult to exclude citizens from the benefits, and it is difficult to force them to pay for the benefits. It is possible that more centralized control and collective action could help lower the cost of fundraising, force all beneficiaries to pay, and ensure that the public benefit of the park or statue is realized.

Costs of Collective Park Management

A notable problem of collective action is that it forces all individuals to pay whether they gain satisfaction from the action or not. So although government action may lower the cost of transactions, ensuring that all beneficiaries pay, it may go too far in charging many who don't benefit at all. Once the government takes over the provision of a good or service, the production decisions become political rather than market-based, and consumers have less influence in keeping the agency accountable.

In other words, government control has costs of its own that must be balanced with potential benefits. Unanimity is a problem because everybody must buy, which changes the production incentives. Government is not under much pressure to quickly respond to changing consumer demands; the exit route for government production is political, not economic. Management is slow to change and moves more closely with the tides of influential special interest groups than with consumer demand. Examples in the NPS abound where politicians have earmarked funds for their desired program while ignoring the wishes of park managers who, presumably, know more about the resources and what visitors want.

In one case, Montana's congressional delegation earmarked $3 million to restore two backcountry chalets in Glacier National Park (*USA Today* 1997). The chalets were used by less than 1 percent of park visitors, who must hike or ski to them between July and September. A few Montanans, however, let it be known that their restoration was of utmost importance. Save the Chalets, a nonprofit group, lobbied for the restoration. They were fortunate to catch the ear of the Montana congressional delegates because they were unable to raise their own funds for the project. One of the restoration's major expenses was a $1 million privy—a self-composting unit with a solar-powered generator to ensure proper composting throughout the year. Glacier's superintendent, on the other hand, had set his top priorities as visitor center improvement and road repair. These projects were unfunded.

Vying to gain votes and political support, politicians are eager to defer costs while showing off benefits such as new facilities and new parks or displaying their effectiveness at solving crises. Championing support for maintenance and repairs is not nearly as appealing or glamorous to politicians, so these essential areas are often neglected.

Tracking long-term stewardship in the national parks illustrates the distorted priorities. Sewer systems are failing in a number of national parks, historic structures are crumbling, roads are becoming dilapidated, and cultural dwellings are being destroyed. In Death Valley National Park the superintendent fears visitors may fall into portals created by gold rushers more than one hundred years ago, and buildings at Gettysburg National Historic Battlefield suffer from neglect because of years of low maintenance and repair. At the same time that Congress is providing dollars for new parks and new structures, many of the deferred maintenance problems are left unfunded until they become a crisis.

When a crisis arises, congressional representatives race to gain credit for allocating funds to the neglected resource. It was not until Yellowstone's aging sewer system spewed raw sewage into the park's trout streams that Congress came to its rescue. The Going-to-the-Sun Highway in Glacier

National Park was closed several times for safety concerns before Congress approved funding to examine the need for road renovations. Though funds are short for day-to-day maintenance, dollars flow unimpeded when high-profile cases can reap political rewards. Rather than investing capital in long-term maintenance and stewardship, Congress directs its attention to short-term projects with high visibility or constituent interest (see Leal and Fretwell 1997; Stroup and Goodman 1992).

Another political route for good visibility and constituent support is in the creation of new park units. When new areas are proposed for inclusion as a national park, the decision is based on the benefits politicians perceive to gain, rather than on the national significance of the area. Though local constituents may gain from the introduction of a new park unit, the additional value to taxpayers hundreds of miles away is negligible. These are often pork-barrel decisions. Numerous national parks are arguably of little national importance.

For example, Keweenaw National Historic Park in the company town of Quincy, Michigan, was established in honor of the copper mining industry. Adding the land and facilities to the NPS and funding the park's restoration have made for a nice local economic development project. With strong constituent support and logrolling in Congress, many similar areas have been added to the NPS roster without great consideration for their national significance. Says James Ridenour, former director of the NPS, a visit to Keweenaw would make a "nice tourist trip . . . but I still have doubts as to the national park stature" (Ridenour 1994, 84). Another park with questionable national stature is Steamtown National Historic Site, a park unit that provides a history of American and Canadian locomotives. As a local development project, it benefits the local economy more than the national park system (Ridenour 1994, 81).

The Presidio, an awesome piece of property at the end of the Golden Gate Bridge overlooking the Pacific Ocean in San Francisco, may be another example. Formerly a military post, it is now managed by the NPS. Buildings on the Presidio site are leased for residential and nonresidential uses. It does have a more natural component as well, including a saltwater marsh, forests, beaches, and coastal bluff. Arguably, at least the building sites could be more effectively managed under local contract than by the NPS. Theoretically, this should be the case, and in reality, the Presidio is a unique congressionally mandated experiment in which a local board, the Presidio Trust, has management control. This is a useful experiment in

devolving management responsibility. The NPS provides oversight, to ensure that management remains within the parameters outlined for national
parks. Nonetheless, although these areas and the many more like them have
local value, their national significance is less clear.

While disrepair plagues many of the crown jewels of the national park
system, NPS dollars flow into the development of new parks and facilities, spreading operating dollars even thinner. A new park in the nation's
capital, Georgetown Waterfront Park, is in the development stage of transforming an industrial area into a world-class park along the Potomac River.
The benefits to local citizens and visitors of the area are clear; the value to
the remaining taxpayers is not. Ridenour (1994, 88) believes that many
of the newer parks are designated more for their political pork than their
national significance. This is less likely to be true of a park with genuine
local or even state management.

Reliance on Appropriated Funds

Whether managed by the states or the national government, parks are normally supported by appropriated funds. This reliance on appropriated funds
can be considered another characteristic of collective action, and one that
imposes some severe costs.

Park managers depend on budgets provided by Congress or legislatures
for present and future funding. The inconsistency of funding from year to
year makes it impossible for managers to know whether projects will be
funded in the future; hence, they have less incentive to allocate funds to
long-term projects. Budgets may be fairly high one year, but an unexpected
event unrelated to parks, such as a natural or political disaster, could significantly reduce budgets the following year.

In return for the appropriated dollars, Congress and legislators often expect park revenues to be deposited in the general treasury. The result is a disconnect between money spent and money earned, making cost control an
abstract concept rather than a fiscal necessity. Between 1918 and 1993, nearly
all fee revenues earned in the national parks reverted to Washington, D.C.,
providing no added benefit to the park unit where they were collected.[8]
Hence, fee collection costs were covered with general appropriations that
could otherwise be spent elsewhere, and managers collecting fees were, in
effect, punished for generating revenues.

Legislation in 1993 allowed up to 15 percent of fee collections to be retained on-site to cover the costs of collection. This was an improvement, although the link between visitor demand and a park's budget was still missing. It was not until 1996 under the Fee Demonstration Program that the link between managers and visitors to the national parks was reestablished. Many state park systems made that link long ago.

Over time, park system budgets are becoming more reliant on nonappropriated funds. In both state and national parks, there are more user fees, and revenues as a share of total budgets are on the rise. Importantly, more of the revenues are being allowed to stay in the parks where they are generated.

The federal Recreational Fee Demonstration Program (Fee Demo) marked a turning, authorizing the NPS and other federal land management agencies to charge higher fees and keep most of those fees at the point of collection rather than sending them to the national treasury. Each of the participating areas is allowed to keep at least 80 percent of the fee receipts. The remaining 20 percent goes to the agency, to be allocated by the director.

Since inception of the program, NPS revenues from fees have doubled, reaching nearly $270 million. Though fee receipts still make up only a meager 12 percent of the operating budget, participating park managers have made good use of the funds. Projects using Fee Demo funds include rebuilding trails, erecting signs, restoring facilities, installing exhibits, repairing sewers, carrying out water quality and resource studies, and undertaking other deferred maintenance work.

State park systems have moved even further toward self-sufficiency, with far greater reliance on user fees. About 43 percent of all state park visits are fee visits, a number that has grown from about 31 percent in 1980 (Fretwell and Frost 2006). At the same time, revenues have grown from 25 percent of the operating budget in 1995 to 36 percent in 2003. These revenues, adjusted for inflation, have grown an average of 7 percent per year. More park systems are charging fees and are allowed to retain those collections in funds earmarked for use by the parks. The direct connection between user and manager encourages fees that are based on the cost to produce an amenity service and to enhance the amenity value.

At the same time that park fees are rising in both state and national parks, the number of visits to many of these parks is increasing. This would seem to challenge the law of demand, but it suggests two suppositions. First, the demand for parks and recreation appears to be growing faster than the fee adjustments. At the national level and in many state park systems, the legislature must permit fee changes. Market prices respond rapidly to changes in supply and demand, but park committees and politicians need time to agree on fee adjustments, and their decisions are politically influenced. Hence, it is likely that as demand grows, fee adjustments are slow to respond.

Second, it may also be true that the fees are enhancing the resource value, thus making the parks more attractive to visitors. When budgets are provided through political appropriations, there is little link between the consumer and producer. Politicians rather than park managers tend to direct decisions, as described above. But when visitor fees fund park management, managers have an incentive to improve what they offer consumers. Indeed, under Fee Demo park managers gloat about being able to use funds to enhance site quality.

Without question, many of the units participating in Fee Demo have improved the quality of recreation. In Natural Bridges National Monument, more than thirteen miles of trails have been repaired, making hikes more pleasant and protecting the area's fragile ecosystem (Fretwell 1999a, 20). Campgrounds in Mount Rainier National Park have begun using automated self-pay machines. The new machines accept both credit cards and cash, expanding the payment service that was previously cash only, at a lower cost. Alternative transportation has been included in several national parks. Scotts Bluff National Monument now provides a shuttle to the summit. Shuttles are also provided in Acadia, Zion, Grand Canyon, and Bryce Canyon national parks. An interpretive exhibit on slavery and emancipation has been added at Appomattox Court House National Historical Park (U.S. Department of the Interior 2003, 36).

It is clear that some state park managers are making the most of the retained revenues, too. In Alabama, the Monte Sano Lodge at Monte Sano State Park, a mountaintop retreat above the city of Huntsville, was recently refurbished to host meetings and weddings. Arizona state parks recently added a more challenging tour in the famous Kartchner Caverns. Demand for the longer tour has been high and has added a steady stream of revenues to the system budget. The Arizona park system has also been adding a number of cabins and yurts to meet the growing demand for park accommodations. Oregon park managers have developed sinking funds that retain a portion of accommodation revenues to be used for repairing and replacing those facilities.

Another illustration of how the increases in discretionary funds are being used comes from the new trend in both national and state park systems toward defining an inventory of existing resources, both natural and manmade. Although a basic inventory of infrastructure resources, including facilities and buildings, has long existed in most park systems, measurements are becoming more precise with regard to current conditions and future needs. In addition, park managers are beginning to inventory the natural resources and their current condition. Such a measure will provide a benchmark for stewardship of these resources. The NPS is beginning to use geographic information system (GIS) mapping to measure stewardship and existing conditions in national parks across the country. All state park systems surveyed are interested in completing a natural resource inventory, and eight have looked seriously at creating a natural resource database (Fretwell and Frost 2006). Although it will be years before the data are consistently available and comparable across landscapes, the inventory will provide new tools for measuring the wealth of nature and holding park managers accountable for their stewardship decisions.

The shift to greater reliance on user fees has helped decentralize park management. It has helped reduce the costs of collective action in our parks and brings them closer to maximizing the wealth of nature that they contain.

Nonetheless, the ideal for park management is not to maximize revenues, but to maximize the wealth of nature. Charging recreation fees provides an important link between park users and park managers. That users are willing to pay fees is a signal to managers about the desired recreational amenities. The fee signal includes the value of the pristine nature that some backcountry users may prefer, but it does not include similar desires for protection by individuals who will never visit the park or backcountry area. Recreation fees, then, must be used with some caution because they may emphasize the need for recreation services over the desire for knowing that pristine wilderness exists.

It is in this existence value that the collective nature of park management can help define parameters to protect areas where the desire for wilderness and other amenities is not readily observable through park use. Interestingly, this is also an area where some private organizations have begun to create a market niche.

The Private Niche

No state or national park system is going to be as responsive to visitors as a commercial or nonprofit organization. As commercial firms aim to make a profit, they pay close attention to the preferences of potential visitors.

Similarly, nonprofits must please members and funders to keep money flowing in. To be consistent with their overall mission, commercial enterprises and nonprofits must meet the desires of actual and potential visitors and donors.

It is good to know that commercial organizations and private nonprofits have not left the field as governments took over more and more parkland. As natural resource protection is becoming more highly valued and as public parklands begin to charge fees that better approximate costs, we should see entrepreneurs providing more private parkland protection. Already, it is evident that more nonprofit groups, clubs, associations, and for-profit firms are entering the market to supply conservation and complementary amenities.

The Nature Conservancy owns and manages nearly 15 million acres.[9] Their goal is to protect areas they have defined as critical wildlife habitat. Some of these lands also provide recreation for members, accommodations, or leases for grazing and other commodity uses deemed appropriate on the landscape. Similarly, the National Audubon Society owns land that is reserved to protect habitat for birds and other wildlife. Again, members may visit some of the lands for bird watching and hiking.

Other groups, too, have spent years in the land conservation field. The Sand County Foundation and North Maine Woods provide conservation and recreation opportunities. Even some for-profit firms are moving toward providing recreation and conservation amenities if they perceive a return on the investment. International Paper Company historically managed 10 million acres of forestland primarily for the production of wood products. Revenues generated from hunting and recreation leases changed the way they did business. To enhance wildlife habitat they reduced the size of the typical clear-cut and left standing trees as stream buffers along waterways and as corridors for wildlife to travel.

In Texas, where there is little public land (97 percent of the land base is private), most wildlife habitat and hunting opportunities are provided on private lands that have fees and lease agreements. With nearly a million hunters in the state, these contracts and the incentives to enhance game habitat are commonplace (Leal and Grewell 1999). The majority of these leases focus on the quality of the hunt, providing exclusive lease rights to small groups of hunters or "clubs." This both reduces congestion, enhancing the hunting experience, and protects the resource by limiting harvest and pressure on the land.

It is becoming evident that private landowners can heighten the quality of a hunt by reducing hunter numbers per acre and increasing the number of trophy-sized animals through habitat enhancement. This has made fee hunting opportunities competitive in states like Montana where hunters have ready access to public lands with no additional fee.[10]

These examples of private landowners protecting and enhancing wildlife habitat are tantamount to the public lands that were intended to provide the same. While many private landowners in states like Texas and Montana provide commercial hunting operations, many nonprofits, like the Audubon Society, The Nature Conservancy, and Defenders of Wildlife, have been successful protecting habitat for songbirds, waterfowl, wolves, and other species.

Though some of these private entities own and manage conservation areas, financial limitations make it impossible for these groups, or the federal government, to own all areas of concern. Alternative methods to land ownership are successfully protecting a variety of wildlife habitat. These innovative solutions include partnerships and contractual agreements between private landowners and other parties, such as nonprofits or governmental agencies interested in conservation.

Conservation easements, for example, provide a tool for land trusts and some government entities to define some of the use rights on a parcel of private land through an agreement with the landowner. Easements may ensure the protection of wetlands, restrict or prohibit development, require continued agricultural use, or place limits on timber harvest (see Chapter 8).

In addition to conservation easements, the Delta Waterfowl Foundation has created another tool to protect waterfowl nesting habitat. Using donations from waterfowl enthusiasts, the foundation pays farmers in the midwestern United States and Canada to maintain and restore wetlands and uplands that provide nesting grounds and cover for ducks. Through this Adopt a Pothole Program, Delta Waterfowl has helped enhance waterfowl habitat since 1991.[11]

Defenders of Wildlife has also been creative in finding solutions to help protect habitat and species in need. To garner support for the 1996 reintroduction of wolves into Yellowstone and to ensure their survival, Defenders of Wildlife offered to compensate ranchers for livestock lost as a result of wolf predation. The Wolf Compensation Trust, as it became known, is financed by private donors; hence those who support wolf recovery help pay the costs. Defenders of Wildlife has compensated ranchers in excess of $500,000 since the initiation of the program.[12] Wolf reintroduction into the northern Rocky Mountain region has been so successful that the U.S.

Fish and Wildlife Service is considering removing the wolf from the federal threatened and endangered species list.

Federal agencies also provide a multitude of conservation incentives to encourage private landowners to protect critical habitat. Many federal programs provide direct payment to farmers and landowners. The Conservation Reserve Program (CRP), for example, pays farmers to convert cropland to vegetative cover. The Farm and Ranch Lands Protection Program uses federal dollars for purchasing development rights that encourage continued agricultural use. The Wetland Reserve Program helps finance landowners to convert cropland for wetland restoration. The Landowner Incentive Program supplies funding and technical assistance for landowners who protect habitat for at-risk species. The Private Stewardship Program offers grants and assistance for private conservation efforts that protect critical wildlife habitat. Although the benefits of these programs may be widespread, increasing nesting habitat for migratory waterfowl, for example, some of the benefits and many of the costs may be of a more local nature, hence better provided at a more local level. CRP, for example, while enhancing duck habitat has also contributed to lower agricultural output in some regions and hence a declining demand for inputs, placing a disproportionate burden on local communities (Sullivan et al. 2004). The use of federal subsidies can promote conservation that many Americans desire, but secondary consequences must also be considered. Solutions created at the local level and paid for by those who receive the greatest benefits are likely to be more efficient than federal-level solutions designed by agencies that pay little of the cost.

The private entities discussed provide examples of the most devolved level of park and conservation management. These institutions are quick to respond to consumer demands—they will go out of business otherwise. They also avoid many of the problems associated with political management and special interest influence. Some free riders likely exist even here, but certainly, some citizens gain value in knowing that The Nature Conservancy, Audubon Society, International Paper Company, and others are protecting habitat and conserving nature even if they are not paying members or users.

Conclusion

State and national parks cover nearly 100 million acres across the United States. Some of these parks have national value; the value of others is more local in nature. Parks of national significance provide some benefits to citizens on the whole, and as a result, management at a national level can help lower the costs of free riders. But federal management comes with its own costs, distorted incentives, and political influence.

Most parks, both state and national, are more local in nature, with the bulk of benefits being received by people in the surrounding region or town. As such, these parks are better managed at a more local level. This reduces the costs of bureaucratic management and political influence and raises accountability to a public that is more aware of the local park conditions. Decentralized management can often enhance the wealth of nature.

Unfortunately, it is unlikely that any national parks will be devolved to state authority given the current political winds. It is encouraging, however, that at both the state and national levels, park institutions are adjusting over time, albeit slowly. The link between managers and consumers is becoming stronger as fees are being retained on-site. The evidence indicates that this is providing greater quality recreational and park sites. It is also encouraging that there is greater private provision of park amenities.

As long as park managers are confident that they will continue to be able to use fee receipts, they are likely to invest more toward enhancing park value. These managers, who know the deferred maintenance and infrastructure problems that exist within the parks and depend on user fees for operations, want to whittle away at the maintenance backlog that politicians have long ignored. Many park user fees are being invested in infrastructure to help make visitors more comfortable and protect resources.

Though state park managers cite funding as the number one park concern, and park-generated revenues consistently increase available funding, not a single park manager surveyed advocated total self-sufficiency in state park systems. Indeed, if parks are providing public goods, there is reason to believe that some public funding should support their management. The true value of the public goods provided is difficult to measure. Nonetheless, the rise in privately protected park and conservation lands and the growing link between beneficiaries and producers are helping to lower costs while enhancing the overall wealth of nature. Many parks, state and national, can continue to benefit if park management is further decentralized, the influence and cost of political decisions is lowered, and the power of the consumer is increased.

Notes

1. Government Land Ownership, the National Wilderness Institute, data on file with author.

2. This was expanded to 640 acres in 1877 under the Desert Land Act.

3. See Anderson and Leal (1997), 24, for a discussion of the profit motive for the creation of many early national parks.

4. In 2004 the Property and Environment Research Center (PERC) completed a survey, "Funding in the State Parks," of the fifty state park systems. The response rate was 62 percent (thirty-one states). Every respondent noted insufficient funds as their major concern.

5. National Park Service Organic Act 16, online at http://www.nps.gov/legacy/organic-act.htm, visited July 3, 2007.

6. Data collected in PERC's 2004 Funding in the State Parks survey.

7. American Park Network, History of the Statue of Liberty, online at http://www.americanparknetwork.com/parkinfo/sl/history/liberty.html, visited March 9, 2005.

8. Several legislative reforms have allowed revenues to be deposited into a special treasury account available for appropriation to the parks. Congress and the Office of Management and Budget, however, have historically used these accounts as an offset to lower appropriations (see Mackintosh 1983).

9. The Nature Conservancy, How We Work, online at http://www.nature.org/aboutus/howwework/conservationmethods/privatelands/, visited March 23, 2005.

10. Montana is the fourth largest state in the nation, and one-third of it is under federal or state ownership.

11. Delta Waterfowl Foundation, Adopt A Pothole, online at http://www.deltawaterfowl.org/ddp/aap.php, visited October 28, 2005.

12. The Bailey Wildlife Foundation Wolf Compensation Trust, online at http://www.defenders.org/wildlife/wolf/wolfcomp.pdf, visited October 31, 2005.

References

Anderson, Terry L., and Donald R. Leal. 1997. *Enviro-Capitalists: Doing Good While Doing Well*. Lanham, MD: Rowman & Littlefield.

———. 2001. *Free Market Environmentalism*. New York: Palgrave.

Anderson, Terry L., and Reed Watson. 2008. Environmental Federalism: The Optimal Locus of Endangered Species Authority. In *Endangered Species Act and Federalism: Effective Species Conservation Through Greater State Commitment*, ed. K. Arha and B. H. Thompson. Washington, DC: Resources for the Future.

Boudreaux, Donald J., and Roger E. Meiners. 1998. Existence Value and Other of Life's Ills. In *Who Owns the Environment?* ed. Peter J. Hill and Roger E. Meiners. Lanham, MD: Rowman & Littlefield, 153–185.

Cheung, Steven N. 1983. The Contractual Nature of the Firm. *Journal of Law and Economics* 26 (April): 1–22.

Fretwell, Holly Lippke. 1999a. Forests: Do We Get What We Pay For? *Public Lands Report II*. Bozeman, MT: PERC, July.

———. 1999b. *Paying to Play: The Fee Demonstration Program*. PERC Policy Series PS-17. Bozeman, MT: PERC, December.

———. 2000. Federal Estate: Is Bigger Better? *Public Lands Report III*. Bozeman, MT: PERC, May.

Fretwell, Holly Lippke, and Kimberly Frost. 2006. *State Parks' Progress Toward Self-Sufficiency*. Online at http://www.perc.org/perc.php?id=833. Visited July 3, 2007.

Friedman, Milton. 1962. *Capitalism and Freedom*. Chicago: University of Chicago Press.

Krutilla, John V. 1967. Conservation Reconsidered. *American Economic Review* 57 (September): 777–786.

Leal, Donald R., and Holly Lippke Fretwell. 1997. *Back to the Future to Save Our Parks*. PERC Policy Series PS-10. Bozeman, MT: PERC, June.

Leal, Donald R., and J. Bishop Grewell. 1999. *Hunting for Habitat: A Practical Guide for State-Landowner Partnerships*. Bozeman, MT: PERC.

Mackintosh, Barry. 1983. *Visitor Fees in the National Park System: A Legislative and Administrative History*. Washington, DC: National Park Service.

Myers, Phyllis, and Sharon N. Green. 1989. *State Parks in a New Era*. Washington, DC: Conservation Foundation.

Ridenour, James M. 1994. *The National Parks Compromised*. Merryville, IN: ICS Books.

Stroup, Richard L., and Sandra L. Goodman. 1992. Property Rights, Environmental Resources, and the Future. *Harvard Journal of Law & Public Policy* 15 (Spring): 427–454.

Sullivan, Patrick, Daniel Hellerstein, Leroy Hansen, Robert Johansson, Steven Koenig, Ruben Lubowski, William McBride, David McGranahan, Michael Roberts, Stephen Vogel, and Shawn Bucholtz. 2004. The Conservation Reserve Program. *Economic Implications for Rural America*. Agricultural Economic Report No. AER834, October.

U.S. Department of the Interior. 2003. *Recreational Fee Demonstration Program, Progress Report to Congress Fiscal Year 2002*. Online at http://www.nps.gov/feedemo/reports/2002annual.pdf. Visited March 23, 2005.

USA Today. 1997. Costly Outhouses Monuments to Red Tape. December 15.

PART THREE

Property Rights
to Facilitate Change

CHAPTER FIVE

Homegrown Property Rights for the Klamath Basin

TERRY L. ANDERSON AND LAURA E. HUGGINS

> Practical people who live in the Klamath Basin are developing homegrown political entities. . . . They are trying to solve local and regional problems within a framework of federal and state regulations, using local expertise.
>
> WILLIAM KITTREDGE, *Balancing Water*

In May of 2001, farmers in the Klamath Basin of southern Oregon and northern California symbolically defied a federal ban on irrigation by dumping buckets of water into the bone dry "A" Canal. An estimated crowd of thirteen thousand people from all walks of life gathered to show support for the farmers passing fifty buckets, one representing each state, along a mile-long line. The crowd cheered as Jess Prosser, an eighty-five-year-old Tule Lake homesteader, dipped out the first bucket of water from Lake Ewauna in Klamath Falls, Oregon, and poured the water into a bucket held by his son, John. Waiting to pass it along the line was John's six-year-old son James. Bucket brigades have been a symbol of community action against threatened disaster throughout the history of the American West. People of the Klamath Basin who farm for a living consider a lack of water a disaster threatening their livelihoods.

Environmentalists also view the Klamath Basin as a disaster, but in their opinion it is because farmers have been diverting too much water for too long. Scientists have cautioned for years that salmon would be wiped out if the Klamath River's water volume did not double and have said that the sucker fish in Upper Klamath Lake also need more water. The potential impact on the fish brings local Indian tribes into the conflict, too, as the Klamath Tribes have relied on fishing as a way of life for hundreds of years.

The tensions in the watershed are exacerbated when the rains dry up and drought sets in, as happened in 2001. The root cause of the problems, however, is not the finite amount of water, but the uncertainty over who has what rights to that water. Who has first rights to water when there is not enough to meet all the demands—farmers who have prior appropriation water rights, irrigators who have contracts for water delivery from the Bureau of Reclamation, Native Americans who have treaty rights for fishing and hunting, or environmentalists who claim water for fish species under the Endangered Species Act? It is this question that has farmers, environmentalists, Indian tribes, and government agencies locked in a battle in the Klamath region.

Until property rights to the water are settled, the battle will rage on. The Oregon courts have announced that the time has come for water adjudication (the process by which water rights are verified, documented, and quantified) in the Klamath Basin. This process, however, is expected to take years. In the meantime, community involvement and cooperation from the basin's water interests could create greater regional control and provide solutions that allow the various players to avoid negative-sum games as they fight over the water.

This chapter examines the potential for local, market-based solutions to incrementally resolve conflicts in the Klamath Basin. It was stimulated by forums organized by the Property and Environment Research Center (PERC) in March and June of 2004. These forums gathered a diverse set of key players from the Klamath region in an effort to discover small steps that might lead to positive outcomes for the various interests in the basin. The people assembled focused on the potential for resolving the question of who has what rights and recognized that this could be achieved at the local level where the actors might "stipulate not adjudicate." With rights stipulated, interested parties have the potential to cooperate in finding win-win solutions for water reallocation among the competing uses rather than wait for rights to be legislated or adjudicated from afar. Such solutions could create reallocations of water, allowing parties to make incremental changes instead of all-or-nothing adjustments of the type that occur when the water is shut off to farmers or streams are left dry. This approach offers a commonsense solution for the Klamath Basin and for communities facing similar shifts in values derived from Mother Nature's assets.

Background

The Klamath watershed is a broad valley extending from the eastern foot-hills of the Cascade Range and Oregon's portion of the Northern Great Basin into the Modoc Plateau in California (see Map 5.1). The basin is classified as high desert, characterized by hot, dry summers and wet, cold winters. The majority of water to the area comes from snowmelt.

Despite the desertlike conditions in the region, an oasis of lakes, rivers, and marshes teams with wildlife. The basin is situated at the convergence

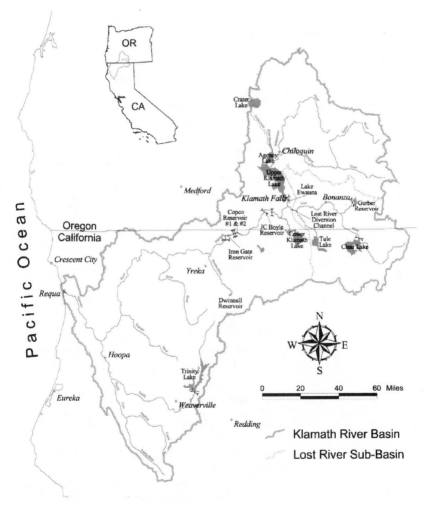

Map 5.1. Klamath River Basin. Compiled by M. Neuman, USBR Klamath Basin Area Office, 10/97.

of the migratory routes of numerous bird species and serves as a critical component of the Pacific Flyway. It is recognized as supporting one of the largest concentrations of waterfowl and the largest wintering population of bald eagles in North America.

For more than one hundred years, settlers, homesteaders, and their descendants have defied the desert by transforming lakes and marshes into farms and pastures. Under the 1902 Reclamation Act (see Table 5.1),

TABLE 5.1

Major water-related events in the Upper Klamath Basin

1826	Trapping for the fur trade lured the first whites to the area as documented by the journal of Peter Skene Ogden of Hudson's Bay Co. The most recent principal inhabitants of the Tule Lake Basin before the arrival of the whites were the Modoc Indians.
1846	Captain John C. Fremont arrived at the shore of Tule Lake on a survey and scouting mission (although technically the land was "Mexican land").
1864	The United States and Klamath and Modoc tribes enter into a treaty establishing the Klamath Reservation.
1902	The Reclamation Act was signed into law by President Theodore Roosevelt. As a result of the law, the Klamath Reclamation Project, an ambitious plan involving three lakes, two major rivers, and an interconnecting network of constructed canals would later be created.
1905	The Klamath Reclamation Project was established with the aim of converting much of the marshy Klamath Lake and Lost River system to agricultural land and wildlife refuges.
1908	Lower Klamath National Wildlife Refuge established.
1917	First project lands opened to homesteaders.
1928	Tule Lake and Upper Klamath Lake national wildlife refuges established.
1948	Final homestead lands distributed.
1957	Klamath River Basin Compact established by Congress to deal with water resource issues in the basin.
1975	Klamath Basin adjudication begins the process of quantifying pre-1909 water rights.
1988	Lost River and shortnose suckers listed as endangered under the Endangered Species Act.
1997	Southern Oregon and California wild Coho salmon listed as threatened under the Endangered Species Act.
2001	Bureau of Reclamation informs project irrigators that water from the Upper Klamath Lake will not be available for irrigation deliveries or wildlife refuges during the 2001 growing season (later releases 40,000 acre-feet of water for irrigation deliveries and 26,000 for the refuges).
2002	Approximately 34,000 salmon die in the Klamath River after full irrigation deliveries in one of the largest adult fish die-offs in Western U.S. history.
2005	The Bureau of Reclamation announces implementation of the 2005 Water Bank for the Klamath Basin. The water bank consists of several programs, including on- and off-project storage, groundwater pumping, and dry-land operation.

the states of California and Oregon ceded lake and wetland areas of the Klamath Basin to the federal government for the purpose of draining and "reclaiming" the land for agricultural homesteading. The act laid the groundwork for transforming an area that was once described as "sunbaked prairie and worthless swamps" into productive farmlands. To do this, the Bureau of Reclamation appropriated all unclaimed waters in the basin, and on February 9, 1905, Congress officially authorized the project for the purpose of luring homesteaders to the region with the promise of cheap land and water.

The Klamath Reclamation Project consists of three reservoirs that store approximately 1,095,000 acre-feet of water in the Klamath and Lost River basins. The project included building seven dams, eighteen canals, forty-five pumping plants, and more than fourteen hundred miles of canals and drains that provide service to water users. The water in the basin is "incredibly managed," according to William Kittredge; it "goes up and down and all around" (quoted in Clarren 2001). The project provides water to about 1,400, totaling approximately 210,000 acres. Furthermore, yearly agricultural output for the upper Klamath Basin averages approximately $320 million, which helps fuel the local economy (Sorte and Weber 2001). The project also provides water to nearly 20,000 acres of national wildlife refuge (Bureau of Reclamation 2004).

Crisis in 2001

In recent years, the drought-prone Klamath watershed has experienced a perpetual crisis over competing demands for water. After near-record drought struck the region in 2001, the Klamath project "water allocation decision" was announced. The decision stated that, on the basis of the biological opinions and the requirements of the Endangered Species Act, no water would be available from Upper Klamath Lake to supply the farmers of the Klamath Reclamation Project. The shutoff of irrigation to most of the fourteen hundred farms on the project was designed to fulfill demands for the shortnose and Lost River suckers in the Upper Klamath Lake and Coho salmon in the Klamath River.

Farmers and ranchers, who accounted for more than 90 percent of the water withdrawals, fought back. At one point the tensions were so high that armed federal marshals were brought in to guard the headgate once used to divert irrigation water. Farmers claimed to have lost an estimated $157 million that season (Hathaway and Welch 2001). Another dry year followed in 2002, but this time federal agencies chose to provide full irrigation deliveries at the expense of fish and wildlife and suppressed warnings of ecological disaster from biologists. The grisly images of dead salmon clogging the Klamath River—broadcast across the country—followed soon after.

The Klamath Basin conflict is ongoing. None of the aggrieved parties—tribes, farmers, environmentalists, government agencies, or even the wildlife—has come out a clear winner in the battle. A series of court cases, however, has determined that (for the present) basin water will be allocated as follows: first to meet the needs of endangered species, second to meet the treaty rights of local tribes and the wildlife on which they depend, third to meet the demands of farmers in the Klamath project, and fourth to meet the needs of wildlife refuges that depend on farm runoff for much of their water.

Who Claims What?

The lineup for rights to water in the Klamath Basin commenced soon after the reclamation program began. Long-term competition for water has severely strained relationships in this high-desert valley. The various interests within the watershed are all vying for what they consider to be their fair share of Klamath Lake and Klamath River water.

In Oregon, like most other western states, water is allocated under the prior appropriation doctrine, which means that the first person to claim and divert water from a stream is the last to be shut off in times of low stream flows. During a drought, the water rights holder with the oldest priority date can demand that his or her water right is honored regardless of the effect on junior users. The prior appropriation doctrine has governed water law in Oregon since 1909 when passage of the first unified water code introduced state control over water use. Before then, water users depended on themselves or local courts to defend their rights to water (Oregon Water Resources Commission and Department 1999).

One of the key problems in the region is that water claims before 1909 have not yet been adjudicated. The formal adjudication process for the basin began in 1975. Approximately seven hundred claims were filed, and about fifty-six hundred contests were submitted to oppose those claims. The contests have been referred to the state Central Hearing Panel, where the proceedings are ongoing (Hathaway and Welch 2001).

NATIVE AMERICANS

Further complicating the crisis in the watershed are the claims held by the Klamath Indians (primarily the Klamath, Modoc, and Snake tribes). On the basis of treaties signed in the 1800s and the 1908 Winters Doctrine (see *Winters v. United States*), the U.S. government is required to protect tribal fishing, hunting, gathering, and water rights. Indian water rights are considered to date from "time immemorial," meaning they predate and have priority over any other water rights.

Although the Klamath Tribes' Indian reservation was officially terminated by the Klamath Termination Act of 1954, the tribes' right to hunt, fish, and gather food on former reservation lands has been legally secured through a series of court cases (see Hood 1972). In 1974, the U.S. Court of Appeals in *Kimball v. Callahan* held that the Klamath Tribes, despite losing land under the Termination Act, retained treaty rights to hunt, trap, and fish—free of state regulations.

Another landmark decision involving water rights for the Klamath watershed, *United States of America and the Klamath Indian Tribe v. Ben Adair* (1984), determined that the Klamath Indians have a right to as much water on reservation lands as they "need" in order to protect their hunting and fishing rights. But how much water is enough? The tribes continue to press for clarification over their water rights. In the latest round of the *Adair* litigation, the court held in *United States v. Adair* (2002) that the tribes had the right to support a "moderate living" standard by way of fishing and hunting. "We want the basic ability to feed our families—no different than the farmers," said Allen Foreman, chairman of the Klamath Tribes, at the 2004 PERC forum. The state of Oregon has the hefty task of trying to decide what this means as it sorts out the heap of claims to the basin water (Meiners and Kosnik 2003).

Although court rulings have upheld the Klamath tribal rights, the adjudication process has yet to quantify those rights. As Jeff Mitchell, former chairman of the Klamath Tribes, stated at the PERC forum, "The water adjudication process is a zero-sum game with only a narrow focus on winners and losers." Mitchell believes that "negotiations, framed and controlled by the basin's water interests, will allow for far greater regional control and a solution sensitive to all interests' concerns."

FEDERAL AGENCIES

Federal laws established at various times under various conditions have laid the legal basis for conflicting claims to the region's limited supply of water. Adding fuel to the fire is the web of regulatory agencies (with assorted missions) trying to manage the watershed. The administrative entities operating in the Klamath Basin include the U.S. Fish and Wildlife Service (FWS), Bureau of Reclamation (BOR), Forest Service, Bureau of Indian Affairs, Bureau of Land Management, National Marine Fisheries Service (NMFS), and even the National Park Service (Crater Lake). These agencies often work at cross-purposes. The BOR, for example, is charged with managing the project to satisfy everyone's water needs, the FWS must manage for the two species of sucker, and the NMFS is responsible for the health of the salmon.

Federal claims to water come from a variety of sources, which contribute to uncertainties within the basin. The Reclamation Act of 1902 states that federal projects should defer to state law with respect to water rights. Yet in 1905, the BOR claimed all available water in the Klamath and Lost rivers for the Klamath project. Because prior appropriation rights were not quantified at the time, this leads to the question of how much water was available in 1905 (Meiners and Kosnik 2003).

The Klamath River Basin Compact of 1957 (see Table 5.1) was designed to alleviate this historical conflict. Oregon and California created the compact, which went forward with the consent of the United States. The compact established a hierarchical priority of use for water appropriations: (1) domestic use, (2) irrigation use, (3) recreational use, including use for fish and wildlife, (4) industrial use, and (5) generation of hydroelectric power. The goal of this arrangement is to better manage the resources in order to reduce the causes of controversy over water distribution and use. The compact seemed to be minimizing conflicts in the basin. Then along came the Endangered Species Act (ESA).

In 1988, the FWS listed the shortnose and Lost River suckers as endangered under the ESA. In 1997, southern Oregon and northern California coastal Coho salmon were listed as threatened. Listing under the ESA sets into motion a cascade of legal steps designed to promote a species' survival and recovery. As the Klamath farmers discovered, the ESA trumps all other water claims. When a species is listed, "critical habitat" is defined and a "recovery plan" is promulgated. The ESA also authorizes the purchase of habitat, prohibits federal agencies from engaging in actions that might jeopardize a listed species, and prohibits individuals from "taking" the species.

Section seven of the act prohibits federal agencies from engaging in any activity that will "jeopardize" the continued existence of a species and requires agencies to consult with either the FWS or NMFS if a harm might occur. The U.S. Supreme Court has held that the ESA is substantive and the duty to prevent jeopardy is absolute.[1]

Long before the ESA was implemented, the federal government was claiming water for two federal wildlife refuges in the Klamath watershed. A year after the Klamath project headgates opened, President Theodore Roosevelt created the nation's first waterfowl refuge on Lower Klamath Lake, and in 1928 the Tule Lake National Wildlife Refuge was established. The wildlife refuges have federal reserved water rights to the amount of water that was unappropriated at the time of their creation and was needed to fulfill the purpose of the refuges. Originally intended for the creation of agricultural homesteads, the reclaimed lands surrounding the wetlands in the national wildlife refuges have been used on a lease basis by agriculturalists.

Although other refuges around the country allow for farming, the setup in the basin is unique because of a 1964 act of Congress specific to the Klamath watershed. The Kuchel Act established and defined the purposes of the refuges "to be dedicated to wildlife conservation . . . for the major purpose of water fowl management, but in full consideration to optimum agricultural use that is consistent therewith" (U.S. Fish and Wildlife Service 1997). The act specifies that 25 percent of the land can be used for row crops, and the other 75 percent can be used for cereal grains and hay. The lease lands make up 10 percent of the acres in the Klamath Reclamation Project. Ron Cole, manager of the Klamath National Wildlife Refuge Complex, explained that the Tule Lake Refuge "is joined with farming by the 1964 Kuchel Act. . . . The refuge wants to help find solutions in the basin. There are 200,000 acres in the six federal refuges in the basin, and we are part of the community and the neighborhood" (Cole 2004).

IRRIGATORS

Under authority of the 1902 Reclamation Act, the BOR entered into contracts with various irrigation districts. The water project beneficiaries were required to repay the federal government for some of the costs incurred for the project in exchange for the delivery and use of project water. The Klamath project has a relatively good repayment history—irrigators have paid off approximately 75 percent of the subsidized costs. To farmers and ranchers this repayment record, along with nearly a century of uninterrupted delivery of water, implies that they own the project and are entitled to the water it provides. "We have overcome many obstacles throughout the years, but without this water, this will be the end of a way of life and an entire community," said Jess Prosser, who homesteaded on the Klamath project. "My two sons are now struggling to save the family farm. . . . I want the government to honor the contract that promised me and my heirs water rights forever. This land is our life" (quoted in Jasper 2004).

But what rights do the irrigators actually have? In many cases they began diverting water before there was a formal government to record their claims. With a small number of users in a closely knit community, neighbors knew who claimed what. As communities and demands on scarce resources have grown, however, conflicts over appropriate use have increased (see Anderson and Snyder 1997).

The water shutoff in 2001 led affected irrigators to sue on the grounds that their water was taken without due process and just compensation. The federal district court determined in *Kandra v. United States* that the irrigators' rights were subservient to the requirements of the ESA and the tribal rights (Meiners and Kosnik 2003). The situation became desperate for farmers. "I'm a survivor at this point," said Steve Kandra, whose family has farmed in the basin since the early 1900s. "I had to cover three generations of equity. I had to get the necessary loans and reassure the bankers. We are on our last run" (quoted in Pokarney 2002).

The irrigators, however, may have a claim for monetary damages against the United States for losses resulting from nondelivery of contract water. In *Tulare Lake Basin Water Storage District, et al. v. United States* (2001) the U.S. Court of Federal Claims held that the United States had taken plaintiffs' property without just compensation. This case concerns the delta smelt and winter-run Chinook salmon—two species of fish determined to be in jeopardy of extinction. The efforts by the FWS to protect the fish by restricting water outflows in California's primary water distribution system brought together, and arguably into conflict, the ESA and California's century-old regime of private water rights.

Discovering the proper balance between the ESA and the established water rights system lies at the heart of this case. The plaintiff had contracts to receive specified amounts of water from federal water projects. The BOR reduced the amount of water it delivered to the plaintiff in compliance with the ESA for salmon and smelt. The court found that the contracts conferred on the irrigators a right to use some quantity of water[2] and that the exclusive use of those rights for a listed species resulted in a physical invasion of property for which compensation is owed under the Fifth Amendment.

Emboldened in part by the Tulare Basin court decision, Klamath irrigators filed a lawsuit to compensate farmers for water restrictions caused by endangered species concerns. However, on August 31, 2005, a U.S. Court of Federal Claims judge rejected the major arguments of Klamath Basin farmers, who sought $1 billion from the federal government after regulators virtually cut off irrigation water in the middle of the 2001 growing season to protect endangered fish. The judge held open the door for further arguments by both sides on the legal debate over whether U.S. officials breached a contract duty to provide water to the farmers. Although the judge did say the irrigators may have a claim to water, he also said they "face an uphill battle" (quoted in U.S. Water News Online 2005b). The appeal process is ongoing.

ENVIRONMENTALISTS

New to the demand equation for water in the Klamath watershed are environmental uses. People across the globe are pushing for improved river flows and cleaner water. In fact, never before has the demand for environmental uses of water been so high (Landry and Phoenix 2003). In the 1990s environmental groups correctly sensed an opportunity to increase water flow in the basin to protect wildlife. Several groups sued the BOR for violating the ESA by not consulting with the NMFS before diverting water from the PacifiCorp dam to irrigators. In the spring of 2001, the court sided with fishers in *Pacific Coast Federation of Fishermen's Assns. v. U.S. Bureau of Reclamation* and issued an injunction against certain water deliveries by the bureau to irrigators (Meiners and Kosnik 2003).

Conservationists' primary tool for claiming water rights thus far has been the courts' relying on the ESA as grounds for having a stake in water allocation. For example, three environmental groups unhappy with the government's decision not to list the green sturgeon (a fish found in the lower Klamath River system) as an endangered species notified the federal government that they plan to sue to reverse the decision. The lawsuit is part of a larger strategy to pressure the government to devote more water to fish in the Klamath River, rather than diverting it for agricultural irrigation. Dan Keppen, then executive director of the Klamath Water Users Association, said in a letter to the editor of the Klamath Falls newspaper that these actions are dedicated to forcing farmers out of the basin and "this lawsuit is just another example of this" (Keppen 2003).

Not all environmental groups turn to the courts to establish water rights. The Nature Conservancy is showing leadership to conservation groups through its offer to make water available for fish and farmers in the basin. The Nature Conservancy and the BOR have entered a joint partnership to advance long-term wetland restoration efforts on conservancy property adjacent to the shores of Upper Klamath Lake and to make additional water available from the Williamson River. The group is pushing to reach a workable resolution to the competing water demands. The Klamath Basin work plan provides incentives for farmers to increase the efficiency of their operations and benefits the ecosystem at the same time. "We're encouraged by the focus on voluntary incentives for Klamath Basin farmers," said Mark Stern, the conservancy's Klamath Basin director in Oregon. "Private landowners are key to long-term conservation in the basin" (Nature Conservancy 2003).

It's the Rents!

The new layers of national control that came attached to the ESA sent tremors through the Klamath region. Local billboards in 2001 read "Stop the Rural Genocide," "Call 911, Some Sucker Stole My Water," "Federally Created Disaster Area," and "Feed the Feds to the Fish."

April 6, 2001, has been etched in the minds of basin farmers and residents as a day similar to the sneak attack on Pearl Harbor. "April 6, 2001 is a day which will live in infamy, a day when those in the Klamath Basin Project and their descendants were stripped of all irrigation water," said third-generation farmer Marshall Staunton. "They became part of history as the first bureau irrigators to completely lose an entire irrigation water supply. How they lost the water our nation promised can be summed up in three letters: E.S.A." (quoted in Souza 2001).

Skepticism of the federal government remained despite the president's budget for 2005, which included $105 million for "balancing fish against farms in the Klamath Basin." "Constantly losing more and more of our water is bad enough," said Bill Ransom. "But the realization is that you just live under the constant fear that they could come in like in 2001 and do it again—turn off the water, at any time, right in the middle of a growing season" (quoted in Jasper 2004). This fear and distrust have paralyzed many players in the watershed and act as a contributing factor preventing settlement.

New regulations are a reflection of shifting demands for the West's resources, and with those shifting demands are new values to be had from water resources in the Klamath Basin. Economists call these values *rents,* referring to the returns to the resource over and above its opportunity costs. If there are no opportunity costs, then the entire value of the resource is a rent. Before white people migrated to the region, attracted by the prospects of earning rents through irrigation, local Indian tribes valued the water for producing fish and wildlife on which they subsisted. With no opportunity cost to the water, the first inhabitants were receiving the full rental value of the water. If their rights to the water and its rents had been secure, newcomers would have had to compensate Indians for these rents before shifting the water to irrigation.

As noted above, the early treaties paid lip service to Indian claims by acknowledging water rights considered to date from time immemorial, but there was little defense of these rights for two reasons. First, the marginal value of water to Indians was low.[3] Second, termination of the Klamath Tribes in 1954 reduced their ability to defend their water rights against other uses.

By applying the water to their land, irrigators captured rents from the resource combination. And as the value of agricultural output rose and especially as the BOR lured farmers to the area with subsidized water projects, rents from using water for irrigation increased and with them, water withdrawals. The rents were increased further by electricity prices kept virtually unchanged at 0.6 cents per kilowatt-hour since 1917. To the extent that owners of land and water believed this price would prevail, they captured additional rents associated with low electricity prices.

Today several issues are threatening the rents to agricultural users. First, local tribes are in a better position and have more incentive to defend their claims to water. As noted above, court cases have supported the Klamath Tribes' claim to enough water to support hunting and fishing as agreed to in early treaties.

Second, new demands, especially for in-stream environmental values, are raising the opportunity cost of irrigation water. As in the case of shifting water to irrigation at the turn of the twentieth century, if new demanders had to compensate irrigators for water moved to in-stream uses, the farmers would voluntarily make some transfers and would capture a share of the new rents in the sale price of water.[4]

Reduced deliveries without compensation to farmers in 2001 showed that agricultural water rights and the rents associated therewith were not defendable. Irrigators filed suit claiming damages of $1 billion (later reduced to

$100 million) resulting from the federal government's decision to shut water off in 2001. In February 2005, the Pacific Coast Federation of Fishermen's Associations (PCFFA) entered the fracas with a judge saying that in the court's view, the PCFFA has a protectable interest in the water of the Klamath Basin that is "related to the property or transaction" at issue, one that lies in protecting access to that water and ensuring that it is distributed in a way that promotes fishing interests (see *Pacific Coast Federation of Fishermen's Assns. v. U.S. Bureau of Reclamation* 2001, 2005). Ultimately, the court will rule on who has what property rights for now, and in the process, resources will be gobbled up in the legal battles. And when these battles are over, other demanders will come along and reopen the rent-seeking process.

Finally, water rents exist in irrigation only if the water can be applied to the land, and it can only be applied to the land with some delivery mechanism. If that mechanism is gravity flow, then the cost of the ditch delivery system factors into the rents. If it is pumping, then the costs of the electricity factor in.

All of these issues work together to explain the conflicts over Klamath water and the potential for markets to resolve such disputes. If the rights of Indian tribes had been honored in the first place, and the irrigators or federal government had purchased those rights, there would be fewer grounds for conflict. Similarly, if environmental demanders had to purchase water either from tribes or from irrigators, those "owners" would be compensated for their forgone water use. The ESA, however, created a new set of rights that allow environmentalists to claim a share of the rents, thus generating another source of conflict.

The historically low price of electricity also factors into the conundrum. As previously mentioned, with electricity prices at virtually the same level for nearly a century, irrigators have incorporated this low cost input into their production decisions and into their land values. Low electricity prices encourage irrigators to use relatively more water and more marginal land. The low electricity prices get capitalized into land values, creating what Gordon Tullock professor of law and economics at George Mason University, called the "transitional gains trap" (1975), meaning that it is difficult to transit from one allocation to another because of the artificial rents to which people believe they have a right.

This explains why the recent decision by PacifiCorp (the power supplier to the area) to increase electricity prices more than tenfold received mixed reactions. Irrigators decried the decision, claiming that the company broke its promises and an economic disaster would result. Steve Kandra, president of the Klamath Water Users Association, said that the utility is reneging on its commitment to low-priced electricity and that, as a result, "people are going to suffer" (U.S. Water News Online 2005a). Environmentalists, on the other hand, applaud the decision on the grounds that it will reduce irrigation and increase stream flows. Higher power rates would make it uneconomical to irrigate hillier parts of the basin that are only irrigable by sprinklers and pumps. Jim McCarthy of the Oregon Natural Resources Council estimates that "if even 40,000 acres of these most marginal lands went out of production, using a rule of thumb of 2.5 acre-feet per acre, that's 100,000 acre-feet of water returned to the system" (quoted in Whitney 2005). Just how much and when water will be returned to the system remains to be seen, but the decision by PacifiCorp illustrates how important property rights and prices are in the battle for Klamath water.

Think Local

The web of federal and state regulations that allocates Klamath water has made rent seeking the norm in the basin. Judicial, legislative, and bureaucratic battles determine the allocation of water based on clout rather than economics or ecology. As William Kittredge put it, bureaucrats "often don't have much sense of the local rhythms or ecologies" (2000, 98).

The negative outcomes of rent seeking coupled with the ecological effects of political allocation are leading some to turn to local solutions. Local approaches take advantage of what Nobel Laureate F. A. Hayek called the "circumstance of time and place." As Hayek said, central planners cannot compute "the infinite variety of different needs of different people which compete for the available resources" (Nishiyama and Leube 1984). Contrary to the frequent presumption that only government can solve conflicts, communities in the highland grazing pastures of Switzerland, the terraced rice land of Java, and other villages throughout the world have been successfully managing their water resources for thousands of years (Ostrom 1990). One of the most important tools these groups use is the indigenous knowledge of resources and the customs for allocating them.

In an example closer to home, southern California water users developed a system of tradable rights to groundwater. They also created multiple special districts to manage a series of injection wells (effectively building a dam against saltwater intrusion) along the coast. These districts levy pump charges on all groundwater extractors in the region to pay for replenishing the water. This water rights system has been protecting groundwater basins underlying the Los Angeles metropolitan area for more than fifty years (see Ostrom, Stern, and Dietz 2003).

Explorer John Wesley Powell was one of the first in the West to recognize the importance of thinking locally when he called for organizing political systems around watersheds. Speaking to the Montana Constitutional Convention in 1889, Powell described what he thought would be the optimal geographical units for organizing county government.

> I want to present to you what I believe to be ultimately the political system which you have got to adopt in this country, and which the United States will be compelled sooner or later ultimately to recognize. I think each drainage basin in the arid land must ultimately become the practical unit of organization, and it would be wise if you could immediately adopt a county system which would be convenient with drainage basins. (Quoted in Kemmis 2001, 177)

Though Montana and other western states ignored Powell's suggestions, his insights into the connection between the physical characteristics of natural resources and the optimal geographic region for making water allocation decisions are as profound today as they were in the nineteenth century.

Daniel Kemmis, director of the Center for the Rocky Mountain West, expounds on Powell's philosophy that a watershed can serve as a unifying device once those within it recognize common interests and move to invent institutions appropriate to the community inhabiting each unique watershed (Kemmis 2001). Author Wallace Stegner also predicted that the West would prosper by learning lessons of cooperation. In *The Sound of Mountain Water* he wrote: "Angry as one may be at what heedless men have done and still do to a noble habitat, one cannot be pessimistic about the West. This is a native home of hope. When it fully learns that cooperation, not rugged individualism, is the quality that most characterizes and preserves it, then it will have achieved itself and outlived its origins" (1997 [1969], 37–38). Stegner made this prediction in 1969 on the eve of several national environmental laws that actually further polarized the western region.

Kemmis believes the West is ready to begin inventing institutions suited to specific watershed needs. This belief is based on two strands of thought that are often wound together in Powell's work: cooperation and watershed organization. Both of these elements are gaining momentum throughout the West where shared watershed dilemmas are pushing citizens to form de facto political entities—watershed working groups—as an alternative form of governance (Kemmis 2001). These groups provide a way for local environmentalists, irrigators, fishers, loggers, and recreationalists, all with a stake in the rents, to stipulate property rights.

Stipulate Rather Than Legislate or Adjudicate

The Klamath Basin could easily remain a battlefield where nobody wins except lawyers. The Klamath Water Users Association (KWUA) has already spent approximately $2 million in legal costs over the past ten years. But the KWUA, according to Keppen, "[doesn't] want the courts deciding our destiny because the results come out gray" (quoted in Hall 2004).

The 1990 listing of the northern spotted owl as a threatened species under the ESA illustrates what can happen when the conflict is played out in the courtroom. The listing and subsequent court orders led to a dramatic reduction in timber harvest in Oregon. The polarization over the matter tore communities apart and has managed to leave deep scars in many rural areas—scars that have not yet healed. As Kittredge (2000) notes, citizens in the Klamath Basin have a choice between working together to find ways of resolving disputes over water rents or battling in courtrooms or capitals.

One way that water users in the Klamath can work together is to stipulate water rights locally rather than adjudicating or legislating them at the state and federal level. If locals can establish and clarify legitimate rights to the basin water, cooperation can replace conflict as property owners bargain with one another and share in the gains from trade. Once water claims are clarified, solutions can be forged.

The solutions, however, will not come easily. "There can be no simple solutions to a situation so complex," said James Huffman, dean of the Lewis and Clark Law School, "which is precisely why it is important to underscore the positive role property rights and markets can play" (2004). Simple solutions often come from the top down because someone has to be in a position to mandate an outcome. Property rights solutions typically grow from the bottom up and include all water users.

Citizens of the Walla Walla Basin near the Oregon and Washington border were able to apply market mechanisms by working out a cooperative trade agreement with each other. Not unlike the Indians of the Klamath Basin, the Confederated Tribes of the Umatilla Indian Reservation had established water rights to the Walla Walla Basin, and irrigators were also relying on the water in the basin for their crops. Conflicts over the water began in the 1990s when the federal government mandated that more water be left in the streams to protect endangered salmon.

Instead of devoting time and resources to fighting one another, the tribes and farmers were able to negotiate a solution based on stipulated rights. The agreement was developed by the tribes, irrigators, the BOR, the Bonneville Power Administration, the Oregon Water Resources Department, and the Oregon Department of Fish and Wildlife. The resolution is based on a water exchange that delivers Columbia River water to irrigators. In exchange, irrigators agree to leave water in the Umatilla when fish need it most. The Colombia is not affected because water is eventually returned to the Columbia via the Umatilla River. This solution has created a positive outcome for all of the parties involved by satisfying the farmers and the federal government and by allowing the tribes to continue to fish the Umatilla (Shaw 2004).

Another example where stipulation has led to watershed-wide ecosystem restoration is the Deschutes River Conservancy (DRC), which has effectively used market-driven approaches to restore water to the Deschutes watershed. Geographically, the Deschutes River Basin is not unlike the Klamath Basin, with its mountains, valleys, and plateaus sitting on the eastern slope of the Cascade Range in Oregon.

The DRC's annual water leasing program is just one of the innovative programs implemented by this private group.[5] The approach facilitates reallocation of existing water rights while ensuring that all water needs are met, including agricultural, municipal, and environmental needs. In order to encourage program participation, the leasing program offers payments to water rights holders willing to lease their water in-stream. The incentive is working (see Figure 5.1). Flows in the Deschutes below Bend, Oregon, were on average 40 cubic feet per second the past two years, with roughly 10 cubic feet per second attributable to in-stream leasing. This market-based initiative has proved an effective tool for in-stream flow restoration and has raised awareness of the value of an emerging market for water.

Will a property rights path allowing trades similar to those made in the Walla Walla and Deschutes basins work in the Klamath? There is new hope that the answer is affirmative. In February 2005, ranchers who irrigate from streams above Upper Klamath Lake reached an agreement with the Klamath Tribes for resolving their long-standing disputes over water rights. The ranchers and other landowners agreed to drop their opposition to the tribes'

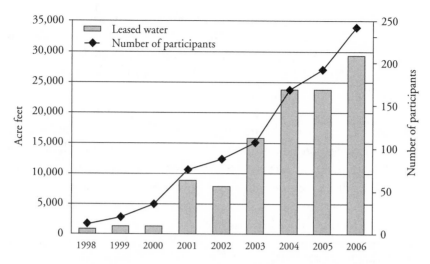

Figure 5.1. Participation in the Deschutes River Basin water exchange
SOURCE: Bruce Aylward, Deschutes River Conservancy, 2007.

claims for water rights that would maintain high stream flows in the Sprague, Williams, and Wood river systems in return for agreement from the tribes not to exercise their water rights in a way that would harm irrigators with water claims established before July 1, 1961. In a four-page agreement, the parties consented to withdraw court challenges to each other's water rights claims; establish a "joint restoration committee" that would identify, evaluate, recommend, and implement stream flow and habitat restoration projects; not seek the listing of additional species under the ESA; and support the development of new water storage. Former state legislator Steve Harper, who spearheaded the effort, said with pride that "no lawyers and no federal bureaucrats" were involved in the meetings (quoted in Darling 2005).

Furthermore, in a process to address concerns about PacifiCorp's four Klamath River dams, twenty-eight groups—including state and federal agencies, three county governments, irrigators, four tribes, and environmental organizations—have come to the table. Every group came with different goals but also with the intent to settle outside the courts. This settlement process according to Greg Addington, executive director of the Klamath Water Users Association, "has helped create unity and goodwill between constituents. . . . It's not often you get two states, the feds and four tribes in the same room" (quoted in Beaver 2007). Details of the settlement process are expected to be released in the summer of 2007. As a result of this settlement Governor Ted Kulongoski of Oregon and Arnold Schwarzenegger of California have agreed to host the Klamath Summit of area governors. "These negotiations will be the basis of any long-term sustainable solution," said Jake Weigler, spokesman for Kulongoski (quoted in Beaver 2007).

Though these agreements do not fully define all rights for all parties, they serve as a starting point for local stipulation—one that moves beyond the Oregon adjudication process mired down in the state's courts. If actors in the Klamath Basin can extend such stipulations further down the watershed to include other water users, there is a greater possibility that they can engage in voluntary exchanges. This route will allow users to take advantage of a variety of market mechanisms, such as water banking, water leasing for in-stream flows, water auctions, and regulatory credit for restoration (see Scarborough and Lund 2007).

Conclusion

Exchange can promote cooperation across interest groups and ideological lines. Such a solution requires clarifying property rights to water in the basin, creating a market in which they can be traded, and minimizing the role of government forces. If reformers can resist the urge to continue rent seeking and can stipulate rights locally, markets can induce marginal reallocations of the water in ways that can meet new demands without creating large rifts in the community.

What is more important—irrigation rights for farmers, productive fishing habitat for the Klamath Tribes, or the protection of endangered fish? There are no easy answers to this question, but if citizens of the Klamath Basin are resilient enough to work through their maze of problems and come out on the property rights path, there is hope that the various interests in the basin can forge a positive outcome—increasing the "wealth" of all parties involved.

Notes

The authors wish especially to thank the following people who participated in a PERC forum in Klamath Falls, Oregon, on June 8, 2004: Leslie Bach, the Nature Conservancy; Mark Campbell, Jeld-Wen Timber & Ranches; Ron Cole, Klamath Basin National Wildlife Refuges; Allen Foreman, Klamath Tribes; Jim Huffman,

Lewis and Clark Law School; Steve Kandra, Klamath Water Users Association; Dan Keppen, Klamath Water Users Association; Jeff Mitchell, Klamath River Inter-Tribal Fish and Water; Fritz Paulus, Oregon Water Trust; Mark Stern, the Nature Conservancy; Douglas Whitsett, Water for Life; and Joe Whitworth, Oregon Trout.

1. For further information regarding specifics of the Endangered Species Act, visit http://www.fws.gov/endangered/esa.html. Many scholars have pointed out the negative impacts of the Endangered Species Act. For a brief discussion on making endangered species the friend, not the enemy, of landowners, see Stroup (1995).

2. Some quantity of water may legally equal a reduced allocation of an irrigator's share of the water, but an allocation of zero water was considered a taking.

3. For a discussion of how the low marginal value of a resource such as land or water can lead one party to forgo its claim to the resource rather than fight to defend it, see Anderson and McChesney (1994).

4. For a discussion of the complexity in bargaining over rents, see Libecap (2005).

5. For detailed information regarding market-based programs implemented by the Deschutes River Conservancy, visit http://www.deschutesrc.org.

References

Anderson, Stephan. 2003. The Nature Conservancy lauds U.S. plan for Klamath Basin. *The Nature Conservancy*. April 4. Online at http://www.nature.org/wherewework/northamerica/states/oregon/press/press989.html. Visited July 2, 2007.

Anderson, Terry L., and Fred S. McChesney. 1994. Raid or Trade: An Economic Model of Indian-White Relations. *Journal of Law and Economics* 37 (April): 39–74.

Anderson, Terry L., and Pamela Snyder. 1997. *Water Markets: Priming the Invisible Pump*. Washington, DC: Cato Institute.

Beaver, Ty. 2007. Groups Closer to Water Settlement. *Herald and News* (Klamath Falls, Oregon). April 25.

Bureau of Reclamation. 2004. Klamath Project. Washington DC: U.S. Department of the Interior, Bureau of Reclamation. Online at http://www.usbr.gov/newsroom/presskit/factsheet/factsheetdetail.cfm?recordid=3000. Visited December 14, 2005.

Clarren, Rebecca. 2001. No Refuge in the Klamath Basin. *High Country News*. August 13.

Cole, Ron. 2004. Resolving Conflicts in the Klamath Basin Through Markets and Property Rights. Unpublished notes. June 8. Bozeman, MT: PERC.

Darling, Dylan. 2005. Water Deal May Aid Restoration Efforts. *Herald and News* (Klamath Falls, Oregon). February 28.

Deschutes River Conservancy. 2007. Interview with Bruce Aylward, Waterbank Director (March 23).

Hall, Barbara. 2004. Resolving Conflicts in the Klamath Basin Through Markets

and Property Rights. Online at http://www.klamathbasincrisis.org/articlesafter
1103/barbhpercnoteso60904.htm. Visited July 9, 2007.

Hathaway, Ron, and Teresa Welch. 2001. Background. In *Water Allocation in the Klamath Reclamation Project, 2001: An Assessment of Natural Resources, Economic, Social, and Institutional Issues with a Focus on the Upper Klamath Basin.* Corvallis and Berkeley: Oregon State University and University of California, 1–13.

Hood, Susan. 1972. Termination of the Klamath Indian Tribe of Oregon. *Ethnohistory* 19(4) (Autumn 1972): 379–392

Huffman, James L. 2004. Property Rights for Klamath Water. *Cascade Update* 11(2). Portland, OR: Cascade Policy Institute.

Jasper, William F. 2004. Water Is for Fighting. *New American Magazine* 20(16), August 9.

Kandra v. United States. 145 F. Supp. 2d 1192 (D.Or. 2001).

Kemmis, Daniel. 2001. *This Sovereign Land: A New Vision for Governing the West.* Washington, DC: Island Press.

Keppen, Dan. 2003. Letter to the Editor. *Herald and News* (Klamath Falls, Oregon). February 21.

Kimball v. Callahan. 590 F.2d 768, 773 (CA9), cert. denied, 444 U.S. 826 (1979).

Kittredge, William. 2000. *Balancing Water: Restoring the Klamath Basin.* Berkeley: University of California Press.

Landry, Clay J., and Laurel E. Phoenix. 2003. Forging New Rights to Water. *Water Resources IMPACT* 5(2) (March): 3–4.

Libecap, Gary. 2005. *Rescuing Water Markets: Lessons from Owens Valley.* PERC Policy Series, No. PS-33. Bozeman, MT: PERC.

Meiners, Roger E., and Lea-Rachel Kosnik. 2003. *Restoring Harmony in the Klamath Basin.* Bozeman, MT: PERC.

Nature Conservancy. 2003. The Nature Conservancy Lauds U.S. Plan for Klamath Basin. Online at http://www.nature.org/wherewework/northamerica/states/oregon/press/press989.html. April 3.

Nishiyama, Chiaki, and Kurt R. Leube. 1984. *The Essence of Hayek.* Stanford, CA: Hoover Institution Press.

Oregon Water Resources Commission and Department. 1999. Water Rights in Oregon: An Online Introduction to Oregon's Water Law and Water Rights System. Online at http://www.wrd.state.or.us/OWRD/PUBS/aquabook.shtml.

Ostrom, Elinor. 1990. *Governing the Commons.* New York: Cambridge University Press.

Ostrom, Elinor, Paul C. Stern, and Thomas Dietz. 2003. Water Rights in the Commons. *Water Resources Impact.* Online at http://www.awra.org/impact/0303impact.pdf. Visited December 14, 2005).

Pacific Coast Federation of Fishermen's Assns. v. U.S. Bureau of Reclamation. 2001. 138 F. Supp. 2d 1228; U.S. Dist. LEXIS 7921.

Pacific Coast Federation of Fishermen's Assns. v. U.S. Bureau of Reclamation. 2005. 9th Cir., no. 03-16718, D.C. no. CV=02=02006-SBA, appealed on February 16, 2005.

Pokarney, Bruce. 2002. Klamath Basin Crisis: One Year Later. *Agriculture Quarterly.* Department of Agriculture, State of Oregon. Summer.

Scarborough, Brandon, and Hertha Lund. 2007. *Saving Our Streams: Harnessing Water Markets.* Bozeman, MT: PERC.

Shaw, Jane S. 2004. Water Trades Work Elsewhere: Why Not in the Basin? *Herald and News* (Klamath Falls, Oregon). June 14. Online at http://www.perc.org/perc.php?subsection=4&id=447. Visited July 2, 2007.

Sorte, Bruce, and Bruce Weber. 2001. The Upper Klamath Basin Economy and the Role of Agriculture. In *Water Allocation in Klamath Reclamation Project, 2001: An Assessment of Natural Resources, Economic, Social, and Institutional Issues with a Focus on the Upper Klamath Basin.* Corvallis and Berkeley: Oregon State University and University of California. Online at http://extension.oregonstate.edu/catalog/html/sr/sr1037/base.pdf.

Souza, Christine, 2001. Klamath Basin Growers Fight for Irrigation Water. *California Farm Bureau Ag Alert.* April 18.

Stegner, Wallace. 1997 [1969]. *The Sound of Mountain Water.* New York: Penguin.

Stroup, Richard L. 1995. *Endangered Species Act: Making Innocent Species the Enemy.* PERC Policy Series, No. PS-3. Bozeman, MT: PERC.

Tulare Lake Basin Water Storage District, et al. v. United States. 59 Fed. Cl. 246 (2003).

Tullock, Gordon. 1975. The Transitional Gains Trap. *Bell Journal of Economics* 6(2): 671–678.

United States of America and the Klamath Indian Tribe v. Ben Adair. 723 F.2d 1394 (9th Cir. 1983), cert. denied 474 U.S. 1252 (1984).

United States v. Adair. 187 F. Supp. 2d 1273; 2002 U.S. Dist. LEXIS 3397.

U.S. Fish and Wildlife Service. 1997. Integrated Pest Management Plan for Lower Klamath and Tule Lake NWRs. Online at http://library.fws.gov/Pubs1/IPM/Guide.html. Visited July 2, 2007.

U.S. Water News Online. 2005a. A Utility's Plan to End a Longtime Power Subsidy Could Mean Less Water Going to Agriculture. March. Online at http://www.uswaternews.com/archives/arcpolicy/5axxxutil3.html. Visited December 14, 2005.

U.S. Water News Online. 2005b. Judge Rejects Klamath Farmers' Water Claim. Online at http://www.uswaternews.com/archives/arcrights/5judgereje9.html. Visited December 14, 2005.

Whitney, David. 2005. Klamath Farmers, Fish at Crossroads. *Sacramento Bee.* February 27.

Winters v. United States. 207 U.S. 564, 28 S.Ct. 207, 52 L.Ed. 340 (1908).

CHAPTER SIX

Fishing for Wealth in Coastal Fisheries

DONALD R. LEAL

Commercial fisheries in the United States figure prominently in both the national and regional economies. In 2005, commercial fishers harvested 4.4 million metric tons of fish valued dockside at $3.9 billion, a decrease of 58.8 million pounds (down less than 1 percent) and an increase of $176.7 million (up 5 percent) compared with 2004 (NMFS 2005). By producing and marketing a variety of fishery products for domestic and foreign markets, U.S. commercial fisheries contributed $32.9 billion to the U.S. gross domestic product in 2005. Alaska led all states in dockside value of landings with $1.3 billion, followed by Massachusetts, $425.4 million; Maine, $391.9 million; Louisiana, $253 million; and Washington, $206.5 million.

That said, many fisheries face formidable challenges in terms of their sustainability and ability to coexist with the growing demands from recreational anglers,[1] marine eco-tourists (e.g., whale watching and reef diving), and ocean ecologists. From 1999 to 2003, seven species of groundfish off Washington, Oregon, and California were declared overfished by the National Marine Fisheries Service. So were several crab fisheries in the Bering Sea off Alaska, and the federal government embarked on a $100 million vessel buy-out program to reduce the size of the crab fleet. From 1990 to

2006, red snapper in the Gulf of Mexico suffered enormous waste under a management-induced fishing derby. In addition, conflicts between fishing interests and other ocean groups have intensified in recent years. Calls for expanding marine protected areas (MPAs) in which fishing is restricted or eliminated have been met with heavy resistance from fishers. Right-to-fish laws are now being proposed in state legislatures and in Congress (e.g., Rogers 2003; Tennyson 2004).

This chapter argues that institutional change based on more fully delineated property rights in coastal fisheries can reverse the secular trend of wealth dissipation. Furthermore, such a change should be structured to allow for recognition of growing demands for ocean amenities.

Government Regulation: Largely a Failure

U.S. coastal fisheries have been managed under a host of governmental regulations in an effort to counter the tendency for ocean fish stocks to be overfished under the classic "tragedy of the commons."[2] These include restrictions on the size and power of fishing vessels, the types of fishing gear (e.g., net mesh size), the area where fishing is allowed, the length of the fishing season, the amount of fish a vessel is allowed to keep per fishing trip, the number of fishing trips a vessel can take in a season, and the landing size for fish. Such restrictions attempt to prevent overfishing by raising the costs of fishing.

The Pacific salmon fishery is a prime example. In the early twentieth century, regulators prohibited the use of traps first employed by Native Americans, who caught the salmon when they returned to spawn. With the elimination of traps, fishers pursued salmon in the open ocean. The substitute for traps became very expensive. When the number of participants and the length of the season were restricted, vessel owners bought bigger boats and more sophisticated gear. They also hired more crew. To counter these changes in fishing ability, regulators then established other layers of restrictions in an attempt to prevent overfishing. The approach generated economic inefficiencies, as more capital and labor were applied to catch approximately the same amount of fish. As fishers were forced to fish longer in less productive areas with more expensive equipment, the economic wastes generated reduced the net value of the fishery (Crutchfield and Pontecorvo 1969).

Fishing restrictions can result in other problems, such as favoring one group over another. Economist James Crutchfield (1973, 115) examined the regulatory policies in the 1960s and 1970s and concluded that the regula-

tory process had "generated an ever-increasing mass of restrictive legislation, most of it clothed in the shining garment of conservation, but bearing
the clear marks of pressure politics." Most of the restrictions, Crutchfield
concluded, reflect "power plays by one ethnic group of fishermen against
another, by owners of one gear against another, or by fishermen of one state
against another state."

Despite the fishing restrictions, overfishing remains, sometimes with
catastrophic results. For example, fish stocks in New England's groundfish
fishery collapsed in the 1990s despite a host of fishing restrictions (NMFS
1999, 1–7). Most U.S. fisheries have not reached such a state, but the risk of
collapse is a real possibility. Just over 40 percent of the 215 U.S. fish stocks
scientists assessed in 2003 were overfished or were being fished unsustain-
ably (NMFS 2004a). Many of the remaining 60 percent could easily become
overfished because regulators have been unable to prevent the tendency of
a fleet to increase its fishing power—that is, the ability to catch more fish
in less time. Nor have they been able to eliminate the excessive number of
fishing vessels and excessive effort in many fisheries.

Such excesses can be financially devastating. For example, the number of
full-time vessels in the Gulf of Mexico shrimp fishery more than doubled
between 1966 and 1991, even as annual net revenues per vessel decreased
about 75 percent to approximately $25,000 (in 1990 dollars). The actual
annual catch of shrimp by full-time vessels was virtually unchanged. Two
economists suggest that one-third of the fleet of more than sixteen thousand
vessels and boats operating in 1988 could have efficiently harvested the same
amount of shrimp (Ward and Sutinen 1994).

Restricting the number of participants in a fishery by limiting the available licenses—called *limited entry*—has become common in recent years as
a modification of the regulatory approach. Unfortunately, this approach has
rarely been enough to prevent a rise in fishing power as a limited number of
fishers invest in new ways to catch more fish in less time. Consider the British Columbia halibut fishery during the 1980s. The maximum number of
vessels in the fishery was limited to 435 in 1980, but over the next ten years
the number of crew and amount of gear increased, resulting in greater fishing power. By 1990, with a season limited to six days, fishers caught almost
50 percent more halibut than they caught in 1980, when the season was
sixty-five days long (Grafton, Squires, and Fox 2000, 684, 686).

Limited entry also falls short when a fishing fleet suffers from overcapacity and nothing is done to reduce the size of the fleet. Such is the case in the

multispecies groundfish fishery off Washington, Oregon, and California. In 1994, the Pacific Fishery Management Council authorized a limited entry system to restrict the number of boats in the groundfish fishery to current participants, but it did nothing to reduce overcapacity (Ad-Hoc Groundfish Strategic Plan Committee 2000, 5). Over the next ten years, the fishery faced new fishing restrictions because of severe depletion of species such as bocaccio. A formerly abundant West Coast groundfish, the bocaccio population has plummeted by more than 95 percent since the late 1960s, the result of the fish being overfished and caught as bycatch—the incidental catch of nontargeted species—in other fisheries. Although bocaccio can no longer be commercially targeted, scientists believe it could take at least a century for the population to recover (Garrison 2002, 217).

Individual Transferable Quotas

In recent years a growing number of fisheries around the world have adopted individual transferable quotas (ITQs) (e.g., see Hannesson 2005). Unlike any of the previous regulatory systems, which "address only the symptoms," property rights approaches like ITQs "fundamentally tackle the cause by altering basic incentive structures" in fisheries (Wilen and Homans 2000, 4). Functionally, ITQs not only limit the number of participants in a fishery, they limit the amount of fish that each fisher / quota holder can catch. Under ITQs, each quota holder is entitled to catch a specified percentage of the total allowable catch (TAC) set each season by fishery managers. Thus, an individual who holds a 0.1 percent share in the Gulf of Mexico red snapper fishery is entitled to catch 3,000 pounds for the season if the TAC is 3 million pounds.

Typically, ITQs are initially assigned to quota holders on the basis of their percentages of the total catch during a designated prior period of fishing. Thus, if an individual caught 0.1 percent of the total harvest over the designated years of 1988, 1989, and 1990, he or she would be initially assigned that quota share. Because the quotas are transferable, current holders can adjust the size of their fishing operations by buying and selling quotas. Those wishing to enter an ITQ fishery can buy or lease quotas from current quota holders who want to reduce their participation. Those wishing to leave the fishery can sell their quota to other fishers.

ITQs are attractive for two main reasons. First, each quota holder faces the certainty that his or her share of the TAC will not be taken by someone else. Thus they remove the destructive race for fish, with its inducement for bigger and faster boats and ever more sophisticated fishing gear (U.S. Commission on Ocean Policy 2004, 244). With ITQs, fishers do not compete for shares of the TAC, so there is much less incentive to race against other fishers. Second, because ITQs are tradable, the problem of fleet overcapacity and corresponding excess fishing effort dissipates as more efficient fishers—those who adopt cost-reducing or value-enhancing methods—buy out those who are ready to retire or pursue other work.

New Zealand and Iceland now use ITQs to manage nearly all of their commercial fisheries, and Canada and Australia use ITQs in quite a few of their fisheries. Greenland and The Netherlands use ITQs for some fish species. The United States uses ITQs for halibut, sablefish, surf clams and ocean quahogs, wreckfish, and several species of Alaskan crab. In addition, ITQs were applied to the commercial side of Gulf of Mexico red snapper in 2007, and plans are under way for applying them to West Coast groundfish and Alaska rockfish. Overall, ITQs have generated higher incomes for fishers, improved product quality for consumers, reduced fleet excesses, and nearly eliminated instances in which the actual overall catch exceeds the TAC set by fishery managers (e.g., see Arnason 1996; National Research Council 1999; Repetto 2001).

Wilen and Homans (2000) point out that ITQs and similar approaches are providing important insights into the types of impacts and sources of wealth dissipation that have come out of traditionally regulated fisheries. One example is the Alaska halibut fishery. Under the old regulatory regime, federal managers tried to prevent the overall catch from exceeding the TAC by shortening the length of the fishing season. The seasons got shorter and shorter, but with shares of the TAC up for grabs, fishers tried to catch as much as they could, as fast as they could, in a race for fish. Under these conditions, the actual catch often exceeded the TAC (Dinneford et al. 1999). By the early 1990s, halibut fishers were limited to fishing during just two to three twenty-four-hour fishing openings a year. Not only did profits fall and consumers receive mostly frozen fish, but halibut fishers had to fish in hazardous weather.

Under ITQs, the season increased from two to three one-day openings a year to just over eight months a year. The extended season allowed fishers to respond more effectively to consumer demand for fresh fish, resulting in higher dockside prices (GAO 2002, 21). Safety improved because fishers were no longer forced to fish during stormy weather (Hartley and Fina

2001, 34). Gear loss and halibut mortality due to gear loss declined substantially, resulting in much lower gear replacement costs and less resource waste (Hartley and Fina 2001, 34). In the 1995–1999 period, the overall catch did not exceed the TAC (Dinneford et al. 1999). The number of vessels active in the fishery declined from 3,412 in 1994 to 1,612 in 1999, largely because of buying and selling quotas (NMFS 2000). All told, higher returns and good prospects led to a dramatic rise in the value of quotas. In 1995, the first year of ITQs, the aggregate value of quotas was estimated to be just over $295 million. In 1998, the aggregate value of quotas had grown to nearly $495 million—a 67 percent increase in four years (Leal 2002, 13).

In the more challenging multispecies British Columbia groundfish fishery, ITQs also proved beneficial. Before individual vessel quotas (IVQs)—a variant of ITQs in which vessels are assigned individual quotas for as many as fifty-five groundfish species—were introduced, the fishery was suffering from fleet overcapacity and vessel per-trip catch limits that resulted in high bycatch and discard mortality,[3] declining income for fishers, and economic instability throughout the industry (Jones 2003, 79–86). Under IVQs, crew and vessel earnings increased. The year-round season enabled fishers to service the market with high-quality fresh fish. The elimination of trip limits resulted in improved operational efficiency. In addition, the number of processors increased from twelve to fifteen companies, helped along by a partial allocation of the TAC to newly formed processor / fisher teams.

Conservation also improved markedly. Before IVQs, bycatch and discard mortality were increasing. Under IVQs, fishers successfully altered fishing strategies to reduce bycatch and discard mortality significantly (Jones 2003, 82–83). Before IVQs, fishery managers were unable to manage groundfish species individually, and as a result target catch levels for many individual stocks were often exceeded. With IVQs implemented in 1997, fishery managers were able to focus on a stock-specific basis, with IVQs for each of the fifty-five stock-specific target levels. From 1997 to 2001 annual catch levels were consistently below target levels.

ITQs also have the potential to foster stewardship. In New Zealand, where ITQs are legally recognized property rights, fishers play an active role in fisheries management. Through self-imposed levies, quota holders channel their own money into companies whose primary mission is to increase the abundance of scallop, orange roughy, oyster, rock lobster, snapper, and other commercially valued fish stocks. For example, the Challenger Enhancement Company invested in its own research vessel, the *FV*

Tasman Challenger, as well as in efforts to reseed scallop stock (Arbuckle and Metzger 2000). Through self-imposed regulations and enforcement, quota holders play a pivotal role alongside governmental managers in helping the stock reach optimal size for higher returns.

Despite the success of ITQs, implementing them in the political arena can be difficult. Such has been the case in the United States. In 1996, Congress imposed a moratorium on ITQs in other federal fisheries. For many non-ITQ fisheries plagued by overcapacity and declining fish stocks, the problems had not reached a crisis and politicians opted for the status quo. Problems eventually reached a crisis stage for several fisheries by the next decade, and the moratorium was allowed to expire October 1, 2002. In 2006, Congress passed the Magnuson-Stevens Fishery Conservation and Management Reauthorization Act, which among other things will help double the use of ITQs or similar approaches in U.S. federal fisheries by 2010.

Private Harvesting Agreements

Another rights-based approach that has emerged in recent years is the private harvesting agreement. Such an agreement typically entails fishers allocating harvest shares among themselves after government has limited entry in the fishery. In addition, the government may facilitate such agreements by identifying within a fishery individual fishing sectors that share a common trait. The government limits the number of license holders in each sector and then determines each sector's share of the TAC. One sector may be the fleet that delivers fish to onshore processors, and the other sector may be the fleet that catches and processes fish onboard a vessel. Then fishers in each sector allocate harvest shares among themselves as well as carry out certain monitoring and enforcement functions. Typically, all or part of these allocations is transferable, but certain restrictions may exist.

Such agreements share two important features with government-administered ITQ programs. First, participants can be certain that their harvest allocations will not be taken by someone else, so there is less incentive to race for fish. Second, because shares are transferable, agreements can free up excess capacity.

Because these arrangements are formed voluntarily and rely on cooperation, their occurrence depends on certain preexisting conditions.[4] The number of participants within the group must be relatively small, and they must have sufficient common interest to make negotiations feasible. There must be an effective system for verifying that actual catches match individual allocations. There must be substantial penalties for violations of the agreement in order to deter cheating. There must be an effective system for preventing those not party to the agreement from entering the fishery, or else outsiders are "almost certain to be predators on the fishermen who rationalize their harvests" (Sullivan 2000, 1). There must be clear indications to fishers that the benefits of carrying out a harvest agreement outweigh the costs. Finally, there must be a clear signal to fishers that such an arrangement will not be overturned by antitrust law.

These conditions are becoming more common in Pacific Northwest and Alaska fisheries. Open access appears to be on its way out as "fishery sectors are increasingly segregated by species and gear-specific licensing systems, which restrict eligibility to fishermen with recent participation above marginal thresholds" (Sullivan 2000, 2).

In addition, global markets and fish farming have made fish production extremely competitive. To compete in the marketplace, fishers must find ways to deliver a quality product for extended periods. These requirements make continuing a race for fish less attractive and joint harvesting arrangements more so. In addition, sophisticated monitoring and reporting services and increasing use of onboard observers, at least on the larger vessels, support stronger enforcement.

These practical conditions have made private harvest agreements more appealing. Also, there are strong indications that these agreements will not be overturned on antitrust grounds. Although colluding during the marketing phase would be illegal under the Sherman Antitrust Act, these agreements involve cooperation during the harvesting phase, primarily in fisheries whose output is regulated. In addition, the U.S. Department of Justice tends to look favorably on an arrangement in which consumers benefit from lower-cost harvests and higher product quality and recovery (Sullivan 2000, 4–5).

Most of the above conditions were in place in the North Pacific pollock fishery located off Alaska in the late 1990s. This federally managed fishery was characterized by heavy competition in a race for fish. The catcher-processor sector anticipated substantial benefits in ending the race so they sought a quota allocation separate from the allocation to the offshore fleet as a whole. The offshore fleet included both the catcher-processor sector and the "mothership" sector, which has a fleet of catcher vessels that brings it fish for processing. If the catcher-processors had their own allocation of pollock quota, it would be easier to reach an agreement on ending the race if they did not have to negotiate with the mothership fleet as well.

They achieved their objective with passage of the 1998 American Fisheries Act, which divided the fishery's TAC into five separate quotas or allocations. Thirty-three percent of the TAC went to catcher-processors, 3 percent to catcher vessels that deliver to catcher-processors, 9 percent to motherships, 45 percent to the inshore processors, and 10 percent to community development quota holders. The act also allowed fishing interests in 1999 to form producer cooperatives, beginning with the catcher-processors and catcher vessels that deliver to them. Two cooperatives were formed: the catcher-processors formed the Pollock Conservation Cooperative, and the catcher vessels that delivered their catch to them formed the High Seas Catchers' Cooperative.

The catcher-processor sector experienced immediate benefits in the first year of the agreement. The number of vessels was reduced from twenty-eight to sixteen. Catcher-processor companies also acquired all of the shares held by catcher vessels that used to deliver their catch to them before the agreement (Loy 2000). Season length nearly doubled to 149 days, and catch rates were about 60 percent lower than the 1995–1998 average, as catcher-processors slowed the pace of fishing. Sullivan (2000, 7–8) estimates that product recovery in 1999 increased by 20 percent over the 1998 season, production of deep-skin fillets increased about 40 percent and surimi by 9 percent, and lower-valued products such as standard fillets and mince decreased by about 40 percent.

In 2000, more producer cooperatives were formed, and more operations were consolidated. Vessels that caught pollock for onshore processors formed seven producer cooperatives. All but two cooperatives saw a reduction in member vessels (Loy 2000). In the offshore sector, an additional five vessels were voluntarily removed from the fishery. For the fishery as a whole, 31 of 129 vessels dropped out, a 24 percent reduction.

As of 2001 private harvesting agreements in North America were in effect in Mexico's Baja lobster fishery (2000), in the weathervane scallop fishery (2000) and Chignik salmon fishery (2001) off Alaska, in the Pacific whiting fishery off Oregon and Washington (1997), in Oregon's Yaquina Bay herring fishery (1989), and in British Columbia's red sea urchin fishery (1994).

A private harvest agreement was initiated by forty-two roundhaul net fishers beginning in the early 1980s. Unfortunately, the state of California outlawed the use of such nets in the mid-1990s, and all forty-two permits were converted to permits in the gill net herring fishery in the San Francisco Bay. For this fishery the cost of reaching an agreement among 412 participants remains prohibitive, and shares of the herring catch remain up for grabs—that is, fishers race for fish.

ITQs Versus Private Harvesting Agreements

When they are feasible, private harvesting agreements have an important advantage over government-administered ITQs. Agreements mitigate the political problem of allocating shares of the catch among participants—individuals or firms. The government defines the fishing sectors, closes entry, and determines the initial percentage allocation of the TAC for each sector. Although this process is not free from controversy, it appears to be easier to let the sector's participants allocate individual shares than having the government do it.[5]

But once established, ITQs have some advantages: a new entrant can simply buy or lease quotas from a current quota owner willing to sell or lease. With a private harvest agreement, transferring a share to a new entrant will require having or obtaining membership in the cooperative. Also, ITQs are likely to remain in force, especially once they acquire value in the secondary market. By contrast, many private harvesting agreements have a provision requiring members to renew the agreement after a certain period. If the agreement is not renewed, the race for fish and wasteful investment resume. Even when there is no such provision, a harvesting agreement can simply break down when results fall short of expectations. In the northwestern Hawaiian Islands lobster fishery, a harvesting agreement among fourteen permit holders broke down when the anticipated higher revenues of delivering live lobsters to the Asian market never materialized (Townsend 2005, 130–131).

Territorial Fishing Rights

When feasible, another rights-based approach is territorial user rights in fisheries (TURFs). Such an approach has venerable precedent in the Pacific Northwest. Before white settlement, Native Americans established exclusive rights to salmon fishing sites along rivers and streams (Higgs 1982). In some cases, the tribe owned the rights; in others, families or individuals or a combination owned the rights. Intertribal agreements respecting these rights and intertribal trade allowed Indians in the region "not only to subsist largely on salmon but to build substantial wealth" (Nikel-Zueger 2003, 24).

These rights crumbled following white settlement, and coastal fishers began intercepting salmon at sea. With access to the resource open, the resource suffered overfishing. Government regulations—gear restrictions, seasonal closures, and the like—kept salmon populations from serious depletion, but they failed to prevent salmon wealth from being dissipated. "Overfishing has largely been transformed into a problem of overcapitalization and a race for salmon, which ultimately decreases both the quality of salmon and the return from fishing" (Nikel-Zueger 2003, 17).

The property rights that existed before white settlement protected salmon and fostered wealth, but they would not be sufficient to address the demands for salmon today. Recreational fishers both on inland waterways and at sea consider salmon a prized sport fish. In addition, human preference for salmon as food has changed dramatically. In the past, canned salmon was the primary product sold to consumers, and freshness was not an issue in processing salmon for canning. Today, wild, freshly caught salmon is in high demand, and this allows commercial salmon fishers to compete more effectively with farmed salmon producers. But for fishers this shift in food preference requires them to catch salmon in saltwater inlets and bays and in the ocean, before fish begin to deteriorate after entering freshwater. Obviously, property rights to inland fishing sites would not be able to encompass salmon interception in these areas. Given their successful application to mobile species at sea, rights-based approaches such as ITQs or private harvesting agreements among commercial fishers or groups are better suited to meet this new requirement.[6]

For sedentary species, such as oysters, TURFs can be easily defined without the worry that the species will venture beyond property boundaries. Under these circumstances, an entrepreneur holding these rights would have a strong incentive to invest in enhanced marine production because the benefits of doing so could be captured in full. The oyster beds of Washington's Willapa Bay are a prime example. Commercial oyster production began in the bay in the mid-nineteenth century (Wolf 1993, 21–23). After an initial decline in the oyster commons from overfishing, local oyster gatherers began cultivating areas for oyster production and delineating ownership of these areas by marking off boundaries with stakes. With the beds privatized, owners initiated efforts to greatly enhance production (De Alessi 1996, 3–4). For example, methods were developed for culturing oysters in areas normally unsuitable for natural rearing. Such methods included attaching oysters to wooden stakes driven into the ground and on floats or suspended nets. Bed owners also invested in their own hatcheries. These areas were so successful that they served as a source for reseeding oyster beds that had become depleted in Japan.

Other versions of privately enhanced marine production can be found in U.S. coastal areas. Alabama and Florida allow individuals or companies to introduce reef structures in parts of their territorial waters in the Gulf of Mexico. These structures—which range from old cars to prefabricated artificial reefs designed to be durable and blend in with the natural environment—provide more surface area for the small organisms that fish feed on (De Alessi 1997, 78–79). They also provide fish with places to hide from predators. The reefs actually become public property as soon as they are placed in the water, but knowing the location of a reef has given enough security of ownership to spur some private provision. Private efforts would probably increase if states granted marine entrepreneurs options for acquiring fishing and possibly recreational rights in areas around the reefs.

One company, Artificial Reefs, Inc., completed a multifaceted artificial reef structure off the Gulf Coast near Destin, Florida, in 1999, to enhance recreational fishing and provide an area for skin diving. The project was financed with a grant from Florida's Department of Environmental Protection. It could have easily been financed privately if exclusive fishing rights to the state-owned Gulf area where the reef was deployed could be purchased from the state. Owners of such homesteaded areas could catch the fish themselves or lease out fishing rights—even recreational fishing rights.

Experimenting with Recreational Fishing Rights

The conventional view is that fishing for sport has little effect on U.S. marine fish populations. But for species of concern that are overfished, recreational fishing does have a significant impact, as a major study recently completed by marine scientists concluded (Coleman, Figuera, et al. 2004, 1958–1959). Landing records over a twenty-two-year period provide definitive evidence of how recreational fishing affects selected U.S. marine fish stocks.

The percentage of total U.S. finfish landings attributable to recreational fishing was 4 percent in 2002 (averaging 5 percent for the twenty-two-year period). Excluding two major industrial species, pollock and menhaden,[7] the percentage of U.S. marine finfish landings attributable to recreational fishing was 10 percent in 2002. However, it increased to 23 percent when only species of concern were looked at. Regional impacts are more pronounced. In the Gulf of Mexico, 64 percent of the total landings of species of concern were taken by recreational fishers. Along the Pacific Coast (excluding Alaska) that number was 59 percent. For some species of concern, recreational landings outstripped commercial landings by a wide margin, notably for bocaccio on the Pacific Coast (87 percent recreational), red drum in the South Atlantic (93 percent), and red snapper in the Gulf of Mexico (59 percent).

The current approach to regulating recreational fishing has come under attack recently because it fails to prevent overfishing and creates other problems (e.g., see Grimm 2004; Woodward and Griffen 2003, 239–261). This approach focuses on daily bag limits, size limits, and seasonal closures, without restricting the number of individuals allowed to fish or their fishing effort. In this open-access scenario a popular species can still be overfished because fishing pressure is free to grow from increases in the number of anglers or fishing effort. In addition, regulations that rely on daily bag limits and size limits increase the incidence of regulatory discards, which for certain species increases fishing mortality.[8]

The Gulf of Mexico red snapper recreational fishery illustrates the problems. Starting in 1997 federal regulators began closing the sportfishing season for red snapper before the end of the calendar year in an effort to keep the actual catch from exceeding the safe catch level set for the year. As recreational fishing pressure grew, regulators were forced to close the season earlier each succeeding year (GMFMC 2001). As the season began shrinking, regulators lowered the daily bag limit and raised the minimum size for landing fish in an effort to slow the pace of landings. It was hoped these changes would keep fishers on the water longer, which would be beneficial to coastal businesses that catered to them. Unfortunately, these changes forced fishers into a destructive catch-and-release fishery in which an estimated one of every two red snapper caught had to be thrown overboard. In their weakened condition many discarded fish became easy prey to sharks and dolphins.[9] And despite the restrictions, the actual recreational catch exceeded the desired safe catch level by a wide margin in three of the five years, beginning in 1996 (GMFMC 2001).

Another problem with current regulations is that they are inflexible; that is, they ignore geographic differences and differences in preferences among sport fishers. For instance, to maximize income from early spring tourists, resort owners in southern Florida want the snapper season opened a month earlier. Fishers with busy schedules and little time to fish want higher bag limits for the few days they fish. Retirees with plenty of time to fish during the year can tolerate lower bag limits. Other fishers want to go to an area where the chance of catching trophy-sized fish is high. They want an area that is exclusive enough to promote trophy catches, and they are willing to pay more for the opportunity.

Conservation-minded anglers, charter boat operators, and coastal communities are understandably appalled with the current system. Fortunately, a novel approach—one that promises to be more effective at conserving fish, less costly to implement, and more responsive to fishers' preferences than the current regulatory approach—is gathering support among stakeholders. This approach, involving angling management organizations (AMOs) (Sutinen and Johnston 2003), is being designed as a pilot project for introduction in selected areas of the Gulf and by the end of the decade, it may also be tried as a pilot project for one or more recreational fisheries off Oregon and Washington as well.[10] The effort to introduce AMOs in the recreational red snapper fishery is being spearheaded by Environmental Defense, a key environmental group in the Gulf region working for more effective approaches to environmental and economic problems in commercial and recreational fisheries. The AMO concept stems from the recent trend in fisheries management worldwide toward strengthened harvest rights.

The concept for AMOs is similar to the community development quota (CDQ) programs that were implemented in the halibut and sablefish fisheries after ITQs were introduced during the 1990s. In these programs, fishery managers assigned a portion of the TAC in each fishery to coalitions of Alaskan fishing villages located along Alaska's Bering Sea coast.[11] Each coalition, in turn, allocates the assigned catch among its members and helps enforce the fishing rules. These programs have resulted in greater participation in fisheries management and improved conservation, such as reduction of bycatch.

In the Gulf, a group of charter fishing boat owners, a coalition of local communities from a region, a group of fishing clubs, or a national group of sportfishing enthusiasts would be candidates for organizing an AMO. The AMO-forming coalition or group members would be assigned ownership in the AMO through share ownership. AMOs can be for-profit entities with shareholders entitled to dividends from annual profits. Others can be nonprofit organizations in which modest client fees are charged to cover the expense of managing their quota. Nonprofit AMOs with low fees could reserve some or all of their quotas for low-income individuals, with allocations carried out through a lottery.

Each AMO would receive a fixed share of the yearly recreational quota set by regulators. AMO owner/shareholders would have a substantial amount of flexibility in deciding how to use and manage their quota allocation. For example, a southern Florida AMO may allow its clients to fish its quota a month or so earlier than a northern Florida AMO to take advantage of a busy period for tourists. Another AMO may decide to set a higher-than-average limit on landings per client to appeal to fishers who fish only once or twice a year. Yet another AMO may decide to cater to fishers who want trophy fish and limit a client's catch in a trophy area to one or two fish.

Trades of fish quota among AMOs would be allowed, and more. Since anglers and managers may be uncomfortable with unconstrained trading, there might be a few restrictions to start, such as a cap on the quota share an AMO can hold. Given the implementation of ITQs in the commercial side of the red snapper fishery in 2007, trades would also be allowed between AMOs and commercial snapper ITQ holders. Quota trading among different AMOs and between recreational and commercial sectors would provide a nonpolitical, less confrontational way for allocating the TAC among various user groups.[12]

Regulators would be responsible for making sure each AMO adheres to its quota allocation so a reliable means for tracking landed fish, such as the issuance of fish tags, must be in place. Random "sting" operations with officers posing as clients could be carried out to discourage cheating or sloppy monitoring by the AMO. The consequences of an AMO exceeding its quota for the season by minor amounts would be a reduction in quota the following season, with an opportunity for the AMO to earn back its full quota with better adherence to quota in future years. Major violations, such as persistently exceeding quota by large amounts, would result in a loss of quota altogether.

The attractiveness of the AMO concept is in its ability to prevent overfishing at lower managerial costs, in its flexibility in meeting more demands from recreational fishers, and in its ability to avoid the inherent conflicts of allocating catches among disparate groups through the political process. With a strong incentive to protect and enhance their quota value, AMO owners assume important duties for effective management while having the freedom to innovate.

In addition to AMOs, ITQs are another viable approach for recreational fisheries that have significant participation of charter-based operations. These are operations that employ one or more boats, captains, and crew to take out groups of recreational fishers for a fee. By allocating a seasonal quota for each operator, one can control this sector's overall catch level each season. Like commercial ITQs, quotas can be traded so charter operators can adjust the level of operations as desired. New operators can enter by buying or leasing quotas from current operators. For fisheries with commercial ITQs, quotas can be traded between these sectors as well. A pilot program of ITQs for British Columbia salmon has been carried out for selected salmon fisheries for the commercial sector. Canadian proponents anticipate that ITQs for salmon charter operators could be incorporated into the system down the road (McRae and Pearse 2004). A similar system could be designed for commercial and charter-based salmon fisheries off northern California, Oregon, and Washington as well. In addition to their proximity, these fisheries share many of the same characteristics as the British Columbia salmon fisheries

One U.S. coastal fishery that was close to adopting a system of ITQs for commercial and charter-based operators was the Alaska halibut fishery. There are a significant number of charter operators (well over a thousand vessels) in the fishery, and their proportion of the seasonal catch has been steadily rising during the past ten years. A proposal to adopt ITQs in the charter-based portion of the halibut fishery was passed by the North Pacific Fishery Management Council in April 2001 (Criddle 2005). It was never implemented, however, because of concerns that the program did not include a plan to lower entry barriers for prospective charter operators and captains who worked for charter companies for acquiring ITQs. As of 2007, an analysis of a moratorium on expansion within the charter fleet and possible development of a revised ITQ program has been initiated.

Marine Protected Areas

Concerns over the effects of fishing have sparked a move in the United States to set aside ocean areas as marine protected areas (MPAs). These areas vary in terms of fishing restrictions, with the most limiting being a year-round ban on all fishing. Advocates see the MPA as a conceptually simple, easily enforced way of improving fish production and reversing the trends that have resulted in more than 40 percent of the U.S. fish stocks assessed by scientists as overfished or experiencing overfishing in 2003. Advocates of MPAs perceive them as providing a wide range of other benefits, including scientific knowledge, education, ecological protection, source production (e.g., spawning areas), spillover benefits, and intrinsic existence values.

In practice, however, MPAs have fallen short of expectations. For example, the Tortugas Shrimp Sanctuary (3,652 square nautical miles) was established to protect a portion of Florida's primary pink shrimp nursery grounds. Fishery managers expected the spillover benefit of increased shrimp yield in nearby areas open to shrimping after the sanctuary was established. Such was not the case, however, because of weak compliance (Coleman, Baker, et al. 2004, 14). During the years immediately after implementation, there was a high incidence of shrimp being illegally caught within the sanctuary, which prevented any spillover benefit. Evidence indicates that the situation has not improved. Recent declines in pink shrimp, which managers attribute to loss of sea grass and other environmental factors, have encouraged fishers to continue poaching shrimp within the sanctuary.

As another example, the Gulf of Mexico Fisheries Management Council established in 1990 the Longline/Buoy Gear Restricted Area (72,000 square nautical miles), which prohibited the use of longline/buoy gear for harvesting reef fish in designated nearshore waters around the Gulf. The intent was mainly to reduce fishing effort on groupers. Since implementation, longline fishing for groupers in waters beyond the MPA has intensified substantially and populations have seriously declined (Coleman, Baker, et al. 2004, 14). At the same time, overall fishing effort for grouper within the MPA has not declined because recreational and commercial fishers using other gear have increased their effort there.

The above case illustrates a hard lesson: MPAs will inevitably fail to reduce fishing effort because they do not solve the fundamental problem in fisheries—the tragedy of the commons. Unfortunately, MPA advocates overlook this lesson. Coleman, Baker, et al. (2004, 18) identify seven MPAs that were established in the Gulf of Mexico with the primary intent of reducing fishing effort and observe that, "rather than reducing effort, MPAs inevitably displace it, whether spatially or temporally." Moreover, when the shift in effort is to other fisheries, the result can be an increase in the number of fish stocks that become overfished.

Another hard lesson, illustrated in California, is that MPAs can be used for declaring large ocean areas off-limits to fishing. Such attempts have costly repercussions for fishers and thus can be expected to face stiff opposition. In

1999, the California legislature passed the Marine Life Protection Act, which mandates the establishment of state-run MPAs in the state's 3.6-million-acre coastal waters. When the system is fully in place, up to 20 percent of these waters (about 720,000 acres) could be closed to most types of fishing. Not surprisingly, commercial and recreational fisher groups protested loudly against the potential for such sweeping closures (Benfell 2001). The state's massive deficit closed off the millions of dollars that would be required to monitor and enforce the closures, and the plan was temporarily put on hold (McLaughlin and Rogers 2004). In April 2007, a portion of the closures were implemented.

MPAs have a role to play in improving ocean health, but there must be guidelines that improve their effectiveness and help mitigate abuse in the political arena. For example, areas open to fishing around an MPA must have an effective means, such as ITQs, that prevents intensification of fishing effort and possible overfishing. The ocean environment is dynamic and certain objectives, like rebuilding a severely depleted stock, are temporary, so any MPA created for a particular objective should be subject to periodic monitoring to see whether the objective is being met. If it is, the MPA should be reassessed to see whether it can be eliminated, with some form of ITQ management adopted to prevent depletion in the future.

Before an MPA is established, there should be the assurance that compliance will be high. Resources available for government enforcement are stretched thin, and alternatives will become necessary. The use of vessel monitoring systems (VMSs), through satellite tracking of vessels, can provide 90 percent compliance within area boundaries (Coleman, Baker, et al. 2004, 19). Increasing use of VMSs in fisheries will free government resources for other uses. Another way to maximize resources for MPAs is to encourage the use of private MPAs. In New Zealand, fishers have been reaping the rewards of investing in marine conservation through the formation of private management companies. These companies carry out their own stock assessments and, with backing of the New Zealand government, regulate harvests and establish their own no-take MPAs (e.g., see Arbuckle and Metzger 2000).

To mitigate political abuse, MPAs must not be used to reallocate resource use among different groups. In other words, creation of any zone for strictly sightseeing, recreational diving, or recreational fishing in an MPA must be offset by creation of areas for commercial fishing only. In addition, MPAs with no fishing restrictions should be implemented if and only if less costly alternatives—for example, ITQs with a series of declining annual TACs—cannot accomplish the desired objective.

Carrying out these recommendations will ensure that our ocean fisheries are jointly profitable and sustainable, and that marine protection is subject to the proper checks and balances to avoid political divisiveness and abuse.

Conclusion

The current regulatory approach to U.S. fisheries fails to prevent overfishing and generates enormous waste. The good news is that through more fully delineated property rights in fishing these problems can be solved. On the commercial side, ITQs and private harvesting agreements have brought about substantial benefits for the commercial side of a growing number of fisheries around the globe. For sedentary species, TURFs can do the same if entrepreneurs are allowed exclusive rights to areas they invest in for marine production. On the recreational side, property rights approaches have yet to be tried, but one promising concept waiting in the wings is the AMO. The AMO concept promises to provide better conservation, lower monitoring and enforcement costs, and a means for avoiding the inherent conflicts from politically allocating the catch while increasing the wealth of nature. For recreational fisheries with significant participation of charter-based operations, ITQs are a viable option.

To meet ecological demands, MPAs are seen as a conceptually simple, easily enforced way of reversing the trend of overfishing in U.S. fisheries. In practice, however, MPAs have fallen short of expectations. The main problems are unobtainable goals (e.g., reduced fishing effort), weak compliance, lack of performance monitoring, and potential for political misuse. With appropriate guidelines and with opportunities for more private participation, MPAs can become an effective tool for enhancing ocean systems.

Not to be overlooked are the property rights lessons that span different natural resources. A close cousin of ITQs for fish is the system of water rights in the West. Specific quantities or quotas of water are being allocated among different uses through water markets, including water purchased or leased from irrigators for the purpose of providing more water in the stream for trout and salmon. So too, one can imagine markets for ITQs being expanded to include fish quotas purchased from commercial fishers for some ecological or recreational purpose. The latter possibility can be seen in quota trades between AMOs and commercial fishers. In such cases, trades will be carried out if both sides benefit, thereby fostering greater overall wealth from nature.

Notes

1. On the recreational side, an estimated 17 million saltwater fishers spend more than $25 billion per year on fishing-related activities and products in the United States. See Kenney (2003).

2. The term *tragedy of the commons* is taken from Garrett Hardin's (1968) influential article describing the tendency for a jointly exploited resource held in common to become depleted over time. In the case of the fishery, ocean fish stocks are the commons. For a classic article on the fishery, see H. Scott Gordon (1954).

3. With trip limits set for each vessel, fishers are forced to discard fish when the amount of fish caught exceeds the limit set for a fishing trip. Discarded fish can succumb to poor handling or to predation because of their weakened condition when they are returned to the sea.

4. See also Ostrom (1990), 90.

5. For example, it took less than half a day to finalize a private harvesting agreement in the Pacific whiting fishery and little over a month in the North Pacific pollock fishery. After ITQs were deemed the preferred option by the Mid-Atlantic Fisheries Management Council, it took another ten years to implement them in the Atlantic surf clam fishery.

6. For a discussion, see Nikel-Zueger (2003), 18–24.

7. Pollock and menhaden comprise half of U.S. landings. Both have little, if any, recreational value. Pollock is used to produce frozen fish products, and menhaden is used almost exclusively to produce fish meal.

8. Discards are not included in the analysis of national and regional effects of fishing, so the results in Coleman, Figuera, et al. (2004) underestimate likely impacts.

9. Snapper discard mortality caused by shortened seasons, bag limits, and minimum size limits on the commercial side of the fishery alone amounts to more than 2 million pounds each year—a huge amount in a fishery that lands just 4.5 million pounds a year (NMFS 2004b).

10. Information based on a phone conservation with Kathy Viatella at Environmental Defense, January 21, 2005.

11. For example, 7.5 percent of the TAC was assigned to six CDQ groups, organized from fifty-six eligible Alaskan communities. These groups managed their harvest quotas and allocated returns.

12. Criddle (2005) shows that a system of ITQs for both charter-based sportfishing and commercial fishing produces higher total benefits than strictly commercial ITQs in the Alaska fishery. He also points out that ITQs trading across the two sectors would avoid the current conflict when catch allocations between the two sectors are made by political means.

References

Ad-Hoc Groundfish Strategic Plan Committee. 2000. *Pacific Fishery Management Council Groundfish Fishery Strategic Plan: Transition to Sustainability.* October. Online at http://www.pcouncil.org/groundfish/gflibrary/stratplan.pdf. Visited November 5, 2001.

Arbuckle, Michael, and Michael Metzger. 2000. *Food for Thought: A Brief History of the Future of Fisheries' Management.* Nelson, New Zealand: Challenger Scallop Enhancement Co. Ltd.

Arnason, Ragnar. 1996. Property Rights as an Organizational Framework in Fisheries: The Case of Six Fishing Nations. In *Taking Ownership: Property Rights and Fishery Management in the Atlantic Coast,* ed. Brian Lee Crowley. Halifax, Nova Scotia: Atlantic Institute for Market Studies, 99–114.

Benfell, Carol. 2001. Fishermen Oppose New Off-Limits Zones. *Press Democrat,* July 10.

Coleman, Felicia C., Pamela B. Baker, and Christopher C. Koenig. 2004. A Review of Gulf of Mexico Marine Protected Areas: Successes, Failures, and Lessons Learned. *Fisheries* 29: 10–20.

Coleman, Felicia C., Will F. Figuera, Jeffery S. Ueland, and Larry B. Crowder. 2004. The Impact of United States Recreational Fisheries on Marine Fish Populations. *Science* 305: 1958–1960.

Criddle, Keith R. 2005. Property Rights and Multiple-Use Fisheries. In *Evolving Property Rights in Marine Fisheries,* ed. Donald R. Leal. Lanham, MD: Rowman & Littlefield, 85–110.

Crutchfield, James A. 1973. Resources from the Sea. In *Ocean Resources and Public Policy,* ed. T. S. English. Seattle: University of Washington Press.

Crutchfield, James A., and G. Pontecorvo. 1969. *The Pacific Salmon Fisheries: A Study of Irrational Conservation.* Baltimore, MD: John Hopkins University Press, for Resources for the Future.

De Alessi, Michael. 1996. *Oysters and Willapa Bay.* Center for Conservation Case Study. Washington, DC: Competitive Enterprise Institute, March 1.

———. 1997. How Property Rights Can Spur Artificial Reefs. *Freeman* 47(2): 77–79.

Dinneford, Elaine, Kurt Iverson, Ben Muse, and Kurt Schelle. 1999. *Changes Under Alaska's Halibut IFQ Program, 1995 to 1998.* November. Online at http://www.cfec.state.ak.us/research/H98_TS/h_title.htm. Visited June 12, 2001.

Garrison, Karin. 2002. Extinction of Ocean Fish: A Growing Threat. *Endangered Species UPDATE* 19(5): 217–221.

General Accounting Office (GAO). 2002. *Individual Fishing Quotas: Better Information Could Improve Program Management.* GAO-03-159. Washington, DC, December.

Gordon, H. Scott. 1954. The Economic Theory of a Common Property Resource: The Fishery. *Journal of the Political Economy* 62(April): 124–142.

Grafton, R Quentin, Dale Squires, and Kevin J. Fox. 2000. Private Property and Economic Efficiency: A Study of a Common-Pool Resource. *Journal of Law & Economics* 43(October): 679–713.

Grimm, David. 2004. Sportfishers on the Hook for Dwindling U.S. Fish Stocks. *Science* 305(August): 1235.

Gulf of Mexico Fisheries Management Council (GMFMC). 2001. *Regulatory Amendment to the Reef Fish Fishery Management Plan to Set a Red Snapper Rebuilding Plan Through 2032.* Tampa, FL: Gulf of Mexico Fisheries Management Council.

Hannesson, Rögnvaldur. 2005. The Privatization of the Oceans. In *Evolving Property Rights in Marine Fisheries*, ed. Donald R. Leal. Lanham, MD: Rowman & Littlefield, 25–48.

Hardin, Garrett. 1968. The Tragedy of the Commons. *Science* 162: 1243–1248.

Hartley, M., and M. Fina. 2001. Changes in Fleet Capacity Following the Introduction of Individual Vessel Quotas in the Alaskan Pacific Halibut and Sablefish Fishery. In *Case Studies on the Effects of Transferable Fishing Quotas on Fleet Capacity and Concentration of Quota Ownership*, ed. Ross Shotton. FAO Fisheries Technical Paper 412. Rome: Food and Agriculture Organization of the United Nations. Online at http://www.fao.org/DOCREP/005/Y2498E/y2498eof.htm. Visited February 2, 2003.

Higgs, Robert. 1982. Legally Induced Technical Regress in the Washington Salmon Fishery. *Research in Economics History* 7: 55–86.

Jones, Laura. 2003. *Managing Fish: Ten Case Studies from Canada's Pacific Coast.* Vancouver, Canada: Fraser Institute.

Kenney, Justin. 2003. *Fact Sheet: Restoring America's Fisheries.* Washington, DC: Pew Oceans Commission. June.

Leal, Donald R. 2002. *Fencing the Fishery: A Primer on Ending the Race for Fish.* Bozeman, MT: PERC. Online at http://www.perc.org/pdf/guide_fish.pdf.

Loy, Wesley. 2000. Dividing the Fish. *Pacific Fishing*, November, 1–5.

McLaughlin, Ken, and Paul Rogers. 2004. State to Hit Pause on Plan for No-Fishing Zones. *San Jose Mercury News*, January 13.

McRae, Donald M., and Peter H. Pearse. 2004. Treaties and Transition: Towards a Sustainable Fishery on Canada's Pacific Coast. Unpublished manuscript available from the authors.

National Marine Fisheries Service (NMFS). 1999. *Our Living Oceans: Report on the Status of U.S. Living Marine Resources, 1999.* U.S. Department of Commerce, NOAA Technical Memorandum NMFS-F/SPO-41. Online at http://spo.nwr.noaa.gov/olo99.htm. Visited July 10, 2000.

———. 2000. 2000 Report to the IFQ Fleet (July). Restricted Access Management Program, Alaska Region. Online at http://www.fakr.noaa.gov/ram/rtf00.pdf. Visited June 12, 2001.

———. 2004a. *Sustaining and Rebuilding: National Marine Fisheries Service 2003 Report to Congress on the Status of U.S. Fisheries.* U.S. Department of Commerce,

NOAA, National Marine Fisheries Service. Online at http://www .nmfs.noaa. gov/sfa/statusoffisheries/statusostockso3/Report_Text.pdf. Visited November 4, 2004.

———. 2004b. *Gulf of Mexico Red Snapper: Red Snapper SEDAR Data Workshop Report.* St. Petersburg, FL, June 17.

———. 2005. *Fisheries of the United States—2005.* February. Fisheries Statistics Division. Online at http://www.st.nmfs.gov/st1/fus/fus05/fus_2005.pdf. June 26, 2007.

National Research Council. 1999. *Sharing the Fish: Toward a National Policy in Individual Fishing Quotas.* Washington, DC: National Academy Press.

Nikel-Zueger, Manuel. 2003. *Saving Salmon the American Indian Way.* PERC Policy Series, No. PS-29. Bozeman, MT: PERC.

Ostrom, Elinor. 1990. *Governing the Commons.* New York: Cambridge University Press.

Repetto, Robert. 2001. The Atlantic Sea Scallop Fishery in the U.S. and Canada: A Natural Experiment in Fisheries Management Regimes. Discussion paper, Yale School of Forestry & Environmental Studies, April 15.

Rogers, Paul. 2003. No-fishing Zone Takes Effect Today. *San Jose Mercury News,* April 9.

Sullivan, J. M. 2000. Harvesting Cooperatives and U.S. Antitrust Law: Recent Developments and Implications. Paper presented at the International Institute of Fisheries Economics 2000 conference, "Microbehavior Macroresults," July 10–15, Corvallis, OR. Online at http://oregonstate.edu/dept/IIFET/2000/abstracts/sullivan.html. Visited April 8, 2002.

Sutinen, Jon G., and Robert J. Johnston. 2003. Angling Management Organizations: Integrating the Recreational Sector into Fishery Management. *Marine Policy* 27: 471–487.

Tennyson, Janet. 2004. Senate Introduces Freedom to Fish Act to Protect Saltwater Access. Press release by American Sport Fishing Association. Online at http://www.asafishing.org/asa/newsroom/newspr_040104.html. Visited June 29, 2007.

Townsend, Ralph E. 2005. Producer Organizations and Agreements in Fisheries. In *Evolving Property Rights in Marine Fisheries,* ed. Donald R. Leal. Lanham, MD: Rowman & Littlefield, 127–148.

U.S. Commission on Ocean Policy. 2004. *An Ocean Blueprint for the 21st Century,* chapter 19, Achieving Sustainable Fisheries. Online at http://www.ocean commission.gov/documents/prepub_report/chapter19.pdf. Visited November 2004.

Ward, J., and J. G. Sutinen. 1994. Vessel Entry-Exit Behavior in the Gulf of Mexico Shrimp Fishery. *American Journal of Agricultural Economics* 76(4): 916–923.

Wilen, James E., and Francis R. Homans. 2000. Unraveling Rent Losses in Modern Fisheries: Production, Market, and Regulatory Inefficiencies? Paper presented at the Western Economics Association 74th International Conference, Vancouver, BC, June 30–July 3.

Wolf, Edward C. 1993. *A Tidewater Place: Portrait of the Willapa Ecosystem.* Long Beach, WA: Willapa Alliance.

Woodward, Richard T., and Wade Griffen. 2003. Size and Bag Limits in Recreational Fisheries: Theoretical and Empirical Analysis. *Marine Resource Economics* 18: 239–262.

CHAPTER SEVEN

The Mining Landscape

Bootleggers, Baptists, and the Promised Land

ROGER E. MEINERS AND ANDREW P. MORRISS

Since at least 1849, mining in the United States has been based on free access to mineral resources on public land. The mining booms of the nineteenth century brought great wealth to the western United States, producing newly rich towns from San Francisco, California, to Butte, Montana. For more than a century mining was the dominant industry in some western states. Given its economic power, the industry had little to fear from state governments; those same states reliably supported the mining industry in Congress to preserve mining companies' access to federal lands.

Today, a new form of gold—the wealth of nature—is present in those same areas of the American West, and it goes beyond mineral deposits. Increasing demands for recreational uses make views as valuable, and sometimes more so, as gold. The rise of an industry built around nature tourism is bringing new wealth to parts of the West. This industry surpasses mining in some dimensions, including the generation of tax revenues and employment.

Because much of the West remains in a quasi-colonial status because of federal ownership of a large percentage of land in many states, the allocation of resources between these two industries is a highly political question.

Landowners do not simply assess the costs and benefits of mining and tourism and choose the activity they prefer. Instead, because property rights are unclear or politically determined, even landowners with some private property rights must contend for control of neighboring parcels of public land. Political groups seek to impose their preferences over public lands (and private property as well) via Washington. And people living outside the West increasingly demand a voice in the allocation of "public" resources in the West. Hence, for much of the West, politics dominates property rights.

In this chapter, we assess the impact of these changes on mining institutions and conclude that the rise of the tourist industry in the West threatens the political protections upon which the mining industry has relied. As a result, mining interests in the United States will be increasingly subject to expropriation through regulatory measures.

The Context

Mining represents a declining economic sector in the United States. The number of mining establishments, annual payroll, sales, and number of paid employees all dropped from 1997 to 2002. This decline was mitigated by the spike in mineral prices in subsequent years, but mining is still not a large industry for the country. Nonetheless, it remains an important sector for some states. Nevada, for example, received more than $10 billion in 1998 in direct and indirect revenue from the nonfuel mineral mining industry (National Mining Association 2002). For most states, however, tourism exceeds mining in economic impact. Table 7.1 compares the economic impact of the two industries for the top five mining states.

The mention of mining often carries with it the romantic image of the hardy prospector, with his pick, mule, and pan, and the lucky strike that transforms him into a cigar-smoking gentleman patron of the arts in a western boomtown. Never entirely realistic, this portrait does not capture the nature of today's capital-intensive, regulated industry operating on thin profit margins and dependent on multiple income streams from ore that is often literally the waste of earlier generations of miners. We briefly outline the state of the mining industry in the economy to place it in context. An understanding of the mining industry requires more than knowledge of its place in the economy, however, because the legal regime under which mining operates is as significant a feature of the landscape as the shape of the ore veins.

TABLE 7.1

Mining and tourism: Total economic impacts (2002)

State	Mining				
	Employment	Direct economic gain (millions of dollars)	State and local tax revenue (millions of dollars)	Federal tax revenue (millions of dollars)	Production (millions of dollars)
Arizona	11,240	2,408.9	141.7	102.7	2,130.2
California	13,506	2,802.2	113.0	56.3	3,440.0
Montana	4,625	360.6	79.6	124.4	788.5
Nevada	10,470	1,990.8	146.6	168.8	2,900.0
Wyoming	11,177	2,004.6	509.8	396.5	3,387.0

State	Tourism			
	Employment	Direct economic gain (millions of dollars)	State and local tax revenue (millions of dollars)	Federal tax revenue (millions of dollars)
Arizona	144,200	9,934.3	688.4	662.7
California	820,200	68,218.4	4,763.1	5,139.9
Montana	25,900	1,960.8	102.6	136.9
Nevada	336,300	20,243.5	1,102.1	1,560.5
Wyoming	27,700	1,604.1	88.0	118.7

SOURCES: Tourism statistics from Travel Industry Association of America, Research Department, Impact of Travel on State Economies, 2004 Edition (Washington, DC); mining statistics from National Mining Association, online at http://www.nma.org/statistics/state_statistics_2002.asp# (visited February 1, 2005).

Defining the Mining Landscape

Hardrock mining is a capital-intensive industry in which large quantities of low-grade ore must be extracted and processed to produce a mixture of useable minerals (Lacy 1998, 49; Rinke 2000, 825; Humphries and Vincent 2001). These investments yield results: annual metal mining output in the United States in 2002 was approximately $8.3 billion (U.S. Census Bureau 2005). Hardrock metal mining (which does not include coal, gravel, or sand mining) occurs largely west of the Mississippi and is concentrated in five western states (Humphries and Vincent 2001). The combination of these factors gives the mining industry three characteristics critical to understanding its economic position: the vulnerability to political risks, the high cost of locating new deposits and production once located, and the location of most domestic mineral deposits on federal land.

POLITICAL RISK

Mining is particularly vulnerable to political risks. The combination of capital intensity, the limited and fixed locations, and the production of wealth renders the industry vulnerable to expropriation; once a mine is developed it cannot be moved. Historically, this vulnerability has been exploited by governments outside the United States that have partially or completely expropriated mining interests (Vagts 1978, 36). As a result, the more secure property rights environment in the United States drew mining investment into U.S. operations (Otto and Cordes 2002, 1–48).

Relatively secure property rights do not eliminate opportunities for rent seeking. The United States is able to exploit its advantages as a provider of "unlikely-to-be-directly-expropriated" property rights in mineral deposits to "charge" mining concerns higher indirect taxes through environmental and other regulations than could a country with less stable property rights. Oliver Williamson (1983) has explained that when there is insecurity about the strength of property rights, there is less incentive to invest or to have investments that are less asset-specific. In private relationships, parties may help bind themselves to a relationship by making themselves "hostage" to an exchange (Williamson 1983). But when the other party to an exchange is the sovereign, the risk is more political, rather than purely legal or economic.

Mining is vulnerable to partial "regulatory expropriation." Immobile capital investments prevent businesses from escaping regulatory burdens imposed after the investments are made. This has important effects on the structure of firms in the industry. The National Research Council concluded that regulation of mining already has reached the level at which "it is only the larger, more established firms that can afford to make the investment in time, extensive data collection, complex analyses, and expensive environmental protection measures that the state and federal regulations currently require" (NRC 1999, 33).

State-level political risks to the mining industry are mitigated by the industry's relatively large size in those states where it is present, giving it political clout commensurate with its economic impact, but the political risks to the industry from the national government are exaggerated by the regional nature of the industry. Since most states have little or no interest in the mining industry, and since mineral resources are largely on federal land, states without mining interests can easily form a majority coalition in favor of converting federally owned resources into a form that "shares" the mineral wealth nationally. Indeed, the regional nature of the conflict over the mining industry dates back to the first national mining law in 1866, with Easterners seeking federal revenue and Westerners seeking free access to mineral resources (Mayer and Riley 1985, 48–53).

As a regional, capital-intensive industry, mining lacks a mass political base to protect it. Hardrock mining (which excludes coal mining and nonmetal mining such as gravel and clay) hit peak employment in 1916, when 195,438 people—almost one-half of 1 percent of the U.S. labor force—worked directly in the industry. Today, hardrock mining directly employs only about 31,000 people, or one-quarter of one-tenth of 1 percent of the labor force.[1] Only the protection provided minority interests by the structure of the U.S. Senate has prevented the nonmining states from forcing a resource transfer from the mining states to the rest of the country (Morriss, Meiners, and Dorchak 2003, 567–568).

As mining's share of state economies declines, and other industries that define their interests as sometimes opposed to mining, such as tourism, grow in western states, mining's political protection from both state and national regulatory burdens and property rights insecurity erodes. This erosion stems from mining's dependence on maintaining within-state political alliances both to block state attempts at regulatory expropriation and to keep sufficient national Senate political power to block the efforts of nonmining states at redistribution.

Because one critical aspect of the legal landscape is the security of mining firms' property rights, and because secure property rights are critical to inducing investment in long-term operations (Bohn and Deacon 2000; Otto and Cordes 2002, 1–51), instability in the regulatory environment reduces the relative advantage of investing in U.S. mining operations. Mining is thus an economically vulnerable activity with little protection from political risks: it generates enormous wealth yet has significant capital at risk; it has a limited regional political base; and the industry's workforce is small, eliminating a potential source of political support.

COST OF LOCATION AND PRODUCTION

Although the rewards to locating a mineral deposit can be significant, the cost of location is also substantial. Because economically viable deposits are relatively rare, locating new deposits is a lengthy process that typically costs $150,000 to $250,000, with another $500,000 to $1 million necessary to determine whether to proceed with the site (Lacy 1998; NRC 1999, 23).

Production is also complex and expensive (NRC 1999, 25–26). A successful mining operation requires large capital investment in extraction, significant intellectual capital (patents, trade secrets), and the ability to ride out fluctuations in commodity prices and currencies. Successful operators of mining operations are therefore likely to be companies with large amounts of capital at risk, increasing their vulnerability to expropriation.

As a result of the high costs of location and production, "mining has one of the lowest returns on investment of major industries" (NRC 1999, 24). Critics of the mining industry often do not take these costs into account, focusing on the gross value of the mineral deposit rather than on the net value. Distinguishing between net and gross costs is critical to the decision of whether to invest in mining operations in a particular jurisdiction. Because net mineral values are discounted for the probability of regulatory expropriation, changes in the legal regime governing mineral rights can reduce the net value below the economically sustainable point.

FEDERAL LAND

Most of the unclaimed mineral reserves in the United States are located on federal land. This largely follows from mining's dependence on western locations: since the federal government owns a large share of the land in these states, most undeveloped mineral resources are also located on federal land. The predominant federal ownership of untapped (and unknown) mineral resources means there is a dominant provider of unmined land suitable for mineral exploration.

The federal government "sells" mineral rights primarily through the General Mining Law of 1872.[2] The crucial institutional features of that statute are that transfers of mineral rights from the public domain to private ownership are self-initiated and nondiscretionary. Someone who has located a mineral deposit can, with minimal expense, procure full title to the mineral estate alone or to both the mineral and surface estates (Morriss, Meiners, and Dorchak 2004, 756–758). This is an important distinction between the Mining Law and the most commonly mentioned alternatives—leasing and auctions (Prince 1998, 395).

The most significant restriction that must be overcome for obtaining a mineral patent is the requirement of discovery of a valuable deposit—"the *sine qua non* of a valid mining claim" (Outerbridge 1998, 30-15). The patent process itself is straightforward and focuses on collecting the information necessary to document the claim through a survey of the land, giving notice to other potential claimants, and verifying the mineral deposit. Once the patent is issued, the claim becomes private property, which "removes any opportunity the federal government has to collect revenues on the minerals extracted, because the government no longer has title to either the minerals or the land" (General Accounting Office 1989, 11). Of course, the government may still tax the property as it does all other property, through income taxes on income collected from economic activity, property taxes on the value of the land, and so forth.

There are good reasons to believe that the policy of providing free access to resources to those who discover them is the most appropriate means of determining when and how to develop resources located on public land (Morriss, Meiners, and Dorchak 2004; Gordon and Van Doren 1998). The policy has withstood more than a century of attacks by interest groups seeking to redistribute mineral resources (Morriss, Meiners, and Dorchak 2004).

Hardrock mining remains regionally concentrated and protected only by the combined institutional power of western state senators. This protection becomes increasingly costly as the economic interests of those western states diversify. As Tables 7.1 and 7.2 demonstrate, tourism is now more important than mining in terms of state and local tax revenues in four of the top five mining states, and far exceeds mining's employment impact in all five states. Because mining depends so heavily on deposits located (until privatized) on federal land, a change in the balance of power in western states leaves the industry increasingly vulnerable both to limits on future expansion to new deposits and to regulatory expropriation of existing investments through increased regulation of current operations.

TABLE 7.2

Mining impacts as a percentage of tourism impacts

State	Mining as a percentage of tourism		
	Employment (%)	State and local taxes (%)	Federal taxes (%)
Arizona	7.8	20.6	15.5
California	1.6	2.4	1.1
Montana	17.9	77.6	90.9
Nevada	3.1	13.3	10.8
Wyoming	40.4	579.3	334.0

SOURCES: Tourism statistics from Travel Industry Association of America, Research Department, Impact of Travel on State Economies, 2004 Edition (Washington, DC); mining statistics from National Mining Association, online at http://www.nma.org/statistics/state_statistics_2002.asp# (visited February 1, 2005).

The Institutional Advantages of Free Access

The free access principle provides several important institutional advantages, which we have described in an earlier work and summarize here (Morriss, Meiners, and Dorchak 2004). The fundamental problem is to explain the seeming gift of public resources to private interests, a problem ably exploited by former Secretary of the Interior Bruce Babbitt's melodramatic ceremony in which he produced a mock government check for $10 billion made out to a mining patent holder at a press conference marking the issuance of a patent under the law. The primary solution until recently has been to look to the historic purpose of the Mining Law: "to promote mineral exploration and development on federal lands in the Western United States, offer an opportunity to obtain a clear title to mines already being worked, and help settle the West" (Humphries and Vincent 2001).

LEGAL RATIONALE

The "promotion of settlement and exploration" explanation is partially true. The Mining Law grew out of the experiences of the mineral rushes, particularly the gold rushes that began with the California Gold Rush of 1848–1849 (Morriss 1998, 620). As a practical matter, there was little alternative to free access in California in 1848–1849, although the later Canadian experience suggests that, albeit it with the application of considerable resources, the federal government might have controlled access to at least some mineral resources (Greever 1963, 359–367). Nonetheless, free access was a logical outgrowth of the effective status of mineral resources on federal land as un-owned common pool resources during much of the late nineteenth century, much as ocean fish in unclaimed waters are today (Adler 2002, 11–18).

Although this explanation is true, it does not take into account the institutional advantages offered by the free access principle. The United States had experience with selling public resources to generate government revenues. The government rejected sales in favor of free access during the nineteenth century, in part because of the problems sales produced (Lacy 1995, 17–18). However, the settlement rationale does not explain the persistence of free access well beyond the point at which the federal government achieved effective control over its landholdings in the West. Finally, it does not explain the persistence of privatization through free access as a common element of federal land policy across much of the nineteenth century and well into the twentieth.

Critics of the Mining Law have one ready answer to this persistence: most conclude it must be because of the power and influence of the recipients of this great "giveaway" (Leshy 1987, 17; Kysar 2003, 707). We contend instead that the open access to public resources is an evolved institution (de Soto 2000, 105–151; Hayek 1978, 85–88) whose persistence is best understood as a response to incentive problems (Morriss, Meiners, and Dorchak 2004, 764–789).

ECONOMIC RATIONALE FOR OPEN ACCESS

The essence of the supply side of a private market is that as long as one is willing and able to invest in an enterprise, putting aside those restricted by entry regulation, one may invest in the hope of being successful. One prospects the market to discern whether a profitable opportunity may exist to, for instance, make cabinets, build houses, run a flower shop, or be a glass blower. To enter the mining business, one prospects potential lodes.

There are benefits for all if any business—whether a mine or other business—is successful. Goods and services are produced for consumer use. Individuals are employed and earn wages. For governments, businesses and their employees pay taxes that fund government activities and provide resources for politicians and bureaucrats to allocate.

Among the economic lessons of the past century is the fact that barriers to entry impede competition and so reduce the benefits of market competition. Eliminating such barriers has improved markets, from transportation to pharmaceuticals. There are few advocates of increasing entry barriers into markets as a general matter, and those who promote them in specific areas bear a heavy burden of demonstrating that the barriers provide a social benefit.

Adding a barrier to entry is what some mining critics attempt to do by insisting that when a lode is discovered, the government should be paid a high claim fee based on the estimated profit of the lode, or that the government should be paid a royalty based on the volume of minerals extracted. This is no different from advocating that any business should have to pay a premium to the government when a new facility is located in what is believed to be a particularly desirable location, so that the government is rewarded for "allowing" a profitable enterprise to stake a claim in the market.

THE GENIUS OF THE MINING LAW

Valuable mineral deposits await discovery, but the current value of these deposits is minimal because their location is unknown. Until someone successfully applies resources to the task of locating the deposits, they have little value. Encouraging investments to discover mineral deposits is a critical part of mining law. Any legal regime that reserves a portion of the find for the government (e.g., royalties) provides a lesser incentive for locating resources than those that do not.

The Mining Law transfers title for a nominal fee but only to those who have produced knowledge about the location of a valuable deposit. It is the production of the knowledge about the deposit that creates the value— there is no value without knowledge and, therefore, without investment in creating knowledge. In fact, the language of the Mining Law's grants of rights ("patents") is more than an unconscious parallel to intellectual property rights, for the incentive issues are similar.

Like patent law, the Mining Law rewards the creation of tradable property rights in valuable assets. Rights holders are also able to hold their claims on the mineral assets until they are ready to develop them, rather than being forced to act immediately, which "provides much of the incentive for making the investment in the first place. . . . Exploration expenditures are much more risky [under discretionary grants of time-limited rights], and therefore less likely to be made, because of a time limit that will not permit a deliberate program of investigation and data evaluation and because of the frightening uncertainty of being able to meet the regulatory test for discovery of a commercial deposit of minerals even if encouraging results are obtained" (Parr 1989, 65). The fixed time period for rights awarded under discretionary grant programs reduces the value of the rights because the requirement that development occur forces a calculation of the likelihood that market conditions will support development during that period. This reduces the incentive for investment compared with the longer time horizon offered by the grant of tradable property rights.

Investors must consider not only the current royalty, tax, and other expense rates but also whether those rates are likely to change in the future. In the case of a private landowner and a prospector, a contract negotiated in advance of the prospector's investment can ensure that the discovery of mineral resources does not lead to a sudden change in the expected return on the resources found. Market pressures limit landowners' ability to extract all the gains from discovery, and legal institutions limit ex post opportunistic expropriation value by the landowner. Governments have a problem making credible commitments for the future through contracts (see generally North and Weingast 1989).

In the case of the American West, the federal government's large land-holdings mean it faces little competition in the sale of mineral rights and so is less subject to market discipline than it would be if landholdings were less concentrated. Even more importantly, governments as a class have difficulty making credible long-term commitments compared with private landowners. Of course, both reputation effects and constitutional guarantees can safeguard the actual language of contracts with the government from forced changes. Governments cannot commit, however, not to use other margins to expropriate. For example, the government cannot commit that it will not change environmental regulations in such a way as to reduce the mining company's ability to operate under the terms of its lease. Because mining interests are particularly attractive targets for resource extraction by governments, reducing the threat of expropriation is an important element in creating an incentive to locate.

By vesting the resource locator with title to the minerals and, at the resource holder's option, with fee simple title to the surface estate as well, the government increases the strength of the reputation constraint on its activities. Expropriating a vested property right requires the government to pay for the value of what it expropriates to avoid destroying value in *all* vested property rights—not just mineral rights—under its jurisdiction because uncompensated expropriation reduces the general level of security in property rights generally. By giving owners of mineral rights property rights of equal status to other property rights, the Mining Law provides mining interests with important allies among property owners generally and significantly reduces the gains available to the government from expropriation.

Of course, the government still has margins under which it can harm the mining interest. Special environmental restrictions on mining activity may be imposed on private landowners as well as on lessees or contractors. Again, the clarity of the property rights granted by the Mining Law provides additional protection. Although the regulatory takings doctrine offers some additional check on such forms of expropriation, it is more difficult to establish such claims in the absence of a clearly defined property interest. Creating a general ownership interest in land with mineral resources, as opposed to a lesser interest such as a lease, increases the cost of reneging on a commitment not to expropriate. This increases the value of the incentive to locate, leading to the discovery of more mineral wealth.

The incentives of mineral rights owners to maximize the value of property, including surface rights, also depend on the structure of ownership.

Landowners with secure property rights to both the surface and mineral estates will choose among land management strategies to maximize their net returns from the land. If there are valued uses of the surface estate such as recreation, landowners may exploit them rather than mine or use mining methods that accommodate the surface uses. If property rights are not secure, or the mineral rights owner does not hold surface rights, then the mineral rights owner might not benefit from those uses, and incentives will be skewed as to long-term management strategies. Because land management choices present a continuum of possible strategies, residual claimant status can be a powerful incentive for environmentally sound land management practices on the margin. For example, a landowner who engages in conservation practices that increase wildlife habitat and so enhances recreational values may be rewarded by the marketplace for increasing the value of the land (Fretwell and Podolsky 2003, 156–157).

Secure property rights also promote consideration of alternate uses by extending the time horizon of the rights holders. Where mineral rights are of limited duration, there is an incentive for overly rapid exploitation because resources left at the end of the ownership period are lost. The resource extraction problem, in which a resource is owned only when removed from the land, becomes similar to a commons exploitation problem, and a result comparable to the "tragedy of the commons" is more likely. Lengthening the time horizon is critical to creating incentives for choosing management strategies that produce future payments, as from recreation or hunting, over "rape-and-scrape" short-term strategies that merely maximize immediate extractive value (Yandle and Morriss 2001).

PROBLEMS OF ACTIVE POLITICAL CONTROL

As Richard Epstein notes, "a rule that allows the first possessor ownership of the soil is not likely to lead to a premature exhaustion of the fields. The owner who stakes out a bit of land can then decide how and when to cultivate it and when to let it lie fallow. Indeed, the long-term time horizons give the right incentives against overuse" (Epstein 1995, 62). As a result, mineral law regimes that do not provide outright title produce duration-related problems, as the end period will involve attempts by the outgoing resource owner to maximize the land's wealth at the expense of the residual claimant (Scott 1987, 2033). By creating a single bundle of rights uniting the surface and mineral estates, the Mining Law avoids these temporal division problems.

Moreover, state ownership of mineral resources (which includes leasing of mineral rights since reversion remains in state hands) must confront a critical problem with such schemes. The mineral rights holders are not full residual claimants, nor are the government land management agencies (such as the Bureau of Land Management) that hold the future interest. Public agencies do not reap direct benefits of increasing land value and do not bear the direct costs of reduced land value. Moreover, there are conflicts of interest inherent in government ownership of mineral resources: "The desire to assert control through ownership or equity participation places the government in the position of being both regulator and partner" (Otto and Cordes 2002, 1-43). The results of government equity ownership, common outside the United States, are state enterprises "seldom able to achieve the decisional independence or abilities necessary to mirror private sector performance standards—they were unable to recreate the social insulation from governments and local demands historically provided by foreign investors" (Otto and Cordes 2002, 1-49).

Discretionary authority is a key condition for the existence of corruption (Aidt 2003, F633). "The Mining sector has certain characteristics that make it especially vulnerable to corruption, including: the requirement for large initial capital expenditures; lack of choice in location; . . ." (Marshall 2001, 37). Nondiscretionary privatization of resources, as provided by the Mining Law, also reduces corruption by eliminating the opportunity for someone to demand payment in exchange for a discretionary decision. Indeed, the structure of the Mining Law may well have been a response to earlier corruption problems with the lead leasing program of the 1820s (Clawson 1971, 126–127).

Importantly, the Mining Law privatizes resources by allowing private entities, not the government, to choose both *which* resources are privatized and *when* they will be privatized. This avoids the potential for corruption in the selection and scheduling of privatization. Although the government does not obtain significant revenue directly from the privatization, it obtains income from the mineral resources. As with any profitable enterprise, revenue from resource exploitation may be taxed. Even the staunchest critics of the Mining Law, such as John Leshy, concede this point: "hardrock mineral development under the Mining Law, like any income-producing business, eventually produces some direct or indirect payment to Uncle Sam. The argument for greater revenue return is thus not an overwhelming argument for reform of the Mining Law" (Leshy 1987, 366).

Mineral Rights in the Twenty-First Century

Where does the mining industry stand today? Despite its political vulnerability, the industry has prospered in the United States. This can largely be attributed to the combination of the (perhaps unintentional) institutional virtues of the General Mining Law of 1872 and the procedural rules of Congress that have given western mining states the ability to block attempts to "reform" the law in pursuit of rent seeking by nonwestern interests. As western states' economies become more dependent on tourism and other industries, the mining industry's protection against "reform" of the Mining Law is weakened to the extent that other industries view mining as a competitor.

This threat is exacerbated if a coalition between tourism interests and antimining interests can be forged to impose restrictions on mining that do not affect other landowners. As we suggest below, we do not think the two industries have an *inherent* conflict of interest but one that exists only because of the political nature of the allocation of federal land needed for both industries. While federal lands remain political—that is, while they remain publicly owned by agencies without residual claimant status—such conflicts are likely to grow.

POLITICAL CONTROL OF LAND MEETS INCOMPLETE PRIVATIZATION

In his "bootleggers and Baptists" theory, Bruce Yandle argues that successful lobbying efforts often result when one supporting group—the "Baptists"—takes the moral high ground while the other group—the "bootleggers"—provide political resources to gain competitive advantage (Yandle 1983). The bootleggers and Baptists theory explains how implicitly shared lobbying efforts reduce the cost of gaining political advantage and how ideology can create such implicit sharing. There is potential for a bootleggers and Baptists coalition against the mining industry in the American West, a coalition possible because of the combination of incomplete opportunities for privatization of federal land and political control of the extensive western federal public lands.

IS THERE A CONFLICT BETWEEN MINING AND TOURISM?

Mining and tourism are sometimes, but not always, incompatible land uses. Mining requires excavations, the use of earth-moving equipment, and the processing of ore. For some tourist uses, including wilderness experiences of the "cathedral" variety (Nelson 1997), the presence of a mining operation near a recreational area detracts from the experience.

Mining operations need not be completely in conflict with recreational uses, however. Resource extractions have been successfully conducted in wildlife habitat, most famously by the Audubon Society in Louisiana (Lee 2001). Landowners may change management practices to enhance alternate uses when those uses produce revenue, as has happened in the case of timber company lands (Fretwell and Podolsky 2003). Furthermore, mine sites are also tourist attractions, such as the Homestake mine in Lead, South Dakota.[3] Tours emphasize mining history, engineering feats in creating the mine, technology, and human accomplishments rather than the natural wonders of the Black Hills region.

Problems arise not because the different uses are completely incompatible but because the only way to acquire land in the West for privately conducting either activity is by obtaining a mining patent. Since no other means of privatizing federally owned lands remain, the General Mining Law is the only method of securing title to the land. As noted above, securing title under the Mining Law does not obligate the owner to conduct mining operations, but it does entail expending the resources necessary to document the presence of a viable mineral resource. This is not a complete barrier to privatizing land for nonmining purposes; as critics of the Mining Law frequently point out, land is regularly acquired under the statute for nonmining purposes (General Accounting Office 1989, 24–25). Nonetheless, the Mining Law is incomplete as a means of privatizing federal land.

Given that resources can be claimed by more than one party, claimants with different priorities may seek to make use of the same land. A mining company may wish to develop the mineral resources while recreation groups may wish to preserve the same site for hiking, hunting, or other uses. Although the Mining Law's critics charge that it inappropriately resolves such conflicts by giving mining use a priority over nonmining uses (Leshy 1987, 26),[4] they ignore the freedom provided to landowners who gain title to do as they wish with their property.

The Mining Law provides an absolute preference for *private ownership* of mineral resources over *public ownership* of those resources, but the law says nothing about *what* the private owners must do with the mineral resources once they have acquired them. Rights owners are free not to exploit the mineral deposits on their property as they have full title to the resource and, at their option, to the surface estate as well. Ironically, when mineral rights owners do make alternative uses of their claims, they are often accused of being speculators or of inappropriately using the mining law to privatize public property.

Secure property rights provide owners with the incentives to consider the long-term value of the land. Property owners take into account the impact of their decisions by incorporating the value of the land into the rights holders' wealth. Landowners who damage their property by extracting minerals today gain in the current period from the additional production but lose value from the land's decline in long-term productive potential. These factors are capitalized in the value of property.

The same is not true of resources held by government agencies. Institutional means other than increasing the value of the land are necessary to persuade public land managers to consider alternative uses to resources they control. The Federal Land Policy Management Act (FLPMA) of 1976 attempts to provide this through a complex framework for balancing different land uses. The success of the FLPMA in striking an appropriate balance is open to question.

To the extent that mineral resource rights are severed from surface rights, the mineral rights holder's incentives to mitigate harm to the surface rights or to consider the value of alternative uses of the surface estate must be provided by outside authority, either through contract or regulation. Where the rights are combined and held by a single owner, however, the rights holder has a powerful incentive to make decisions on when and how to extract in light of their consequences for both the mineral resource and the future value of the surface estate. The Mining Law's structure produces a default ownership structure that reduces the costs of attempting to maximize the total value of the mineral and surface resources. The point is not that the Mining Law will "save" every parcel; the value of a method of mineral production that destroys the surface estate may well outweigh the residual value from the surface estate. When it does, the resource owner will not preserve or restore the surface estate. An important benefit of the Mining Law, however, is that mineral rights owners have strong incentives to consider the impact on surface estates.

The question of the environmental impact of mining remains. When mining is conducted on private land, particularly on private land adjoining other private land, there is no reason for concern. Private landowners have powerful incentives to monitor the condition of their land because their wealth is reduced as the value of their land is reduced. Government land managers lack this incentive because they do not suffer wealth consequences of damage inflicted by adjoining landowners. Other than the problem of insufficient incentive for governments to monitor their land, however, there is little reason to think that the general principles of tort, property, and contract are inadequate to deal with the environmental consequences that arise between neighbors or that the environmental statutes (the Clean Water Act, the Clean Air Act, etc.) are inadequate to deal with mining's overall impact on the environment.

BOOTLEGGERS AND BAPTISTS

There is a problem with the Mining Law's effect on land-use decisions. It is not that the law does not privatize enough federal land, with or without mineral resources under it; rather, it is that the Mining Law creates too few residual claimants. Removing some of the doctrinal accretions and statutory complications to patenting joint mineral-surface estates would improve the Mining Law's performance in this regard. As Gordon and Van Doren concluded in their study of the statute: "the 1872 Mining Law serves America relatively well. It could be improved by broadening its reach to all federal land and allowing any interested party to bid for public resources" (1998, 22).

Conflicting land use is not the problem. The problem instead lies in the method for resolving the conflicts. If all land in question were held by private owners, the conflict would be resolved by advocates of the competing uses bidding for control of the resources. Such a contest would not be as favorable toward mining as many suppose. Mining is a low-margin business, and many deposits of mineral resources cannot be economically exploited. Moreover, tax incentives favor preservation uses.

Thus the primary problem is that only certain parcels of federally owned land can be claimed; claiming is possible if the parcels meet the criteria of not having withdrawn from the Mining Law and having a mineral deposit upon them. The second of these criteria requires a considerable investment to determine, and not all parcels will qualify.

This would be a problem if the list of available parcels were fixed, for the assignment of a parcel to the claimable or unclaimable category would not have taken into account the changes in mining technology and mineral prices that determine which parcels are exploitable. The more serious problem is that the allocation of parcels to one or the other is based instead on the political process.

For simplicity's sake, let us assume that any given parcel of land has only three potential uses: mining, dude ranch, or primitive recreation (i.e., without development). For nonwithdrawn land with a mineral deposit, the acquirer can choose among all three options. For nonwithdrawn lands without a mineral deposit, the land cannot be acquired directly but may be leased from the federal land management agency. For withdrawn lands, the land may be used only for primitive recreation. Actual federal land policy is somewhat more complex, but this captures the essence. Nonwithdrawn lands with mineral deposits may thus end up in the hands of private owners if they are willing to pay the cost of documenting the presence of the mineral deposit. These owners, who will have both the surface and mineral estates, will then choose among the possible uses. People who prefer to use the parcel for primitive recreation will be able to bid for the parcel and, if they succeed, devote it to that use.

There is an alternative means of determining the use of the nonwithdrawn parcel. Rather than investing in the knowledge necessary to gain title under the Mining Law (knowledge that could force the advocates of primitive recreation use to face the opportunity cost of satisfying their preferences for that use), proponents of primitive recreation can seek to have the land withdrawn from the Mining Law's coverage. President Clinton's creation and expansion of national monuments under the Antiquities Act of 1906 are prime examples of the political nature of the withdrawal process (Vincent and Brown 2000). Because such withdrawals are extremely difficult to reverse, they offer a ratchetlike effect to steadily increase the area of public land dedicated to primitive recreation and preservation (Vincent 2000).

Indeed, investing in eliminating the Mining Law's "giveaway" is a rational alternative for groups opposed to mining if their goal is a general attack on mining. If they prevail, they can end mining on far more land than they could ever hope to claim on their own, shifting the cost to others (such as the mining company shareholders and employees, who will lose profits and wages, and the general public, who will face higher prices for goods made with mineral resources and who will bear the costs of the reduced economic activity that results) rather than paying the opportunity cost themselves. The Mining Law also provides a potent fund-raising vehicle for environmental pressure groups.[5] If they fail, the groups will leave land unprotected that they could have saved. When such groups are faced with a choice between gambling on "protecting" public land by investing in the political process to hinder mining and the sure thing of protecting some land by investing their resources in the land itself while leaving other land open to mining, they almost always opt for the former.

There thus exists a potentially potent bootleggers and Baptists coalition against the mining industry. The bootleggers are those who profit from their ability to capture the federally controlled public land for their desired use. This group includes businesses that profit from the dedication of the land to open access. Some tourist businesses (guide services, resorts surrounded by public land, etc.) benefit from their ability to use the public land for their businesses; others benefit from blocking potential competitors from acquiring the public land (e.g., a resort that has a section of private land surrounded by public land; mining interests with competing sources located on private land). The bootleggers also include those who do not wish to profit monetarily from the restriction of land use but who simply prefer to impose their preferences on as large an area as possible.

The Baptists in this coalition are the members of some environmental pressure organizations who assert that the West is vanishing under the pressure of development and that the natural heritage of all Americans must be preserved. Although they have no interest in commercial tourist businesses, which they may find tacky, they often end up in an alliance with such interests. (Of course, some of the Baptists may have private reasons for favoring recreation over development. They may live near a particular parcel and so derive personal benefit as well as the larger "religious" benefit from its preservation.)

The result is that land-use decisions are politicized. The well-known defects of political markets and centralized decision making need not be recounted here. The problem is that the combination of the vulnerabilities of the Mining Law and its inadequate scope creates a situation in which the rational strategy is investment in the political process rather than in the land.

Conclusion: Markets, Freedom, and the Wealth of Nature

The solution to the dilemma we describe above is simple: create a means of privatizing federal lands for nonmining uses. Only when competing land uses have equal access to private title to land in the West will the incentive exist for entrepreneurs to design solutions that allow the peaceful coexistence of mining and tourism.

Despite its vulnerability to expropriation, directly or indirectly, the mining industry in the western United States has, by luck or otherwise, been able to avoid expropriation. Because the General Mining Law of 1872 created secure property rights and prevented rent seeking in the allocation of those rights, the industry has prospered. Because mining's economic importance ensured that western politicians would pay attention to the industry's concerns, changes to the General Mining Law that would undercut the institutional features that secured property rights and avoided the corruption that has plagued so many resource allocations elsewhere were blocked. Whether or not politicians grasped the importance of the Mining Law's institutions is less important than the fact that they blocked the changes that would have destroyed those institutions.

Signs indicate, however, that the coalition protecting those institutions is about to break down. Mining will soon no longer have sufficient political weight to allow assertion of its parochial interests to safeguard the institutions. It will be increasingly vulnerable to the bootleggers and Baptists coalition of those seeking to make use of public resources for their own purposes. It is therefore no longer sufficient to rely on the unconscious success of the General Mining Law. The free access principle needs to be expanded beyond land with mineral deposits to provide for the privatization of public land generally. The use of land should be determined freely in the marketplace, rather than through political battles.

Notes

This chapter draws extensively on our earlier work (Morriss, Meiners, and Dorchak 2003; Morriss, Meiners, and Dorchak 2004) and a work-in-progress on the politics of mining law "reform."

1. See Table B-12. Employees on Nonfarm Payrolls by Detailed Industry. Establishment Data, Employment, Department of Labor. Online at ftp://ftp.bls.gov/pub/suppl/empsit.ceseeb12.txt.

2. 30 U.S.C. §22 et seq. See Morriss, Meiners, and Dorchak (2004) for a more complete account of the statute's operation and history.

3. See http://homestaketour.com/. Towns such as Butte, Montana, and Leadville, Colorado, owe what little tourism they have to mining, not to their statuses as scenic locations in the West.

4. There is a germ of truth to the claim of a "promining" bias, but the critics are wrong about both its location and its cure. By allowing only nonwithdrawn federal lands with valuable hardrock mineral resources to be privatized, federal land law prevents nonmining uses from competing for most federal lands. The flaw lies, however, in the absence of a privatization mechanism for lands lacking valuable mineral resources. The Mining Law offers an appropriate regime for resolving disputes within the framework of private ownership of mineral resources. The only

requirement of the Mining Law, historically, was the discovery of a valuable resource and minimal annual work development. With the replacement of even the minimal annual work requirement with a $100 fee, no actual mining activity or even environmentally destructive activity is necessary to maintain and perfect a claim.

5. See, for example, Westerners for Responsible Mining Web page at http://www .bettermines.org/pledge.cfm (visited June 23, 2007), describing the need for individuals to "Join the WRM Action Team" "to help ensure that communities, water resources, and special places in the western states are protected from the adverse impacts of irresponsible mining practices—and a lack of corporate accountability in the hardrock mining industry." See also Richard and Rhoda Goldman Fund, 2003 Annual Report, online at http://www.goldmanfund.org/pdf/Annual_Report_2003 .pdf (visited June 22, 2007), listing a $300,000 grant to the Mineral Policy Center and Oxfam America for the "Campaign for Responsible Gold Mining."

References

Adler, Jonathan H. 2002. Legal Obstacles to Private Ordering in Marine Fisheries. *Roger Williams University Law Review* 8: 9–42.

Aidt, Toke S. 2003. Economic Analysis of Corruption: A Survey. *Economic Journal* 113: F632–F652.

Bohn, Henning, and Robert T. Deacon. 2000. Ownership Risk, Investment, and the Use of Natural Resources. *American Economic Review* 90: 526–549.

Clawson, Marion. 1971. *The Bureau of Land Management*. New York: Praeger.

de Soto, Hernando. 2000. *The Mystery of Capital*. New York: Basic Books.

Epstein, Richard A. 1995. *Simple Rules for a Complex World*. Cambridge, MA: Harvard University Press.

Fretwell, Holly Lippke, and Michael J. Podolsky. 2003. A Strategy for Restoring America's National Parks. *Duke Environmental Law and Policy Forum* 13: 143–186.

General Accounting Office. 1989. *Federal Land Management: The Mining Law of 1872 Needs Revision*. No. GAO/RCED-89-72. Washington, DC: General Accounting Office.

Gordon, Richard, and Peter Van Doren. 1998. Two Cheers for the 1872 Mining Law. *Cato Policy Analysis* 300. Washington, DC: Cato Institute, April. Online at http://www.cato.org/pubs/pas/pa-300.html. Visited March 29, 2004.

Greever, William S. 1963. *Bonanza West: The Story of the Western Mining Rushes 1848–1990*. Moscow: University of Idaho Press.

Hayek, Friedrich A. 1978. *Law, Legislation, & Liberty: Rules & Order*. Chicago: University of Chicago Press.

Humphries, Marc, and Carol Hardy Vincent. 2001. *Mining on Federal Lands*. Congressional Research Service (CRS) Issue Brief IB89130. Online at http:// www.ncseonline.org/nle/crsreports/mining/mine-1.cfm.

Kysar, Douglas A. 2003. Law, Environment, and Vision. *Northwestern University Law Review* 97: 675–729.

Lacy, John C. 1995. The Historical Origins of the U.S. Mining Laws and Proposals for Change. *Natural Resource and Environment* 10: 13–20.

Lacy, Willard. 1998. An Introduction to Geology and Hard Rock Mining, Rocky Mountain Mineral Law Foundation. *Science and Technology Series* 1. Online at http://www.rmmlf.org/SciTech/Lacy/lacy.htm. Visited March 12, 2004.

Lee, Dwight R. 2001. To Drill or Not to Drill? Let the Environmentalists Decide. *Independent Review* 6(2): 217–226.

Leshy, John D. 1987. *The Mining Law: A Study in Perpetual Motion*. Washington, DC: Resources for the Future.

Marshall, Ian E. 2001. *A Survey of Corruption Issues in the Mining & Mineral Sector*. Washington, DC: International Institute for Environment and Development.

Mayer, Carl J., and George A. Riley. 1985. *Public Domain, Private Dominion*. San Francisco: Sierra Club Books.

Morriss, Andrew P. 1998. Miners, Vigilantes, & Cattlemen: Overcoming Free Rider Problems in the Private Provision of Law. *Land and Water Law Review* 33: 581–694.

Morriss, Andrew P., Roger E. Meiners, and Andrew Dorchak. 2003. Between a Hard Rock and a Hard Place: Politics, Midnight Regulations, and Mining. *Administrative Law Review* 55: 551–599.

———. 2004. Homesteading Rock: A Defense of Free Access Under the General Mining Law of 1872. *Environmental Law* 34: 745–806.

National Mining Association. 2002. *Mining in Nevada*. Online at http://www.nma.org/pdf/states_02/nv2002.pdf. Visited February 1, 2005.

National Research Council (NRC). 1999. *Hardrock Mining on Federal Lands*. Washington, DC: National Academy Press.

Nelson, Robert H. 1997. Does "Existence Value" Exist? Environmental Economics Encroaches on Religion. *Independent Review* 1: 499–522.

North, Douglass C., and Barry R. Weingast. 1989. Constitutions and Commitment: The Evolution of Institutions Governing Public Choice in Seventeenth Century England. *Journal of Economic History* 49(4): 803–832.

Otto, James, and John Cordes. 2002. *The Regulation of Mineral Enterprises: A Global Perspective on Economics, Law and Policy*. Denver, CO: Rocky Mountain Mineral Law Foundation.

Outerbridge, Cheryl, ed. 1998. *American Law of Mining*, 2nd ed. New York: Matthew Bender.

Parr, Clayton J. 1989. Self-Initiation Under the Federal Mining Law. In *The Mining Law of 1872: A Legal and Historical Analysis*. Washington, DC: National Legal Center for the Public Interest, 49–71.

Prince, William B. 1998. Mining Law in the United States. *Mineral Resources Engineering* 7: 393–401.

Rinke, Nicole. 2000. The Crown Jewel Mining Decision: Recognizing the Mining Law's Inherent Limits. *Ecological Law Quarterly* 27: 819–839.

Scott, Robert E. 1987. Conflict and Cooperation in Long-Term Contracts. *California Law Review* 75: 2005–2054.

U.S. Census Bureau. 2005. *2002 Economic Census.* Online at http://www.census .gov/econ/census02/data/us/US000_21.htm.

Vagts, Detlev F. 1978. Coercion and Foreign Investment Rearrangements. *American Journal of International Law* 72: 17–36.

Vincent, Carol Hardy. 2000. Authority of a President to Modify or Eliminate a National Monument. Congressional Research Service. *Federal Public Land Management Reports.* Online at http://www.nplnews.com/toolbox/fedreports/ fedreports-crs-modifynm.htm#1. Visited February 1, 2005.

Vincent, Carol Hardy, and Pamela Brown. 2000. National Monuments and the Antiquities Act. Congressional Research Service (CRS) Report RL30528. Online at http://www.ncseonline.org/NLE/CRSreports/Public/pub-15.cfm. Visited February 1, 2005.

Williamson, Oliver E. 1983. Credible Commitments: Using Hostages to Support Exchange. *American Economic Review* 73(4): 519–540.

Yandle, Bruce. 1983. Bootleggers and Baptists: The Education of a Regulatory Economist. *Regulation,* May / June, 12–16.

Yandle, Bruce, and Andrew P. Morriss. 2001. The Technologies of Property Rights: Choice Among Alternative Solutions to Tragedies of the Commons. *Ecological Law Quarterly* 28: 123–168.

CHAPTER EIGHT

The Effects of Public Funding Systems on the Success of Private Conservation Through Land Trusts

DOMINIC P. PARKER

The growth of the land trust movement is one of the most important trends in American land conservation. Land trusts are nonprofit organizations that conserve open space amenities such as scenery, wildlife habitat, and recreational trails on private lands. They operate using a mix of private and public monies and have emerged to address demands for open spaces in a climate of growing personal incomes and rapid development on urban fringes.

The data are striking. From 1984 to 2005, the number of state and local land trusts grew from 535 to 1,663. During the same period, land trusts acquired approximately 11 million acres in outright ownership or in conservation easements. (Conservation easements are partial interests in land that typically prohibit intense subdivision and commercial development.) The growth in conservation easements is especially impressive. Approximately 81 percent of the acres acquired by state and local trusts between 1984 and 2005 are held in easements.

Most local trusts have grown by negotiating with landowners one deal at a time. In exchange for donations of easements, trusts offer landowners a way to conserve their land in perpetuity, an opportunity to reduce their tax burden, and, occasionally, cash payments. This method of conservation is appealing to pragmatic environmentalists seeking cooperative agreements with landowners and to politicians on both the right and left (Dana and Dana 2002). Bipartisan support for land trusts has led to a steady increase in federal and state tax incentives for easement donors in recent years. Now the aggregate tax benefit can sometimes fully compensate a landowner for his or her charitable contribution.

Yet as land trusts move from fringe to center stage, analysts should carefully consider whether tax-code funding best facilitates strategic, cost-effective conservation. Tax laws affect the incentives, focus, flexibility, and conservation methods of trusts. These factors in turn affect their environmental and economic performance.

This chapter identifies several problems related to funding conservation easements through tax incentives. The media have reported on a handful of cases in which land developers have used easements for tax-reduction goals rather than for public benefit (Ottaway and Stephens 2003). Politicians at the federal and state levels are working to address these problems by increasing the oversight of easement appraisals. Unfortunately, most policy makers are ignoring other more fundamental problems.

Tax-code funding fails to provide land trusts with basic economic incentives and constraints that could help direct public monies toward conservation plans most valued by beneficiaries. Absent from this funding approach are rudimentary features of marketlike policy instruments.[1] There is a disconnect between those who pay for "donated" easements and those who benefit, and the tax-code source of funding does not create budget constraints for land trusts to encourage prioritization in their use of public funds. Instead of trying to maximize the conservation benefits of each public dollar spent, land trusts have incentives to compete for more donations of conservation easements. Although competition for cash donations and grants is likely to encourage better performance (see Edwards 1995), competition for easement donations means that trusts that are lenient can acquire more easements than trusts that have focused goals and high standards.

The remainder of this chapter is divided into five sections. The first offers a primer on land trusts and conservation easements. The second describes the primary sources of public funds supporting land trust acquisitions: tax benefits to easement donors and matching grants. The third section presents the economic rationale for governmental funding. The fourth section identifies several problems caused by funding easements through tax incentives. The problems with tax policies range from allowing abuses by a small number of unethical landowners and land trusts to impeding the performance of well-intended trusts. The fifth section highlights the potential advantages that a matching grant approach has over tax-code funding. This public funding system creates an institutional structure for land trusts under which competition for public monies improves environmental performance, markets guide conservation, and trusts are accountable for successes and failures.

Land Trusts and Conservation Easements

Land trusts are nonprofit organizations that preserve or enhance open space amenities on private land, primarily by owning land or holding conservation easements. The nation's largest is the Nature Conservancy, but more than sixteen hundred smaller trusts operate in local regions across the United States. Most enjoy charitable status and exemption from federal and state income taxes and are governed by an unpaid board of trustees (Fairfax and Guenzler 2001).

The Nature Conservancy has the ambitious goal of preserving the biodiversity of plant and animal communities, but smaller trusts typically have more modest objectives. About one-third of land trusts responding to a recent Land Trust Alliance (LTA) survey said they seek to protect open spaces. This is a catchall term for the absence of dense development, but an earlier LTA survey identified a number of more specific goals. For example, more than 50 percent of the surveyed land trusts reported protecting wetlands or watersheds as a goal; nearly 40 percent, preserving wildlife habitat; and approximately one-third, providing trails for recreation.

GROWTH IN ACREAGE

Table 8.1 illustrates the tremendous growth in the acreage held by state and local land trusts from 1984 to 2005. Their acreage in conservation easements and fee simple ownership increased from almost 440,000 acres to 7.9 million acres, not including the Nature Conservancy, which grew from 792,000 acres in 1984 to approximately 4.3 million acres in 2003.[2] To give perspective, the total acreage increased from an area the size of Delaware to an area larger than the size of Vermont plus New Hampshire.

This growth partly reflects the increasing affluence of Americans and their growing interest in protecting open spaces from development. As personal income in the United States grows, Americans are more able and typically

TABLE 8.1

Growth and distribution of state and local land trusts

Geographic region	LTA census acres in conservation easements and fee simple	
	1984	2005
Northeast	139,859	2,895,910
Mid-Atlantic	89,156	857,061
Southeast	30,801	553,172
Midwest	60,467	329,981
Northwest	54,172	938,487
Southwest	51,319	1,641,775
Pacific	14,013	732,795
United States	439,787	7,949,181

SOURCE: 1984 Land Trust Alliance (LTA) data come from Parker and Thurman (2006); 2005 LTA data are from the 2005 National Land Trust Census (available online at http://www.lta.org/aboutlt/census.shtml).

NOTE: Northeast states include Connecticut, Massachusetts, Maine, New Hampshire, New York, Rhode Island, Vermont; Mid-Atlantic, District of Columbia, Delaware, Maryland, New Jersey, Pennsylvania, Virginia, West Virginia; Southeast, Alabama, Arkansas, Florida, Georgia, Kentucky, Louisiana, Mississippi, North Carolina, South Carolina, Tennessee; Midwest, Illinois, Indiana, Iowa, Kansas, Michigan, Minnesota, Missouri, North Dakota, Nebraska, Ohio, Wisconsin, South Dakota; Northwest, Alaska, Idaho, Montana, Oregon, Washington; Southwest, Arizona, Colorado, New Mexico, Oklahoma, Texas, Utah; and Pacific, California, Hawaii, Nevada.

more willing to spend money on the preservation of environmental amenities. Increases in income also increase demand for houses, restaurants, and shopping malls—land uses that compete with open spaces. Thus, land trusts appear to be emerging to broker deals with landowners and developers on behalf of those willing and able to pay to conserve open space amenities in the presence of development pressure.

This implies that land trusts should be more prevalent in regions of the country with rising incomes, but other factors drive land trust growth as well. County-level data of land trust acquisitions from 1990 to 2000 show the strongest land trust growth in counties endowed with significant natural amenities. Various federal land conservation programs are also slowing and accelerating land trust conservation (Parker and Thurman 2006).

CONSERVATION EASEMENTS

The growth in conservation easements is outpacing the growth in fee simple acquisitions by a wide margin. In 1984, 22 percent of Nature Conservancy acres were held in easements compared with approximately 38 percent in 2003. The change is more dramatic for the LTA trusts. In 1984, 33 percent of their acres were held in easements compared with 79 percent in 2005.

Conservation easements are legally binding agreements between land-owners and land trusts (or government agencies). They typically prohibit subdivision and commercial development while permitting agriculture and residential development. The provisions of conservation easements are wide ranging, however, and can prevent landowners from actions such as har-vesting timber commercially, farming, spraying pesticides, altering water courses, building new fences, and harvesting native plants. The restrictions in easements "run with the land"; that is, successor landowners are bound to the terms of the easement agreed upon by the original parties. Further-more, The Internal Revenue Service (IRS) requires that donated easements for which charitable claims are made be held in perpetuity (Mahoney 2002). Perpetual easements cannot easily be amended or extinguished, as discussed below.

Whether easements are purchased by land trusts or donated to them, their value is appraised as the difference between the value of the land with the easement (the encumbered value) and without the easement (the full-market value) (Boykin 2000). Consider a tract of farmland that could be sold for $2 million to a developer who intends to build a residential subdivi-sion. If a conservation easement is placed on the land, keeping the farm from being developed, and the value of the land in agriculture is estimated at $1.5 million, then the value of the conservation easement is $500,000. Although this appraisal methodology is conceptually simple, it can be difficult for ap-praisers to calculate easement values with a high degree of accuracy.

A conservation easement is an important legal innovation that has helped serve the needs of landowners and of those wanting open space amenities. Easements provide a way for landowners to be compensated for keeping their property but leaving it undeveloped. To land trusts, easements can be more attractive than fee simple ownership because they cost less to acquire and they provide a way to negotiate with landowners who are unwilling to wholly give up their land. Easements also save trusts the management costs they might incur if they owned land outright.

What explains the increasing popularity of conservation easements com-pared with land trust ownership? One contributing factor is the emergence of state laws that explicitly accept or acknowledge easements as legally bind-ing agreements. Another factor is that over time, lawyers have developed greater technical expertise in drafting clear easements that are defensible in court (see Parker 2004). Thus, land trusts can now more confidently provide open space amenities via easements, and landowners can be more assured of which land uses easements allow and do not allow. The increase of various tax incentives for conservation easement donors has also contributed to land trust growth. Tax incentives are discussed below.

Public Funding for Land Trust Acquisitions

Land trust acquisitions are financed by a mix of private and public dollars. A few large trusts, such as the Nature Conservancy, raise revenues from tourism and other marketable uses on land they own. Most trusts, however, raise revenues only from private sources through cash donations. They use these monies to pay for operational expenses and for land and easement acquisitions (or to buy conservation leases and management contracts).[3] Trusts rely on public monies as well. Importantly, federal and state tax benefits are available to landowners donating easements to qualified trusts. And public monies are channeled more directly to trusts through a number of grant programs administered by local, state, and federal agencies.

TAX BENEFITS TO EASEMENT DONORS

Federal income tax deductions for donated conservation easements received explicit statutory authorization in 1976, and estate tax benefits were expanded in 1997 (Small 2000). To be eligible, donated easements are required by the IRS to preserve land for one of the following general purposes: outdoor recreation, wildlife habitat, scenic enjoyment, agricultural use, or historical importance.

The extent to which a landowner can obtain a tax benefit from an easement donation depends on income, primarily because the law caps the deduction amount a landowner can claim at 30 percent of his or her adjusted gross income each year for six years. Table 8.2 uses information provided by McLaughlin (2004) to show the effect of income on the benefits to donors of conservation easements. The table assumes that three landowners of differing incomes donate easements appraised at $500,000. The high-income landowner can deduct $450,000 of the $500,000 value over six years. In contrast, the middle-income landowner can deduct $135,000 of the value, and the low-income landowner can deduct only $63,000. In the end, the high-income landowner accrues a tax savings of $157,500 (unadjusted for

TABLE 8.2

Federal income tax benefits to easement donors

	High-income donor	Middle-income donor	Low-income donor
Adjusted gross income	$250,000	$75,000	$35,000
Marginal income tax rate	35%	27%	15%
Charitable donation	$500,000	$500,000	$500,000
Annual deduction	$75,000	$22,500	$10,500
Aggregate deduction over 6 years	$450,000	$35,000	$63,000
Aggregate tax savings	$157,500	$36,450	$9,450

SOURCE: McLaughlin (2004, 32).

NOTE: This table does not reflect the significant increase in tax benefits for easements donated in 2006 and 2007.

inflation) compared with $36,450 for the middle-income landowner and $9,450 for the low-income landowner.

Federal legislation passed in August 2006 increased income tax benefits for easements donated in 2006 and 2007. The new laws raise the deduction landowners can take for donating a conservation easement from 30 percent of their income in any year to 50 percent, and it allows qualifying farmers and ranchers to deduct up to 100 percent of their income. The law also extends the carry-forward period for a donor to take tax deductions for a voluntary conservation agreement from five to fifteen years.[4] This change, if made permanent, makes tax benefits for easement donations less dependent on income.

An easement donor can also claim the appraised value of the donation against his or her federal estate tax burden, provided the donor meets the eligibility requirements for income tax deduction. This benefit is relevant only to landowners wanting to pass to heirs estates valued in excess of an exclusion amount, but it offers significant savings to these heirs. It should be noted that estate tax rules are currently in a period of great flux, so the actual benefits from donating an easement are rapidly changing.

Many states provide additional tax benefits; a number offer income tax credits. According to McLaughlin (2004), these tend to be modest when compared with federal tax benefits. Colorado and Virginia, however, recently enacted generous tax credits that allow donors of easements to sell easement tax credits to other taxpayers. These measures help equalize the tax incentive across landowners of differing incomes.

A final tax incentive may come in the form of property tax relief. According to a study by Defenders of Wildlife (2002), about seventeen states have statutes requiring local assessors to reduce property value assessments so that they are based on the encumbered, not full market, value of land with a conservation easement. This benefit, however, will not provide additional property tax relief to agricultural landowners whose land is already assessed below market value through an agricultural "current use" assessment program (see Parker 2006).

The aggregate tax benefit can be large if landowners have sufficient income to offset the deduction, hold land that is otherwise ineligible for an estate tax exemption, and live in a state offering attractive tax credit programs. Parker and Thurman (2004) show how donating an easement in North Carolina can be almost a break-even proposition for a high-income landowner carrying an estate tax burden. In Colorado and Virginia, which offer sizeable, transferable income tax credits, it may be possible for some landowners to recoup the entire value of an easement donation (see McLaughlin 2004). Keep in mind that these examples are given before the August 2006 increase in federal tax benefits. The examples also assume an accurate appraisal of the easement value. If appraisals are exaggerated, then some landowners can actually profit by "donating" conservation easements.

GOVERNMENT GRANT PROGRAMS

Public monies are also channeled more directly to land trusts through grant programs administered by federal, state, and local governments. Federal legislation authorizes funding for a few small-scale grant programs administered by the U.S. Department of Agriculture (USDA) and the U.S. Forest Service (USFS). Most state and local programs were authorized directly by voters across the country through open space initiatives.

Open space initiatives appeared in approximately one thousand state, county, and local jurisdictions between 1998 and 2003. Voters approved nearly 80 percent of these referenda, raising more than $21 billion for open space conservation (Kotchen and Powers 2006). The majority of these referenda were local, with relatively few at county and state levels. Most of the funding mechanisms involved increasing property taxes, either through surcharges or rate increases.

In most jurisdictions, local land trusts can apply for funds authorized by open space initiatives to acquire land and conservation easements. There may be competition among land trusts when multiple trusts operate in the relevant jurisdiction. In Gallatin County, Montana, for example, an Open Lands Board administers a $10 million open space bond that voters approved in 2004. The Gallatin Valley Land Trust, the Montana Land Reliance, and other organizations locate possible conservation projects and develop proposals. The Open Lands Board considers applications and approves them on the basis of how closely the proposals come to meeting the purpose of the initiative and other factors.

Federal programs also give land trusts the opportunity to apply for matching funds. The Farm and Ranch Lands Protection Program (FRPP) was enacted by Farm Bill legislation in 1996 and was reauthorized and expanded in 2002. Through this program, state and local government agencies and land trusts make proposals to the USDA's Natural Resources Conservation Service (NRCS). Proposals are ranked on the basis of FRPP criteria and other factors. The NRCS may pay up to 50 percent of the appraised value of the easement, and cooperating entities make up the difference through monies they raise or by soliciting easement donations from landowners. Annual funding has varied since 1996; $70 million was authorized for 2006 (NRCS 2006). The Forest Legacy Program (FLP) is administered by the USFS. This program also channels funds for easement purchase to trusts on a competitive basis. Eligible entities are required to cover 25 percent of the costs through private, state, or local sources (the USFS may pay up to 75 percent). The USFS has aided the purchase of more than one million acres in thirty-three states since 1990. The FLP spent approximately $55 million on projects in 2006 (USFS 2006).

How does the amount of federal spending for land trusts through grant programs compare with the implicit amount of federal spending for easements through tax incentives? Unfortunately, information about foregone federal revenues through tax reductions is not available. Parker (2005) roughly estimates the cost to be between $5 billion and $18 billion for easements donated between 2001 and 2003. Both the upper and lower bound figures dwarf federal spending through the FRPP and FLP, but the range is comparable to the annual amounts that local communities have pledged for land conservation through open space initiatives.

Making Free Riders Pay: The Economic Rationale for Public Funding

Why does government subsidize land trust acquisitions through tax incentives and grant programs? To understand the economic rationale it is useful to first consider a hypothetical situation in which trusts operate in a purely free-market environment. In this simplified model, there is demand to preserve open space amenities on private land in a geographic region (e.g., a county, township, or municipality).

The extent of demand for conservation depends on the characteristics of the people living in a region and on the characteristics of the land. Characteristics of people that affect demand include income and preferences for bucolic scenery, wildlife viewing, and outdoor recreation. Characteristics of land that affect demand include development pressure, natural amenity endowments, and the amount of government land in a region (see Parker and Thurman 2006).

In this free-market scenario, some demanders of amenities give cash donations to land trusts. Trusts respond to customer demands by making strategic conservation plans. Trusts execute their plans by negotiating with landowners for outright ownership, easements, leases, and management agreements. As a result of these negotiations and ongoing monitoring and enforcement efforts, trusts provide cash donors with amenities they demand. In the absence of governmental funding, however, fewer open space amenities may be conserved through voluntary donations than is desired by those who are willing and able to pay. There is a free-rider problem because those who don't contribute to land trusts cannot easily be excluded from enjoying the amenities trusts provide. This free-rider problem is most pronounced in the case of scenery and wildlife habitat provision because it is difficult to exclude nonpayers from access to viewsheds and everyday wildlife viewing[5] (see Anderson 2004).

Of course, land trusts find ways to mitigate free-rider problems and therefore succeed in raising private dollars. A few trusts package amenities with private tourism and charge user fees. The Nature Conservancy, for example, owns and operates several nature reserves with overnight lodging for guests. A vacation stay at the conservancy's spectacular eighteen-thousand-acre Pine Butte Swamp Reserve in northwest Montana offers mountain hiking, horseback riding, and the potential for viewing grizzly bears in their natural habitat. More commonly, trusts try to privatize benefits to cash donors by giving them conspicuous recognition. The Gallatin Valley Land Trust in Bozeman, Montana, for example, devotes nearly half of its newsletter space to listing the names of various donors. These private efforts by land trusts reduce the free-rider problem, but to what extent is unclear.

Tax-Code Funding: A Solution with Flaws

Offering tax benefits to donors of land and conservation easements is one way to address the free-rider problem. Under this financing system, general taxpayers finance trust acquisitions through foregone claims to government tax revenues.

With tax-code funding, land trusts take on an important role: they solicit and bank donations of conservation easements. This process can involve an assortment of constraints, distortions, and perverse incentives. The problems with tax policies range from allowing tax abuses by a small number of unethical landowners and land trusts to impeding the performance of legitimate trusts. As we shall see, tax-code funding weakens the ability and incentives of trusts to strategically provide amenities in cost-effective ways.

"PUBLIC BENEFITS" AND THE EASEMENT APPRAISAL PROBLEM

Appraising conservation easements can be more of an art than a science and thus is open to abuse. When calculating the full market value of land without an easement, appraisers should account for any preexisting zoning regulations, which might have already reduced the value of the land, and they should provide realistic estimates of the demand for intense development on the land. But these factors may be difficult to assess, and appraisers working on behalf of landowners wanting tax breaks have incentives to overestimate full market value. When calculating the encumbered value appraisers should take into account the fact that buyers of land value scenery and wildlife and are often willing to pay extra for these amenities, so the value of the land may remain high even with the easement. But these factors are difficult to quantify, and here too appraisers working for landowners wanting tax breaks have incentives to underestimate the encumbered value.

Another problem is the vague public benefits criteria for donated easements. For a donated easement to be eligible for federal tax benefits, it must convey a "significant public benefit" (Miller 2006). But measuring the conservation benefits from a tract of open land is difficult, and different parties can have wildly different opinions about "significance."

Given the ambiguities in the law and the appraisal process, it is easy to see how opportunistic land developers can profit by setting up land trusts to hold conservation easements. According to expert testimony before the U.S. Senate Committee on Finance (Maybank 2005), a number of developers are encumbering the fairways of golf courses with easements. Their tax benefits have been large. In South Carolina, for example, developers claimed at least $125 million in charitable contributions over golf courses between 2001 and 2003 (Maybank 2005). These claims accounted for nearly 50 percent of the claimed value of all easement donations in the state but are being accepted by only a small number of land trusts.

The golf course scheme seems to violate the spirit of the law, but such tax abuses are difficult to prosecute and may not even be illegal. Although golf courses surrounded in part by housing developments may offer only pockets of scenic access to the general public, it can be argued that they provide good habitat for birds and animals. And although this type of development scheme might maximize profits to developers because homes on golf courses demand premium prices (see Limehouse and McCormick 2005), it can be argued that the alternative use of the land is a dense development project that could generate more profits for the land developer. Regardless of whether the golf course scheme is technically legal, few taxpayers wanting open space amenities would choose to direct their money toward such deals.

The IRS is trying to address the use of easements on golf courses, but the general problem is not specific to only golf course developments. Tax abuse can occur whenever charitable gifts of assets with debatable value are tax deductible. In the case of conservation easements, there is often a range of easement values that are technically defensible, and appraisers working for landowners have incentives to pick values on the upper bound of what is defensible (see McLaughlin 2004). The appraisal problem is exacerbated because the IRS has not held land trusts liable for erroneous or fraudulent valuations (McLaughlin 2004). Freedom from liability weakens trusts' incentives to encourage reasonable appraisals. Indeed, land trusts under this institutional structure can benefit from exaggerated easement appraisals because such appraisals give landowners more incentive to donate.

THE PERPETUITY AND LANDSCAPE CONSERVATION PROBLEM

Federal IRS rules require that donated conservation easements be held in perpetuity. Most environmentalists and land trusts laud this requirement, but it is inconsistent with centuries of common law, which tends to discourage perpetual constraints on land use (Mahoney 2002). The reason is that restrictions that freeze land use to a landowner's present desires may become antiquated and inefficient over time (Meiners and Yandle 2001).

As economic and ecological conditions change, the benefits and costs of conserving different parcels will change. It is doubtful that every easement land trusts currently hold will continue to yield conservation benefits in the face of population growth and migration, changing demands on agricultural land, changes in climate, and changes in preferences toward the preservation of wildlife species.

Fortunately, obsolete easements currently held by land trusts need not really last forever. IRS rules allow for extinguishment if a change in conditions makes it "impractical or impossible" for the easement to serve its intended purpose. If an easement is extinguished and sold for development, the proceeds from the sale are to be reinvested in a conservation purpose similar to the one initially intended by the easement. The IRS inserted this provision to safeguard the public's investment in conservation easements (McLaughlin 2005).

These IRS allowances make it less likely that isolated tracts of easement land with little conservation value will remain enforced for hundreds of years. Even so, the difficulties of transferring land to more productive economic and ecological uses are substantial. Courts will have to determine whether an easement can no longer "practically" or "possibly" fulfill its initial purpose. But courts will be obligated to consider the desires of the easement donor, who presumably had strong personal connections to the land. Furthermore, neighboring landowners may lobby to keep the easement as it is even if public benefits are few and the conservation value of the easement, if reinvested elsewhere, is substantial. Such neighbors probably do not have formal legal standing, but they benefit from adjacent open space and may be able to forestall extinguishment through political means.[6]

Because conservation easements are perpetually nontransferable, land trusts have fixed assets that cannot be easily extinguished and converted into cash to be reinvested in conservation elsewhere. This makes it difficult for trusts relying on easement donations to provide trails or to conserve habitat for wildlife requiring large tracts of land because they must persuade a group of neighboring landowners to donate. Landowners who do not benefit from tax deductions or who do not want perpetual restrictions have a strong incentive to say no. Thus, land trusts relying exclusively on easement donations are best suited to provide generic open space instead of recreational amenities and large tracts of wildlife habitat. In contrast, trusts with a purchasing budget can buy connector parcels where needed—they have the advantage of being able to offer landowners cash (see Parker 2006).

This landscape conservation problem is further exacerbated by dynamic land market effects. When land trusts accept a donated easement, the value of development on adjacent land may increase in response. This can encourage new development on neighboring parcels, which would sabotage trust efforts to conserve contiguous tracts (see Costello and Polasky 2004; Armsworth et al. 2006). The upshot is that land trusts can be left with islands of conservation easements that are alone inadequate for conserving open space amenities of significant value.[7]

THE DISCONNECT PROBLEM

Especially because conservation easements are perpetual, cost-effective conservation hinges critically on which donated parcels land trusts choose to accept. To be cost-effective conservationists, land trusts should protect only those donated parcels where the expected conservation value of the easement is equal to or greater than the full cost to all taxpayers. Otherwise, taxpayers are not getting their money's worth.

It is, of course, difficult to measure the full benefits and costs of conserving a specific piece of land. So it is unrealistic to expect that land trusts will make perfect economic decisions when choosing whether to accept donated easements. However, both economic theory and empirical evidence indicate that individuals, businesses, and nonprofits make more prudent environmental decisions when they bear the full costs and can obtain the full benefits of their decisions (see Anderson and Leal 2001). The disconnect problem with respect to land trusts is that trusts have incentives to pay less attention to the costs to taxpayers generally than to the costs to the local beneficiaries of the trust.

Local trusts want to obtain easements that preserve the scenic beauty or open space in their local areas. The problem is that tax financing gives them incentives to accept conservation easements whenever the benefits to locals outweigh the costs to locals—even if the costs to distant and dispersed taxpayers are high and the benefits are low.

A numerical example given by Parker and Thurman (2004) helps illustrate the issue. They consider a farm parcel at the edge of a growing city in North Carolina that is worth $2 million if sold to developers and $1.2 million if future use is restricted to farming through a conservation easement. They assume the landowner is nearing retirement and not eligible for an estate tax exclusion, has sufficient income to claim the value of the entire deduction over a six-year period, and is eligible for the state income tax credit in North Carolina. Assuming an accurate appraisal, it will cost the landowner $69,000 to donate an easement, and it will cost U.S. and North Carolina taxpayers $506,000 in lost tax revenue.

Suppose that the easement provides scenery and a few environmental services worth $200,000 to nearby residents and $100,000 to all other U.S. citizens. (To be sure, quantifying these values is difficult. Using numbers, however, helps to illustrate what can happen when those who benefit most are asked to pay the least). In this simple hypothetical case, a land trust with an effective marketing campaign might be able to collect from nearby residents the $69,000 needed to compensate the landowner. The land trust accepting this donation would be making local beneficiaries better off by $131,000 (their $200,000 valuation minus their $69,000 contribution). Yet the trust would be making society worse off by $275,000.[8] This figure is calculated by subtracting the benefits of the easement to society ($300,000) from the cost ($506,000 + $69,000).

At first glance, the root of the disconnect problem seems to be the vague language in the "public benefits" criteria under current tax law. A way to try to address the problem is to clarify tax law to require that easements eligible for federal write-offs be over lands with specific important ecological and aesthetic features. In contrast to easements that merely provide scenic views for locals, these easements are more likely to provide significant benefits to the whole of society and therefore to merit a contribution from national taxpayers. However, amending the eligibility criteria would probably do little to fix the disconnect problem in practice. It would be difficult for the IRS to audit a more stringent requirement because aesthetic and ecological qualities are fundamentally difficult to evaluate.

Furthermore, lands with these qualities attract easement donations from wealthy second-home buyers who would not actually develop the land into cookie-cutter homes or shopping malls if they didn't have the easement. Tax benefits for conservation easements provide them with a cheaper way of buying a second home for their personal enjoyment.[9] Land trusts operating as a strategic broker on behalf of national taxpayers would probably not choose to target these lands because the costs to taxpayers would probably not justify the benefits. After all, the open space isn't really threatened. Yet tax-code funding gives trusts incentives to increase the acreage they hold even when the costs to distant and dispersed taxpayers are greater than the benefits.

OTHER PROBLEMS

Two additional incentive problems come from extending tax benefits to easement donors. First, land trusts are more apt to conserve amenities through easements than through leases and contracts because easements receive special tax privileges. Yet depending on the task at hand, these and other lesser-used tools may sometimes be more appropriate (see Elmendorf 2004). Short-term leases and contracts let trusts experiment with land management strategies without committing to perpetual land conservation. This flexibility can be important when trusts are trying to enhance habitat or actively manage resources on the land.

Second, competition among trusts for easement donations can encourage a race-to-the-bottom in easement terms and enforcement. This reasoning presumes that trusts have incentives to increase their raw acreage because acres are a tangible measure of success. Trusts can compete for easement donations by agreeing to lax land-use restrictions in the easements they accept. For example, if Trust A is competing with Trust B for a landowner's donation, Trust B can agree to allow more development, logging, mining, or farming on the land. Trust B's strategy will be especially effective if the value of the additional uses it will allow are difficult to appraise. In such instances, the landowner can receive the same tax benefit from donating to Trust B but will be less restricted. Similarly, Trust B can be more attractive to some easement donors if it has a reputation for not enforcing its easements. The upshot is that Trust B can attract more donated acres than Trust A. Yet this outcome is not advantageous to public beneficiaries who implicitly pay for easement donations.

Fixing the Problems: Tax Reforms or Matching Grants?

The problems with tax-code funding are fundamental; fixing these requires reforms that change the core incentives of land trusts. Successful reforms would create an institutional structure for land trusts under which competition for public monies improves environmental performance, markets guide conservation, and trusts have flexibility in their use of public monies. Two approaches to reform are considered below. The first focuses on modifying the federal tax code; the second involves substituting tax-code funding with matching grants.

TAX REFORMS

Federal tax reforms have already been introduced. These are coupled with August 2006 tax laws that make easement donations less dependent on income (see the above discussion). More stringent penalties are now imposed on landowners and appraisers if the IRS deems easement appraisals to be grossly misstated. The IRS can also implement new requirements for appraisers who are qualified to value conservation easements. And the IRS has warned donors that it will audit charitable donations more stringently and more often—especially high-value donations of property.

The new tax laws should help alleviate a few of the problems described here. Increased oversight and regulation of appraisals should discourage egregious overvaluations. Allowing landowners to claim a higher percentage of their income and extending the carry-forward period for a donor from five to fifteen years should help to mitigate the landscape conservation problem related to relying on donations. This increases the pool of landowners with whom trusts can negotiate when pursuing objectives. However, the law does not relax perpetual restrictions on easements and therefore does nothing to help easement holders respond to changing conditions by exchanging remote easements for easements more useful to a land trust's mission.

The new tax law will also probably exacerbate the disconnect problem and other problems discussed here. Increasing tax benefits to landowners drives a further wedge between those who pay for trust conservation (federal taxpayers) and those who primarily benefit (residents of locales where trusts are active). And increased tax benefits to easement donors will most likely increase competition among land trusts for easement donations. The result can be more lenient land trusts prospering over trusts with stricter standards. The new law will increase tax privileges that conservation easements already enjoy relative to conservation leases and contracts. As a consequence, conservation easements will continue to crowd out these other conservation instruments that may be better suited to some land trusts' missions.

Parker (2005) and Pidot (2005) put forth additional ideas for reforms. I have recommended relaxing perpetual constraints on the alienation of conservation easements so that land trusts accredited by the LTA can sell donated easements back to landowners at its discretion. Land trusts should be legally obligated to reinvest the proceeds in land conservation projects, and stiff penalties would have to be applied to land trusts that did not reinvest the money or that charged too little for easement buybacks. Current IRS rules that specify how much money trusts will receive if courts choose to extinguish an easement already provide a working model. These rules require that the proportional value of the easement to the full market value at the time of a donation serve as a basis for pricing extinguished easements in the future (see McLaughlin 2004).

The upside of relaxing perpetual restrictions on alienation is that it would let LTA-accredited land trusts respond to changing conditions to ensure that conservation easements continue to yield net benefits over time. Because an easement would be more liquid, the general public's financial contribution toward the easement could ultimately be reinvested in land that is more aesthetic or ecologically more important. The potential drawback is that landowners and rogue land trusts could collude by holding conservation easements for speculative purposes to avoid paying higher property taxes while land appreciates. Yet requiring LTA accreditation would help to weed out this type of behavior.

Pidot (2005) identifies a range of issues related to conservation easements. To deal with appraisal and taxation problems, he suggests that the IRS rely on an expert advisory panel to review donated easements (as is done for donated artwork). Appraisers would know that their calculations would be made public, and this would discourage dubious valuations. Pidot's solution to the "public benefit" problem is similar. He proposes a process for "public input into [conservation easement] design, location, and benefits" (page 15). Easements would not formally require public approval, but the review process would expose easement terms and purposes to interested parties.

Pidot's solution to problems related to perpetuity would require legal action on the part of states where legislation that enables conservation easements is vested. States would enact procedures for termination and amendments, and some public authority would play a role in all terminations. Importantly, Pidot states that an easement "should be able to be significantly modified or terminated only if it no longer benefits the public, regardless of the economic benefit to the landowner of extinguishing the easement" (page 26).

If Pidot's recommendations were enacted, easements acquired by trusts would be more transparent, and the process for amendment and termination would be more predictable. This is in contrast to the current situation in which the general public does not know how much they have paid for conservation easements (through foregone tax revenues) and what they will receive in return. Higher transaction costs are a drawback of each reform, but these may be unavoidable if greater transparency and public involvement are goals. Furthermore, policies that require more care in establishing standards and procedures now can save on the high transaction costs future generations may face in dealing with outdated and obsolete easements (see Mahoney 2002).

COMPETITIVE MATCHING GRANTS

The reforms discussed above do not create marketlike incentives and constraints for land trusts. An alternative to tax reforms would require a substantial overhaul of the public funding system but may hold more promise for more effective land trust conservation. Federal tax-code funding for conservation easements could be abandoned and replaced with an equivalent level of funding through federal competitive grants requiring trusts to raise matching funds from private sources and through local governments. This may seem a radical step, but the potential benefits to the general taxpayer, who is already paying for conservation easements, should be considered.

To put the idea into perspective, consider that donated easements cost government treasuries billions of dollars (see Parker 2005). The question is whether the federal government's share of this cost could have been used more effectively if the money had been channeled to trusts through a competitive matching grant program.

To obtain matching federal funds, trusts would submit proposals to a lending board patterned after the National Science Foundation, composed of experts in the field of land conservation (or the grant program could be patterned after the already existing FRPP and FLP except for key differences described here). The board would approve grants based on predetermined and discretionary criteria. The grant proposals would specify in detail the open space amenities to be conserved by the trust along with estimated acquisition costs. Eligible proposals should be for amenities with national significance such as wildlife habitat and biodiversity. Trusts could use grant money to acquire leases, contracts, easements, or fee simple land—proposals would be for conservation outputs over a broad spatial scale, and the appropriate tools for cost-effective conservation would vary. Grants would be leveraged with a high ratio of private and local government money, including that raised through open space initiatives.

This approach could have several benefits relative to federal tax-code funding. First, it would allocate federal dollars to areas about which there is some consensus that the value of wildlife habitat and biodiversity is particularly high. Supporters of the trust would pay the most and therefore guide the decision; proposals would also be evaluated by land conservation experts. This process is in contrast to the current situation in which a local landowner who has an interest in donating an easement triggers the process.[10]

Second, competition among land trusts for grant dollars would encourage innovative and prudent conservation plans. (The grant-lending agency should not preclude multiple trusts from cooperating to propose coordinated conservation plans.) This is in contrast to competition for tax-driven easement donations, which can lead to a sort of race-to-the-bottom in conservation planning with trusts competing only to increase acres.

Third, once trusts received grant monies, they would have budget constraints that would encourage them to act as if they bore the full costs of acquiring different parcels. Currently, the source of forgone tax revenue is potentially limitless, as long as the trust can find willing landowners. In contrast, fixed allocations of grant dollars would force trusts to prioritize. The grant approach would encourage trusts to focus on using the funds effectively rather than finding new easement donors, whose property might be of low priority.

A fourth and related advantage is that trusts would have stronger incentives to oversee the appraisal of easements, thereby discouraging exaggerated appraisals. Land trusts receiving federal grants would be using money from their own budgets to buy easements, land, contracts, and leases. They would be motivated to question appraisals that seem high. In contrast, today trusts can benefit from high appraisals because they make landowners more willing to donate.

Fifth, trusts would not need to commit to perpetual land protection on specific parcels. Grant proposals would be for conservation outcomes, and the most effective means for achieving those outcomes could change over time. Instead of seeking easement donors from a small pool of parties motivated by perpetuity and tax incentives, land trusts would have a public funding source that allowed them to negotiate with a larger pool of potential easement sellers. This approach would also put trusts in a better position to make large-scale acquisitions to conserve landscapes while avoiding dynamic land-market feedback effects caused by the spontaneous acceptance of donated easements one at a time.

To be sure, a competitive grant-lending approach has potential drawbacks. The administration costs of this approach could be very high. Layers of bureaucratic paperwork would be created, and this could slow down the ability of trusts wanting federal funds to act quickly in conserving land. Yet this drawback needs to be evaluated in comparison with the transaction costs of administering tax reforms, which can also be high.

Another challenge for the granting agency would lie in ensuring that trusts were indeed allocating their dollars toward the proposed plan. Some measurable criteria for evaluating plans would need to be established. A process that addresses these issues would be a critical prerequisite to a successful program. Yet the requirement that federal dollars be matched at a high rate by private and local government dollars could provide self-enforcing incentives for sustainable, effective conservation. Federal taxpayers would be funding land conservation plans that had proved their merit in private and local markets. And federal taxpayers who currently do not know how much they have spent on conservation easements and what they have received in return could benefit from the monitoring efforts of private and local donors who will have more at stake in making sure that land trust objectives are met.

Conclusion

Land trusts enjoy widespread support for good reason. They have acquired millions of acres of land for conservation by relying on voluntary transactions with landowners. This model of working with willing landowners is pragmatic and politically sustainable.

The primary funding vehicle for land trust acquisitions are tax benefits for conservation easement donors, and these are growing over time. Yet relying on tax-driven easement donations is probably impeding the effectiveness of land trusts for a number of reasons. First, conservation easements can have debatable value, and tax-code funding gives landowners incentives to seek appraisals that are on the high side of what is defensible. This can lead to the systematic overpayment for easement acquisitions by taxpayers. Second, there is a disconnect between general taxpayers who implicitly pay for donated easements and local land trusts and their supporters who benefit. This disconnect implies that trusts will be less selective in evaluating whether to accept donated easements than they would be if they purchased the easements with locally raised monies. Third, tax-code funding also creates competition among trusts for easement donations, which can result in more lenient trusts succeeding instead of trusts with higher standards.

Tax laws also perpetually constrain the alienation of donated conservation easements. This limits the ability of trusts to respond to dynamic economic and ecological conditions, and perpetuity makes it difficult for trusts to provide amenities such as hiking trails and wildlife habitat over contiguous parcels. Furthermore, tax privileging the perpetual conservation easement may crowd out shorter-term conservation leases and contracts that can sometimes better accomplish land trust goals.

Federal policy makers are aware of the appraisal problems and have enacted reforms in conjunction with a recent increase in tax benefits to easement donors. These include greater regulation of easement appraisals and stricter penalties for overvaluations. Yet policy makers and analysts have paid less attention to the host of other problems identified here.

Parker (2005) and Pidot (2005) discuss additional reforms. These include ideas to alleviate the perpetuity problem and to better ensure that donated easements provide significant public benefits. The reforms proposed by Pidot would make the purpose, goals, and terms of donated easements more transparent by creating a process for public review. A drawback would be higher administration costs, but these may be unavoidable if greater transparency and public involvement are goals.

An alternative approach to reform could create marketlike incentives and constraints for land trusts using public dollars. Rather than implicitly allocating federal monies to donors of easements through the tax code, federal dollars could be awarded to land trusts on a competitive basis through matching grant programs. A few existing, small-scale federal programs provide rough models for how matching-grant programs could be administered.

To be most effective, a federal grant program should require a high ratio of private and local governmental dollars (including those raised by open space initiatives) to each federal dollar granted. This system could help direct federal monies toward the most valuable and most carefully designed conservation projects. Matching grants would give trusts stronger incentives to define their objectives clearly before acquiring land and more freedom to use public monies in effective ways.

Notes

Some of the ideas expressed in this chapter were first presented in Parker (2005).

1. See Chapter 1 for a discussion of the various ways in which environmental policies can have marketlike features.

2. These data come from e-mail communication with Christen McGinness, a

database administrator at the Nature Conservancy (latest correspondence, August 9, 2005).

3. The Nature Conservancy, for example, governed more than four million acres in conservation leases and management contracts in 2000.

4. This information comes from the Land Trust Alliance's Web site at http://www.lta.org/publicpolicy/tax_incentives_updates.htm (visited August 21, 2006).

5. To be sure, scenic values can be packaged with private goods, such as residential housing with mountain views, hiking trails traversing beautiful landscapes, and even a system of toll roads with fees corresponding to the desirability of roadside scenery (see Thompson 2000).

6. McLaughlin (2005) describes the process leading up to a potential extinguishment using the "Audry Farm Easement" example, which is loosely based on a real case reported in the media. In this example, an easement over a farm in a rural area in the Northeast was donated in 1976. By 2005, after the donor had died, the small, isolated parcel of land had been engulfed by development and was generating few conservation values for the public. If the easement were extinguished and sold to a developer, the land trust holder could use the proceeds to protect tracts of land contiguous to other easements it holds. Although extinguishing the Audry Farm Easement seems appropriate to most, the family of the donor and neighboring homeowners dissent and can perhaps prevent extinguishment.

7. Making the tax benefits to easement donors tradable could help with the landscape-conservation problem. A few states, such as Colorado and Virginia, have tradable tax credit programs (McLaughlin 2004). This approach gives cash-poor landowners incentives to donate, providing land trusts with a larger market of landowners from whom to solicit donations. Yet the IRS does not support this approach because it opens more doors for tax abuse (Miller 2006).

8. The assumption here is that government agencies would otherwise spend the $275,000 in ways valued by society.

9. A related point was made in 1979 by Daniel Halperin, then the deputy assistant to the secretary of the treasury department (see McLaughlin 2004).

10. Also, the provisions in conservation easements would reflect private and local demands. For example, if cash donors to land trusts wanted recreational access, then a plan for future public hiking and access would be included in conservation proposals.

References

Anderson, Terry L. 2004. Viewing Land Conservation Through Coase-Colored Glasses. *Natural Resources Journal* 44(2): 361–382.

Anderson, Terry L., and Donald R. Leal. 2001. *Free Market Environmentalism*, rev. ed. New York: Palgrave.

Armsworth, Paul R., Gretchen C. Daily, Peter Kareiva, and James Sanchiro. 2006. Land Market Feedbacks Can Undermine Biodiversity Conservation. *Proceedings for the National Academy of Science* 103: 5243–5244.

Boykin, James H. 2000. Valuing Scenic Land Conservation Easements. *Appraisal Journal* 68(4): 420–427.

Costello, Christopher, and Stephen Polasky. 2004. Dynamic Reserve Site Selection. *Resource and Energy Economics* 26(2): 157–174.

Dana, Andrew C., and Susan W. Dana. 2002. Rogue Land Trusts, Abused Conservation Easements, and Regulation of the Private Land Trust Movement. Working paper. Available from PERC, Bozeman, MT.

Defenders of Wildlife. 2002. *Conservation in America: State Government Incentives for Habitat Conservation*. Washington, DC: Defenders of Wildlife.

Edwards, Victoria. 1995. *Dealing in Diversity: America's Market for Nature Conservation*. Cambridge, UK: Cambridge University Press.

Elmendorf, Christopher S. 2004. Securing Ecological Investments on Other People's Land: A Transaction Costs Perspective. *Natural Resources Journal* 44(2): 529–562.

Fairfax, Sally K., and Darla Guenzler. 2001. *Conservation Trusts*. Lawrence: University of Kansas Press.

Kotchen, Matthew J., and Shawn M. Powers. 2006. Explaining the Appearance and Success of Voter Referenda for Open-Space Conservation. *Journal of Environmental Economics and Management* 52: 373–390.

Limehouse, Frank, and Robert McCormick. 2005. The Demand for Environmental Quality and Green Space: An Application of Golf and Real Estate Development. Working paper WP05-06. PERC, Bozeman, MT.

Mahoney, Julia A. 2002. Perpetual Restrictions on Land and the Problem of the Future. *Virginia Law Review* 88: 739–787.

Maybank, Burnet R. III. 2005. Testimony, Senate Committee on Finance Hearing: The Tax Code and Land Conservation: Report on Investigations and Proposals for Reform, June 8. Washington, DC. Online at http://www.finance .senate.gov/sitepages/hearing060805.htm. Visited September 8, 2005.

Meiners, Roger E., and Bruce Yandle. 2001. Land Trusts: A Return to Feudalism. In *Agriculture and the Environment*, ed. Terry L. Anderson and Bruce Yandle. Stanford, CA: Hoover Press.

McLaughlin, Nancy A. 2005. Rethinking the Perpetual Nature of Conservation Easements. *Harvard Environmental Law Review* 29(2): 421–521.

———. 2004. Increasing the Tax Incentives for Conservation Easement Donations: A Responsible Approach. *Ecology Law Quarterly* 31: 1–115.

Miller, Steven T. 2006. Remarks Before the Spring Public Lands Conference. Washington, DC, March 28. Online at http://www.irs.gov/pub/irs-tege/miller_ speech_3_28_06.pdf. Visited June 29, 2007.

Natural Resources Conservation Service (NRCS). 2006. Farm and Ranch Lands Protection Program. Fiscal Year 2006 Announcement of Program Funding. Online at http://www.nrcs.usda.gov/programs/frpp/pdf_files/FRPP_RFP06_ 05-11-06.pdf. Visited June 29, 2007.

Ottaway, David B., and Joe Stephens. 2003. Developers Find Payoff in Preservation. *Washington Post*. December 21, A1.

Parker, Dominic P. 2006. Easements or Ownership?: An Empirical Analysis of the Organization and Strategies of Land Trusts. Working paper. Available from PERC, Bozeman, MT.

———. 2005. *Conservation Easements: A Closer Look at Federal Tax Policy.* PERC Policy Series, No. 34. Bozeman, MT: PERC.

———. 2004. Land Trusts and the Choice to Conserve Land with Full Ownership or Conservation Easements. *Natural Resources Journal* 44(2): 483–518.

Parker, Dominic P., and Walter N. Thurman. 2006. Crowding Out Open Space: Explaining the Growth in Private Land Conservation. Working paper. North Carolina State University, Raleigh, NC.

———. 2004. The Private and Public Economics of Land Trusts. *NC State Economist* (July/August): 1–4.

Pidot, Jeff. 2005. Reinventing Conservation Easements: A Critical Examination and Ideas for Reform. Policy Focus Report. Lincoln Institute of Land Policy, Cambridge, MA.

Small, Stephen J. 2000. An Obscure Tax Provision Takes Private Land Protection into the Twenty-First Century. In *Protecting the Land: Conservation Easements Past, Present, and Future,* ed. Julie A. Gutanski and Roderick Squires. Washington, DC: Island Press.

Thompson, Barton H. 2000. Markets for Nature. *William & Mary Environmental Law Policy Review* 25: 261–316.

U.S. Forest Service (USFS). 2006. Forest Legacy Program. Online at http://www.fs.fed.us/spf/coop/programs/loa/flp.shtml. Visited August 21, 2006.

PART FOUR

Measuring the Wealth of Nature

CHAPTER NINE

The Wealth of Nature

Costs as Well as Benefits?

F. ANDREW HANSSEN

People value beautiful landscapes. Estimates from hedonic models and investigations of land and housing prices reveal a substantial willingness on the part of many people to pay for unspoiled forests, undeveloped coastlands, and attractive views in general.[1] Of course, one does not need to be an economist to appreciate this; as anyone from western Montana can attest, it is wonderful to live in a beautiful place. Yet policy makers often subsidize extractive activities (mining, for example), which may diminish the enjoyment people receive from the surrounding countryside.

The "wealth of nature" literature seeks to focus attention on the fact that "unspoiled nature" may be a source of economic value in its own right. I use the phrase *unspoiled nature* as shorthand to refer to all forms of enjoyment emanating from "natural" landscapes—hiking, biking, camping, etc. This is not to suggest that extractive use invariably spoils a landscape; indeed, my critique in this chapter focuses specifically on the failure of the wealth of nature literature to address the degree to which such spoiling actually occurs. Be that as it may, the wealth of nature literature points out that for much of this country's history, nature has been considered valuable only to the extent that it provides resources to extract: minerals, timber, grass to feed animals, or fish to eat. However, things are changing; people are increasingly willing to pay to live or recreate or both in areas with attractive natural landscapes. This willingness to pay can be a source of wealth for communities fortunate enough to be located in physically attractive areas. Yet many communities nonetheless continue to emphasize (or at least to tolerate) extractive industries that put this new source of wealth—the wealth of nature—at risk. The prescription offered is straight-forward: emphasize nonextractive activities that do not spoil the landscape, and de-emphasize those extractive activities that do.[2]

For virtually all economists, there is much in the wealth of nature litera-ture to admire. For example, the literature proposes an end to the subsidi-zation of public land use (below-market grazing permits, for example) and the opening up of bidding on public lands to all parties (so that the lands are allocated to the highest value uses).[3] Just as importantly, the literature makes an effective case that natural beauty is something for which people are willing to pay (and indeed do pay) and thus should be taken seriously in policy analysis.[4]

At the same time, some features of the wealth of nature literature deserve criticism. First and foremost, the literature is one-sided when it comes to counting costs and benefits; indeed, this is its greatest weakness.[5] That the general willingness to pay to enjoy natural settings has risen over time is not surprising, given the concomitant rise in American incomes. And as that willingness to pay rises, it appears reasonable to expect that the optimal mix of extractive and nonextractive activities may change. How much and in what ways are open questions, presumably susceptible to empirical analysis. Yet the wealth of nature literature makes no attempt to conduct such analy-ses. Instead, it appears simply to assert that extractive activities should be minimized to the greatest extent possible. Such a conclusion would be eco-nomically justified only if the costs imposed on the enjoyment of unspoiled nature are greater than the value that extractive activities generate in almost *any* quantity. Although this is possible, the wealth of nature literature pro-vides no evidence one way or the other. Indeed, the literature does not even acknowledge the possibility that a certain (maybe very small) amount of ex-tractive activity may yield positive values on net. Such an omission is hard to square with the literature's ostensible focus on economic benefits and costs.

The wealth of nature literature thus moves from a reasonable starting point—an increase in the willingness of people to pay for unspoiled nature—to the unsupported conclusion that nearly *any* extractive uses of the land (e.g., mining, logging, and ranching) should be avoided.[6] But the reasonable starting point is consistent with other conclusions. For example, the costs extractive industries impose on other uses of the land may not always be very high. Furthermore, even where those costs are high, there are also costs to giving up extractive industries, which should be considered as well. Finally, in some instances, extractive industries may actually complement, rather than substitute for, the consumption of unspoiled nature. For example, many of the hiking and biking trails recreationalists use to access state forestland were originally constructed by logging companies (it of course does not follow that publicly funded logging roads were necessarily worth the cost).

In short, the wealth of nature literature makes a valuable contribution to the debate over land use by pointing out that people value unspoiled nature and that attractive landscapes may be important to the economic well-being of particular communities (contrary to the implications of much public policy); however, it fails to take the next step. The central question as far as the appropriate public policy is concerned is not whether unspoiled nature is more or less valuable than given extractive activities *in total*, but rather whether the value of one additional tree logged (for example) is greater or less than that of one additional tree left standing. And that is a question the wealth of nature literature does not address.

The Wealth of Nature Literature

Tom Power is a prominent and careful proponent of the wealth of nature approach. Power (1996) sets as its task the mediation of a "war" between environmental groups and long-time residents of western communities that, says Power, has followed attempts by environmentalists to limit the extractive uses of public (and private) lands. Power maintains that the source of the war is a fundamental misconception about the role of natural resources in local economies. He begins by attacking the widespread (and erroneous) belief that economic well-being is not possible unless a community has tangible products to "export" to the outside world. He goes on to note that many well-educated people are moving into attractive rural areas—and bringing employers (always in search of a qualified workforce) with them—*because* the areas are physically attractive. Environmental amenities are a resource from which community wealth can flow, and should be protected accordingly. Indeed, income from environmental amenities is preferable to income from raw material extraction, says Power, because raw materials–based income is less likely to stay "within the community." The prices of most basic commodities (timber, copper, beef) have been declining over time in any case, and technological change has reduced the number of jobs a given production level in these industries creates. In short, extractive industries cannot be counted on for long-term economic growth, whereas environmental amenities can.

As a result, concludes Power, community well-being is enhanced by emphasizing environmental protection and de-emphasizing extractive production. In other words, there is no reason for conflict between environmentalists and long-time community residents; their respective goals are fundamentally compatible. Power's book is sprinkled with examples of communities that have been able to overcome declining demand for extractive products by emphasizing the physically attractive features of their locations, and cautionary tales of communities that have continued to emphasize extractive industries, to their cost. Power makes several policy recommendations. He argues for the elimination of public subsidies to extractive activities (below-market-price grazing permits, for example). He recommends that the money saved on subsidies be used to help communities make the transition to environmentally friendly activities. Finally, he calls for a more aggressive use of environmental permits by federal, state, and local bodies to limit extractive uses of the land.

In Power and Barrett (2001), a wealth of nature view of the world underlies the analysis, but the objective is somewhat different: to demonstrate that most communities in the rural West are not in the terminal decline so widely advertised. The "folk story" the authors take on is the belief that too-harsh environmental regulations have crippled extractive industries, and that "bad" (i.e., low-wage) jobs have replaced the old "good" (i.e., high-wage) ones as a result. The dearth of good jobs, goes the folk story, is also reflected in the burgeoning number of residents who are forced into part-time work. And to make things worse, rich out-of-staters are moving in, driving up housing prices and forcing an exodus of young community residents. The conclusion from the folk story is straightforward: scrap the regulations hampering timber production, mining, ranching, etc., and thus return to the good old days of good jobs paying high wages.

Power and Barrett take on these points one by one. They provide evidence that the fall in community wage levels is not due to local conditions (much less to the local effect of environmental regulation) but largely to national trends. Furthermore, they note that "low wages" are not necessarily indicative of undesirable living conditions; indeed, in this instance, they cannot be, given that people have been moving into the region. In addition, those who are moving in are very similar to those who are moving out in terms of age, education, and income level; the stereotype of local kids being forced out while rich older couples purchase ranchettes is simply wrong. Finally, they point out that an increase in part-time work does not always signify a dearth of "good" jobs; many people prefer working part time. The policy prescriptions are fewer: principally, to avoid wasting government money fighting inevitable changes in the economic structure of local communities. At the heart of the book's recommendation is an optimism based on confidence that natural amenities will fill any void left by the declines in ranching, logging, and mining.

Ray Rasker is another careful and prolific proponent of the wealth of nature approach. About a decade ago, the Wilderness Society published a monograph by Rasker and several coauthors titled *The Wealth of Nature* (Rasker, Tirrell, and Kloepfer 1992). The study focuses on the region immediately surrounding Yellowstone National Park and encompasses twenty counties in three states (Idaho, Montana, and Wyoming). Its goal is to document the declining importance of extractive industries in communities in this area and the increasing importance of recreation and tourism. The authors argue for stronger policies to preserve the "ecological integrity and beauty" of this region. Their argument is quite similar to Power's. The natural beauty these communities offer is a capital asset ("natural capital") that allows them to attract residents and businesses that presumably would avoid uglier places. The promotion of long-term economic growth within these communities should therefore take the form of protecting this natural capital, rather than attempting to extract resources from it. Although the authors acknowledge that resource extraction may continue to be an important source of income in some communities, they posit that such communities will inevitably suffer from more severe economic downturns than will those that instead exploit the region's natural beauty. The report bolsters its conclusions by providing data on job and income growth. The authors criticize the large subsidies provided to resource extraction and call for more subsidies for recreation and conservation. The report's primary policy recommendations revolve around protecting the environment ("the principal income-generating capital asset of the region," page 2) and promoting policies to make better use of it in its natural state.

Rasker (1995) conducts a similar analysis for the Columbia River Basin, encompassing one hundred counties in parts of Oregon, Washington,

Idaho, Montana, Nevada, Utah, and Wyoming. Rasker's thesis is again that, although logging, ranching, and mining may once have been economic mainstays, "now the magnet that draws new residents and holds the regions' existing inhabitants is environmental quality: clean air and water, handsome scenery, and native wildlife" (page vii). Rasker documents a significant decline in the proportion of personal income generated by resource extraction and farming between 1969 and 1993. He counters the claim that service jobs are always menial and poorly paid by noting recent regional growth in jobs in the medical and high-tech industries. He posits that the key to successful community growth and development is to continue to take advantage of the region's natural beauty by promoting activities that do not degrade that beauty. His specific proposals include de-emphasizing the role of resource extraction, steering clear of centralized attempts to direct economic activity in local communities (which seem always to favor resource extraction), ensuring that any resource extraction that does occur is "sustainable" (i.e., leaves resources for future generations to enjoy), promoting entrepreneurship, diversifying away from jobs in extractive industries to jobs in nonextractive activities (e.g., tourism), and protecting against excessive development as the number of people seeking to move into these communities increases.

Rasker, Gorte, and Alkire (1996) are more specific in their goal; they seek to determine whether logging "creates" jobs, as is widely believed. The authors point out that although the amount of logging done nationally has been growing (by 64 percent between 1950 and 1994), the number of jobs created nationally in the forest products industry has been shrinking (by 15 percent between 1951 and 1996). Furthermore, timber from national forestlands is only a small percentage of the total national timber harvest in any case (between 5 and 6 percent in 1994), and the connection between local timber production and local processing is becoming weaker (so there is no guarantee that local harvests will lead to local jobs).[7] Accordingly, the authors call for a stop to the subsidization of national forest timber harvests, and for the Forest Service to recognize the many other roles that forests play (as watersheds, fish and wildlife habitats, etc.). Underlying the analysis is again a wealth of nature perspective: community well-being is best enhanced by moving away from "extractive" timber production toward nonextractive uses of the land.

Rasker (1994) focuses on the Multiple-Use Sustained-Yield Act, which requires the Forest Service to consider community stability in setting policy, but only to the degree that stability is consistent with sustained yield (of timber, minerals, etc.). Rasker argues that the two assumptions underlying the act—that community stability can be publicly "managed" and that timber, forage, minerals, and energy are so essential to community survival that they should have the central place in community planning—are both erroneous, particularly in light of the "new economy" that has been flourishing in the West. Rasker proposes that three forces have undermined the old way of doing things: (1) the uncoupling of raw materials production from raw materials processing; (2) technological change, which has weakened the link between raw material production and job creation; and (3) the increased mobility of capital. Together, the three forces suggest the importance of focusing on "brainpower" rather than on extractible raw materials.

Rasker reviews the fallacy that community jobs in retailing, banking, and so forth can exist only on the back of a base of raw material exports by showing that jobs in these other sectors (and in the government) have boomed at the same time that jobs in extractive industries have declined. He posits that environmental quality will be key to successful community growth in years to come by helping attract small firms and members of an increasingly footloose workforce. However, he cautions against leaping from dependence on raw material extraction to a single-minded focus on tourism; diversity of activities is the key. He reviews the experiences of a handful of communities that have managed to implement this "new economic paradigm" (page 385) with reasonable success. And he calls for a correspondingly new paradigm for the management of public lands—specifically, a de-emphasis of raw material extraction and an emphasis on preserving the natural beauty of local landscapes. He also suggests that local and state governments engage in complementary investments, such as in education and the telecommunications infrastructure, with the objective of promoting entrepreneurial activity. Rasker briefly summarizes the free-market environmentalism literature and notes favorably that literature's recommendation that more appropriate market incentives be used (e.g., appropriately priced grazing permits, mining leases, and timber sales and the acknowledged right of communities and groups wishing to avoid the extraction of resources to bid for land rights). Rasker argues that this will lead to a better allocation of land—particularly, more land left in its natural state—which will be better for communities in the long run. He acknowledges that some communities will remain heavily dependent on natural resource extraction for the time being but states that future dependence "will not be as heavy as it was in the past" (page 390).

Rasker and Alexander (2003) tie many of these strands together. Their objective is to examine the state of affairs in the greater Yellowstone region today and to summarize the changes that have occurred in that region's economy over the past several decades: the decline of logging, ranching, and mining; the rise of service industries; and the increasing importance of small firms to job creation.[8] The study highlights how well most of the communities within this area have performed despite difficulties in the national economy and attributes the good performance to the Yellowstone region's unusually high "quality of life"—specifically, its beautiful setting. For example, the authors point out the rising importance of retirement and investment income to the region, which explains why the area has seen both rising per capita income and falling average wages. The authors ascribe the falling wages to several factors: decreases in the number of high-paying jobs (in mining, in particular), an increased tendency toward part-time work (augmented by the entry of more women into the labor market), the willingness of people generally to work for less in return for attractive living conditions (a willingness that may temporarily outpace job creation), and the growth of jobs in relatively low-paid service industries. The authors present many pages of tables and figures to bolster their case.

The study posits that the region has been remarkably successful at sustaining economic growth, but that future growth requires protecting the beauty of the landscape, which these days is as threatened by overdevelopment as by extractive industry. The authors note continued resistance from those who see extractive land uses as the only true way to economic development (a view exemplified by the bumper sticker the authors quote on page 3: "True wealth comes from the ground"). However, they acknowledge that "a growing number of residents are not benefitting from economic change" (page 3). The communities that have grown most slowly, say the authors, are those most heavily dependent on farming, ranching, and other forms of resource development. The study concludes by recommending that communities "identify and trade upon their competitive advantages" (page 3)—specifically, natural beauty, friendly residents, and well-educated labor forces. Furthermore, communities should seek to support risk-taking entrepreneurs, to provide access to larger markets—through airports, delivery services, or the Internet—and to continue to build "social and human capital."

Finally, Niemi, Whitelaw, and Johnston (1999) analyze the effect of logging reductions that followed a 1991 federal court ruling in favor of the famous spotted owl. The ruling effectively made twenty-four million acres of federal land in Oregon, Washington, and northern California off-limits to loggers and was followed by intense hue and cry and extravagant estimates of the job losses that would occur. Instead, as the authors document, jobs grew steadily as part of a regionwide economic expansion. The authors explain this with reference to the already declining importance of logging in local communities and to the fact that the enjoyment of natural amenities has become the central contributor to the economic vitality of the region. The authors conclude that logging has actually become a drain on the region's economy, primarily because it reduces the attractiveness of the area as a place to live.

A Critique

The wealth of nature literature makes a number of policy recommendations that many economists would support: stop subsidizing extractive uses of public lands, stop trying to manage "job creation" through governmental programs, recognize the value of nonextractive (i.e., service) jobs, recognize that jobs follow people, recognize that people value unspoiled nature. However, the literature also draws a number of more dubious conclusions. In this section, I provide a broad critique. First, I review a number of questionable points made specifically by one or more of the studies. Second, I discuss the failure of the literature in general to devote proper consideration to basic tradeoffs.

QUESTIONABLE POINTS

First, all of the studies emphasize the importance of "natural capital" to the growth and development of Rocky Mountain communities. However, that capital is not uniformly distributed. What should be done about communities that lack sufficiently attractive settings to provide a viable basis for economic growth? With respect to such communities, the wealth of nature literature has nothing to say. In fact, the literature's line of reasoning would seem to imply that hopelessly ugly areas should be subjected to very intensive extractive use. Furthermore, the literature does not consider the possibility of Tiebout (1956) effects, whereby those who prefer beautiful settings move into some communities, while those who prefer extractive activity move into others. In this case, optimal policy will require that regulations vary among communities.

Second, and relatedly, some studies point out that the communities in the Rocky Mountain West most heavily dependent on extractive industries have grown the most slowly and therefore conclude that these communities should exert serious effort to reduce their dependence on raw material extraction. But there is a problem of causality. A community's continued dependence on raw material extraction may indicate a lack of the natural beauty that wealth of nature studies identify as essential to successful development. In such circumstances, near exclusive dependence on extractive industry may be a community's only option.

Various studies propose that policy makers support "entrepreneurship" as an alternative to extractive industries. Although entrepreneurship is clearly important to economic growth, its source is unpredictable; furthermore, there is little that local policy makers can do to "support" it, beyond the general nostrum of avoiding policies that discourage wealth creation (which has nothing to do with the wealth of nature). And because entrepreneurs need no public sector encouragement to seek profits, recommending that local governments implement policies to attract entrepreneurs is likely to lead to a waste of public resources.

Several studies claim that an economy based on exploiting a region's beauty rather than its "extracted" resources will be less subject to economic cycles (i.e., downturns). This is not necessarily so. Certainly, the demand for raw materials can be, and has been, cyclical. However, so is the economy as a whole, and a region focused uniquely on tourism, for example (i.e., on bringing people in to enjoy the natural amenities), may be very sensitive to economic cycles. Indeed, an economy that depends on tourism may very well be *more* sensitive to economic cycles than an economy that depends on resource extraction because the income elasticity of demand for such things as skiing and fly fishing is probably very high. Some studies (e.g., Rasker 1994) explicitly state that communities should seek economic diversification, and diversification may indeed reduce the severity of economic cycles. Yet even these studies seem more concerned about shifting activity away from resource extraction than with diversification per se.

Ultimately, how well communities dependent upon the wealth of nature survive economic downturns remains to be seen. But the potential sensitivity of recreational activities to wealth created elsewhere is a question that the wealth of nature literature ignores. In fact, engaging in a certain amount of extractive activity (pumping oil, for example) would likely serve as a hedge against economic shocks that reduce the demand for outdoor recreation, while earnings from tourism can offset the risks inherent in relying solely on extracted resources. In other words, if the goal is a proper degree of diversification, the optimal mix probably involves undertaking both extractive and nonextractive activities.

Several authors focus on the importance of keeping money "within the community." For example, attracting retirees is recommended on the grounds that retirees bring money (in the form of pensions) in from elsewhere and spend most of it locally (on food, housing, etc.). However, money is money: whether the community consists of miners spending their salaries or retirees spending their pensions, if the income levels are the same, presumably the level of local spending will be the same (taking the potentially different mix of purchases into account). More to the point, policies aimed at attracting retirees do not increase wealth but simply shift wealth around. Where one community is made better off, another must be made worse off, which cannot be a good public policy approach for the country as a whole.

Almost all the studies recommend eliminating federal subsidies to extractive industries (below-market grazing permits or mining leases, for example) but then simply turn around and recommend the subsidization of other activities instead (e.g., promoting the transition to more environmentally friendly activities, conservation, recreation). In the absence of externalities, subsidies are socially wasteful, be they paid to loggers, entrepreneurs, or environmentalists.

For a number of these studies, a virtue of making natural beauty the basis for economic growth is that such beauty is "sustainable." However, most authors do not explain why "sustainability" is so desirable (or even precisely what sustainability is). For example, why are such extractive activities as logging and ranching not "sustainable," given that they can be repeated indefinitely? And although a vein of ore (or a gas well) may eventually be exhausted (in theory, at least), what is gained by leaving it untouched in the ground? The literature makes no comment—that sustainability is a good thing is simply taken for granted.

Most studies point out that jobs and income have grown despite bans on logging and mining in various places. Although the communities can take comfort from this, it begs the unanswerable question: what would have happened otherwise? Interestingly, former U.S. Forest Service chief Jack Ward Thomas recently went on the record to the effect that the Northwest Forest Plan, which Thomas helped design and which was intended to balance logging in the Northwest with the existence of the spotted owl—the issue analyzed by Niemi, Whitelaw, and Johnston (1999)—is not working as planned. Specifically, Thomas criticized the one-sided emphasis on logging reductions and said: "The promises of the Northwest Forest Plan to the people of the communities [have] taken a back seat to the precautionary principle. We've been so careful to do no harm that we've overlooked the promises to the people."[9]

Finally, much of the wealth of nature literature focuses on jobs: will a given use of the land (recreation versus extraction) lead to more or fewer jobs? The supporters of extractive industries argue that such things as logging and mining are the most durable source of jobs, while the wealth of nature literature counters that, ultimately, natural landscapes will provide more jobs. What both sides ignore is that jobs are simply a cost of getting the goods we want. What makes society better off is getting more output from a given quantity of inputs—that is, economic growth. To the degree that allocating less land to extractive activity makes us wealthier (in the broad sense, meaning happier), we should leave more land in its natural state. But that is independent of whether the net effect on the number of jobs is positive or negative. To cast the argument in terms of jobs—which both sides are guilty of doing to an inordinate degree—is to miss the point.

THE ISSUE OF TRADEOFFS

The most fundamental failing of the wealth of nature literature is the short shrift it gives to tradeoffs. It is very useful to point out that a particular activity has unrecognized benefits or costs (as the literature has done), but setting good policy requires *comparing* those benefits and costs. The entire wealth of nature literature is based on criticizing the costs extractive industries impose on the enjoyment of natural amenities, yet it fails for the most part to acknowledge the existence of offsetting benefits. Indeed, even those studies that concede that extractive industries may contribute to community income in some cases (e.g., Rasker 1995) treat this fact as a misfortune that time and effort will correct. As far as the literature is concerned, it appears that extractive industries are undesirable at best, and downright harmful (in the long run at least) at worst.

There are a few points to consider. First, even assuming that engaging in a given extractive activity renders a community a less attractive place to live, the appropriate response is usually not to *forgo entirely* the extractive activity, but to determine *how much* of it to do. The reason is that at certain levels, the costs a given extractive activity imposes on the enjoyment of a landscape may be quite small. This will in turn depend on the types of public policies that are in place to mitigate adverse effects, and such policies can presumably be adjusted to take into account the "natural wealth" of the locality. Therefore, determining how an extractive activity reduces the attractiveness of a particular locale, at what rate, and in combination with what public policies is essential to developing the proper recommendation.

Second, even if the costs that a given extractive activity inflicts on the landscape are large, the activity also generates benefits (it would not be engaged in otherwise, of course). A more balanced approach must therefore compare what a community (the wealth of nature literature focuses its recommendation at the community level) gains with what it gives up. The argument made by the wealth of nature literature is that greater economic value is generated by leaving landscapes in their natural state than by extracting the physical resources. Presumably, then, if one concludes that greater economic value is generated in a given instance by extraction, the extraction is justified. The literature must therefore grapple with the question of measuring that value, beyond simply documenting the number of jobs held in a particular extractive industry. Furthermore, basing the analysis at the community level creates a bit of a "not in my backyard" problem: the benefits generated by resource extraction (and, indeed, from leaving landscapes untouched) spread far beyond the individual community.

Third, it is conceivable (despite what the wealth of nature literature maintains) that some extractive and nonextractive activities are complements rather than substitutes—that is, each enhances the value of the other. One possible example is ranching: many people consider ranches beautiful. Another is logging: many hiking and biking trails, as well as access roads, were originally constructed by loggers (albeit at public expense). In this case, the various activities can be undertaken in tandem. In sum, policy analysis requires a more nuanced view than is provided by the wealth of nature literature.

Conclusion

A concise summary of the wealth of nature viewpoint is contained in Rasker (1994, 380):

> Like the rest of the region, Montana's economy needs be viewed as more than a repository of raw materials for production. For communities throughout the West, the key assets are not only the natural capital of the land, but also the intellectual capital of its residents and a friendly, small-town atmosphere—the quality of life. These amenities are economic assets in very

much the same way timber and mineral reserves are. They serve an important function, to retain existing people and business, and to attract potential entrepreneurs.

This is a very sensible statement. The problem is that although the author proposes that natural capital should be considered an economic asset "in very much the same way timber and mineral reserves are," in fact, the wealth of nature literature does not treat timber and mineral reserves (or other extractible resources) as if they are economic assets. Instead, it discusses such resources as if they only impose costs and provide few benefits. Clearly, both extractive (mining, logging, ranching) and nonextractive (enjoyment of the landscape) activities can generate value. The task is identifying the degree to which, and the manner in which, these activities affect each other, and thus the degree to which they can (or cannot) coexist.

Why is establishing that optimal mix of extractive and nonextractive activities so difficult? The answer appears to lie with the institutions governing land use. The simple fact is that laws and policies that make it difficult (or impossible) for resources to be traded will discourage the efficient use of those resources. It is in criticizing such laws and policies that the wealth of nature literature makes its greatest contribution. Take the example of a rancher who has the right to graze his or her cattle on a parcel of public land. Suppose the value of that parcel in an ungrazed state is higher to an environmental group than its value to the rancher as grazing land. A simple market transaction—the environmental group purchases the grazing rights from the rancher—makes everyone better off. However, in the real world, grazing rights are often allocated through the political process, so that the environmental group can gain control of the grazing rights only by changing the law. And because a change in the law is likely to make the rancher worse off, he or she will strenuously resist it. If the rancher has sufficient political clout, the parcel will remain in the lower value use (i.e., in grazing). Allocating the rights through the political process short-circuits what should be a mutually beneficial transaction.

Institutions establishing secure and tradable property rights are thus crucial; without them, welfare-enhancing exchanges will not occur. Indeed, economists have increasingly come to agree that the enormous variation in wealth we see across countries results not so much from a lack of resources as from an inability to put those resources to their most productive uses—in other words, from bad legal, political, and social institutions. The political, legal, and social institutions in most poor countries discourage invest-ment in, and the proper use of, a country's resources. To take one example, Deacon (1994) analyzes 120 countries and concludes that insecure property rights lead to deforestation and that the effect of population growth on de-forestation is greatest where property rights are insecure.

A key message from the wealth of nature literature is that we need to do a better job promoting institutions that give people the ability and incentive to transfer land (and other resources) when the highest value use changes. Promoting such institutions is a challenging task; nonetheless, people have been finding ways to do it, as attested to by the many successful communi-ties profiled in the wealth of nature literature.

Notes

I would like to thank Rob Fleck and participants at PERC's Wealth of Nature Con-ference in 2005 for helpful comments.

1. See, for example, Bartik (1988), Cheshire and Sheppard (1995), Benson (1998), Johnston (2001), Koskela and Ollikainen (2001), and Thornes (2002). In a some-what related study, Espy and Lopez (2000) examine the effect of airport noise on residential property prices, making the broader point that amenities come in many forms (for example, quiet settings, good schools, lively nightlife, etc.).

2. See, for example, Rasker, Tirrell, and Kloepfer (1992) and Power (1996).

3. See, for example, Rasker (1994, 394).

4. See Power and Barrett (2001) and Rasker, Tirrell, and Kloepfer (1992) for compelling accounts.

5. Perhaps the most extreme example is a study by Loomis and Richardson (2000) that seeks to estimate the economic value of protecting roadless areas in the continental United States. The authors identify a large range of benefits—rec-reational, jobs in local communities, option values, existence values, bequest val-ues, scientific study, biodiversity conservation, carbon storage, water quality, edu-cational, and so forth—and assign dollar values to them. However, the authors provide *no estimate at all* of the opportunity costs—of what must be given up to achieve these benefits. Therefore, one is left unable even to speculate on the appro-priate policy implications.

6. For more detail, see the literature review in the following section of this chapter.

7. National forests provided a much higher percentage of U.S.-harvested soft-wood timber as recently as the mid-1980s—see Adams, Jackson, and Haynes (1988).

8. Recall from Rasker, Tirrell, and Kloepfer (1992) that the greater Yellowstone region comprises twenty counties in Idaho, Montana, and Wyoming.

9. *Bozeman Chronicle*, June 28, 2003, A6.

References

Adams, Darius, Kristine C. Jackson, and Richard W. Haynes. 1988. *Production, Consumption, and Prices of Softwood Products in North America: Regional Time Series Data 1950 to 1985*. U.S. Forest Service, Resource Bulletin PNW-RB-151.

Bartik, Timothy J. 1988. Measuring the Benefits of Amenity Improvements in Hedonic Price Models. *Land Economics* 64: 72–83.

Benson, Earl D. 1998. Pricing Residential Amenities: The Value of a View. *Journal of Real Estate Finance and Economics* 16: 55–73.

Cheshire, Paul, and Stephen Sheppard. 1995. On the Price of Land and the Value of Amenities. *Economica* 62: 247–267.

Deacon, Robert T. 1994. Deforestation and the Rule of Law in a Cross-Section of Countries. *Land Economics* 70: 414–430.

Espy, Molly, and Hilary Lopez. 2000. The Impact of Airport Noise and Proximity on Residential Property Values. *Growth and Change* 31: 408–419.

Johnston, Robert J. 2001. Estimating Amenity Benefits for Coastal Farmland. *Growth and Change* 32: 305–325.

Koskela, Erkki, and Markku Ollikainen. 2001. Forest Taxation and Rotation Age Under Private Amenity Valuation: New Results. *Journal of Environmental Economics and Management* 42: 374–384.

Loomis, John B., and Robert Richardson. 2000. *Economic Values of Protecting Roadless Areas in the United States*. Washington, DC: Wilderness Society.

Niemi, Ernie, Ed Whitelaw, and Andrew Johnston. 1999. *The Sky Did Not Fall: The Pacific Northwest's Response to Logging Reductions*. Eugene, OR: ECONorwest.

Power, Thomas M. 1996. *Lost Landscapes and Failed Economies: The Search for a Value of Place*. Washington, DC: Island Press.

Power, Thomas M., and Richard N. Barrett. 2001. *Post-Cowboy Economics: Pay and Prosperity in the New American West*. Washington, DC: Island Press.

Rasker, Ray. 1995. *A New Home on the Range: Economic Realities in the Columbia River Basin*. Washington, DC: Wilderness Society.

Rasker, Ray, and Ben Alexander. 2003. *Getting Ahead in Greater Yellowstone*. Bozeman, MT: Sonoran Institute.

Rasker, Ray, Julie Fox Gorte, and Carolyn Alkire. 1996. *Logging National Forests to Create Jobs: An Unworkable Covenant*. Washington, DC: Wilderness Society.

Rasker, Ray, Norma Tirrell, and Deanne Kloepfer. 1992. *The Wealth of Nature: New Economic Realities in the Yellowstone Region*. Washington, DC: Wilderness Society.

Rasker, Raymond. 1994. A New Look at Old Vistas: The Economic Role of Environmental Quality in Western Public Lands. *University of Colorado Law Review* 65: 369–399.

Thornes, Paul. 2002. The Value of Suburban Forest Preserve: Estimates from Sales of Vacant Residential Building Lots. *Land Economics* 78: 426–441.

Tiebout, Charles. 1956. A Pure Theory of Local Expenditures. *Journal of Political Economy* 64: 416–424.

CHAPTER TEN

Counting the Wealth of Nature

An Overview of Ecosystem Valuation

TIMOTHY FITZGERALD AND
A. MYRICK FREEMAN III

The value of that part of the natural world that contributes to human well-being or welfare through the provision of ecological goods and services can be called the *wealth of nature*. We define the wealth of nature as the asset value that human beings derive from natural resources, whether that value emanates from converting natural resources into commodities or using them to produce services or amenities.[1] Counting this wealth is a daunting task because nature makes such diverse contributions to human welfare. Where ownership of natural assets is well defined and markets for ecosystem services exist, welfare analysis is generally straightforward. However, many of the most crucial natural service streams do not flow through markets. There are many complicated substitution and complementary relationships among ecosystem service flows that may be difficult to unravel. Accounting for the wealth of nature can thus be a difficult chore, but it is imperative if humans are to efficiently allocate natural resources in the face of increasing scarcity.

Daily and Ellison (2002) and Anderson and Leal (1997) have documented examples of private efforts to preserve and provide various ecosystem services. These examples demonstrate responses to the incentives created by existing property rights regimes, prices, and costs. Entrepreneurship in new types of private property rights for environmental goods and services has expanded the use of market forces; excellent examples include individual fishing quotas for fisheries and tradable emissions permits. This entrepreneurship has helped find efficient solutions to problems that previously seemed intractable. However, we will argue that new rights may be difficult to establish for other natural goods and services either now or in the foreseeable future. Although this might be construed as a market failure on any number of grounds, it does not imply that the service streams are not very valuable to people. The purpose of this chapter is to explore some of the issues involved in estimating these values and aggregating them into a measure of the wealth of nature.

It is reasonable to suspect that extra-market environmental goods and services are not provided in optimal quantities. This leads us to the question of appropriate policy interventions to achieve a better allocation of ecological resources. This may include addressing market failures. Some might presume that government will provide ecosystem services as a standard response to a public good problem since contracting is apt to be prohibitively expensive. However, Boyd and Banzhaf (2005, 18) point out that "it is a misconception to assume that governments [a priori] know how to provide ecosystem services." Properly constructed valuations of service streams can greatly inform the policy-making process and help agents make optimal decisions. The question is: how can we include market and nonmarket values in a single accounting?

In the past several years, ecosystem valuation has emerged as a means of calibrating the effects on human welfare of changes in nature. A flurry of recent work has sharpened these tools dramatically.[2] The Science Advisory Board of the U.S. Environmental Protection Agency has an ongoing project to assess existing methods and develop new tools for valuing ecosystem services.[3] This chapter will outline the use of ecosystem valuation as a tool for calculating the wealth of nature. Since ecosystem valuation is rooted in the principles of applied welfare economics, it can include both market and nonmarket goods and services, making it uniquely suited to tackling the massive task of valuing ecosystem services.

We will focus on the services produced by ecological systems rather than the flows of materials from nonrenewable resource stocks, although these flows also make important contributions to human welfare. The stream of net benefits from nonrenewables does not depend on current ecological processes and conditions. In the next section, we describe ecological systems and the services they provide. We then turn to the concept of economic value and the measurement of the economic values of ecosystem services. The heart of the chapter is the section in which we discuss what is involved in moving from the valuation of individual service streams to the valuation of the stock of natural capital, that is, to the measurement of the wealth of nature. The final questions we address are some of the policy implications of viewing nature as a set of economically productive assets. Specifically, should public policy take the maximization of the wealth of nature as its objective? And can markets be counted on to produce the right levels of ecosystem services? We conclude with suggestions for further research.

Ecological Systems and Their Services

Homo sapiens is just one of the millions of different species that inhabit Earth. All of these species are related with each other and their surrounding environment through ecosystems. Ecosystems are complicated sets of relationships among organisms that can be very difficult to unravel. For scientific interpretation we rely on ecologists. It is worthwhile to take a moment to sketch the major characteristics of ecosystems that are pertinent to economic valuation.

An ecosystem can be defined as "a spatially explicit unit of the earth that includes all of the organisms, along with all of the components of the abiotic environment within its boundaries" (Likens as cited in Christensen and Franklin 1997, 4). It is a human construct whose size and scope depend on how an investigator draws the spatially explicit boundaries around the objects of interest. The unit of analysis can be as small as the gut of an insect or as large as the delta area of a major river system such as the Amazon. For the purposes of economic valuation, choice of scale is an important consideration. Each ecosystem is characterized by its spatial dimensions, its species composition, the functions or processes that it carries out, and the services that it provides to people. Ecosystems are dynamic networks of relationships—biological, chemical, and physical—between species and their physical surroundings. Ecology is "the scientific study of the interrelationships among organisms and between organisms, and between them and all aspects, living and non-living, of their environment" (Allaby 1998, 136). This definition emphasizes the interconnections, or "web," of ecology. The economic implication of this web is profound.

Because of these many links, drawing explicit boundaries around an eco-system involves rather arbitrary choices. At the margins, every ecosystem is closely commingled with its neighbor. For this reason, it may be difficult or even impossible to definitively demarcate the borders of ecosystems. Con-sidering the Sahara desert, there is little question as to what we are talking about: the arid sandy wastes and attendant species are easily identified as part of the world's largest desert. Yet around the edges, for example where the Sahara borders the Sahel, the distinction between two ecosystems might be hard to make. Similarly, migratory or mobile species may provide ser-vices over a broad spatial range. This might make it more difficult to define, much less enforce, property rights to those service streams.

This difficulty in delineation also presents some problems for economic analysis. For example, scientists may not agree about the native ranges of tallgrass and shortgrass prairies; some add additional ecosystems such as mixed prairie. Such disputes are directly attributable to the dynamic nature of both ecosystems and ecology in addition to the need for human interpre-tation. Without the benefit of clearly defined boundaries, determining eco-nomic value becomes increasingly difficult. Since any welfare comparison requires two well-defined states of the world, ecological uncertainty makes coherent economic valuation more difficult. Ecologists are working at being able to answer the types of questions economists would find useful. When those answers emerge, a significant barrier to valuation will be removed.

As dynamic systems, ecosystems are best considered as a collection of physical, chemical, and biological flows. Although it is tempting to think of an ecosystem as a thing, it is in fact a collection of concurrent changes. Taken in this framework, it is much easier to see that ecosystems provide a series of flows that can be captured by humans. These flows are referred to as *ecosystem services*.

Ecosystem services have been defined in various ways. The Environmen-tal Protection Agency has defined them as "those ecological functions or processes that directly or indirectly contribute to human well-being or have the potential to do so in the future" (U.S. EPA 2004, 4). Ecologist Gretchen Daily writes:

> Ecosystem services are the conditions and processes through which natural ecosystems . . . sustain and fulfill human life. They maintain biodiversity and the production of ecosystems goods, such as seafood, forage, timber . . . and their precursors . . . In addition to the production of goods, ecosystem services are the actual life-support functions, such as cleansing, recycling,

and renewal, and they confer many intangible aesthetic and cultural benefits as well. (Daily 1997, 3)

These definitions all share an anthropocentric focus; that is, ecosystem services are explicitly services to people. Daily (1997, 3–4) goes on to list examples of ecosystem services:

· Purification of air and water
· Mitigation of floods and droughts
· Detoxification and decomposition of wastes
· Pollination of crops and natural vegetation
· Control of the vast majority of agricultural pests
· Dispersal of seeds and translocation of nutrients
· Maintenance of biodiversity, from which humanity has derived key elements of its agricultural, medicinal, and industrial enterprises
· Protection from the sun's harmful ultraviolet rays
· Partial stabilization of climate
· Moderation of temperature extremes and the force of winds and waves
· Support of diverse human cultures
· Provision of aesthetic beauty and intellectual stimulation that lift the human spirit

Other authors (e.g., Costanza, d'Arge et al. 1997) have added such things as erosion control, decomposition of wastes, habitat or refugia for species and preservation of biodiversity, and production of food and raw materials.

We can see that ecosystem services include many things people take for granted but without which well-being would be reduced and, perhaps, even life itself would be threatened. Some of these services affect humans directly, as in the cases of food and raw material production. These direct services can be either market or nonmarket services, depending on the structure of property rights and transaction costs. Other services affect people only indirectly, as in the cases of nutrient recycling and soil regeneration. In these cases, it is crucial to establish the link between the ecosystem service being valued and the channel through which it affects people.

The Millennium Ecosystem Assessment (2003) adds to this conceptual framework by identifying four categories of service streams: provisioning, regulating, supporting, and cultural. *Provisioning services* are the flows of goods such as food, fiber, fuels, and so forth that stem from the primary and secondary productivity of ecological systems. These service streams are usually easily identified and the most apt to be governed by market interactions. A useful distinction can be made between *regulating* and *supporting services*: "Regulating services are the benefits people obtain from the regulation of ecosystem processes, including air quality maintenance, climate regulation, erosion control. . . . Supporting services are those that are necessary for all other ecosystem services" (Millennium Ecosystem Assessment 2003, 8). While supporting services provide the tools (oxygen), regulating services do the work (atmospheric regulation). Supporting services are sometimes called ecosystem functions. Although these functions are undoubtedly critical, their value is susceptible to double-counting as we tally up other service streams. But taking account of these supporting and regulating services helps us to paint a more complete picture of the contribution of nature to human well-being. Finally, *cultural ecosystem services* provide benefits through recreation and other highly subjective activities such as spiritual enrichment and aesthetic experience.

The wealth of nature is a subset of the total wealth of a society, where total wealth is the sum of physical (or manufactured) capital, human capital, and natural capital. For much of the history of empirical economics, a major focus has been on the definition and measurement of physical capital and identifying its contribution to human welfare. The importance of human capital in explaining the growth of income in the developed economies has been recognized during the past fifty years. In the past twenty years, the concept of natural capital has attracted the attention of environmental economists and especially people working in the self-described "transdisciplinary field of ecological economics" (Costanza, Cumberland et al., 1997, xi). By natural capital, we mean the natural systems that produce flows of valuable materials and services to people along with the stocks of nonrenewable and renewable natural resources. Ecological economists have made a major contribution to environmental economics by emphasizing the role of ecosystem services in sustaining a productive economy. For example, they have said that stocks of renewable and nonrenewable resources should be considered as natural capital and that the services of natural capital are essential inputs into production processes. Until relatively recently, standard models of the economics of production posited only labor and manufactured capital (and sometimes energy) as inputs. The new models recognize the implicit tradeoffs between different forms of capital.

The formation of both physical capital and human capital requires that consumption be postponed so that resources can be diverted—in the case of physical capital, to the construction of tools, buildings, machines, and so forth; and in the case of human capital to education, training, enhancement of skills, and research. In contrast, much of the stock of natural capital is essentially a "gift of nature." It is possible to augment some forms of natural capital, but such investments have an opportunity cost in the form of forgone consumption, or forgone investments in manufactured and human capital.

The earth's stock of natural capital consists of both natural resource systems, such as forests and commercially exploitable fisheries, and environmental systems, such as air sheds and watersheds. These systems are valuable assets because they yield flows of valuable services to people, either directly or when combined with other inputs such as manufactured and human capital and labor. For example, a forest provides a wide range of services, including materials, such as wood and fiber and forage for cattle and sheep, and the amenities associated with a variety of outdoor recreation activities. A forest also regulates stream flow, controls erosion, absorbs atmospheric carbon dioxide, and provides habitat for a variety of species, thus protecting biodiversity. Increasing the flow of timber can lead to a decrease in the amenity values associated with mature forests and an increase in the loss of habitat for forest-dwelling species. There is also likely to be an increase in runoff and erosion and degradation of aquatic habitat that is downstream from harvested areas. Similarly, an estuary and its adjacent upland provide services such as support for commercially exploitable fisheries; space for residential, industrial, and commercial structures; and the absorption of waste products from local runoff and from upstream sources along rivers and streams. An estuary also provides amenity services associated with a variety of recreational activities, including fishing, boating, and bird watching.

As these examples suggest, the relationships among ecosystem services from any given ecological system can be complex. There can be substitution relationships among pairs of services: obtaining more of one service means making do with less of another. But there can also be complementary relationships in which two ecosystem services can be viewed as joint products. For example, a species of bird might provide pollination of a commercial fruit species and control of insects that damage some other commercially valuable plant. Some species that generate more than one service stream (such as insect control and recreational benefit) may have both substitutes and complements in the production of their services. Unraveling the pertinent economic relationships from the weblike interconnections of ecological systems may be tedious, but it is essential.

In summary, ecological systems provide a variety of service flows that help to sustain and enhance human well-being. The relationships among these service flows are complex; the levels of these flows are affected by a variety of human activities. We can do things that degrade these natural systems, in effect diminishing our natural capital. We can also do things that increase the capacity of these systems to provide certain kinds of services, in effect investing in natural capital. Thus our relationship to ecological systems can be viewed as an economic problem involving scarcity, opportunity costs, and tradeoffs. In order to manage this relationship, we need information on the economic values of ecosystem services, a topic to which we now turn.

What Is Economic Value?

The term *value* generally means importance or desirability. How to define importance or desirability has generated considerable debate among economists, ecologists, and philosophers.[4] Policy makers need to compare the flows of ecosystem services that are associated with alternative policies. Since human impacts are an integral part of ecosystems, policies are needed to manage them. People interested in making these comparisons might approach the issue from quite different perspectives. For example: "The term value . . . can have different meaning to those with different interests. To an ecologist, the value of a salt marsh might mean the significance or importance of the marsh to the reproductive capacity of a certain species of fish. To a coastal engineer, the value of a salt marsh may be associated with its contribution to shoreline stabilization" (Lipton et al. 1995, 10). We need a way to make comparisons across disparate types of outputs (for example, reproductive success of a fish species versus shoreline stabilization). This is the role and purpose of economic valuation, which is "to make the disparate services provided by ecosystems comparable to each other, using a common metric" (Millennium Ecosystem Assessment 2003, 128).

In economics, value is a measure of the contribution of something to human welfare. Thus the economic value of an ecosystem service is its contribution to human welfare, where human welfare is measured in terms of each individual's assessment of his or her own well-being. On the assumption that people are rational and make choices so as to maximize their well-being subject to a set of constraints, we can interpret the tradeoffs that people make as they choose less of one good and substitute more of some other good as revealing the value that people place on these goods. If one of the goods has a monetary value, the revealed values are monetary values.

Economists value things only in comparative terms. Economic measures of value are comparative in the sense that they express in monetary terms the difference between two well-defined states of the world—for example, a state in which a specified quantity of a good or service is available and a state in which it is not available. In this context, talking about the value of "nature" presents two problems: the description of "nature" is not specific, and what the world would be like without "nature" is unclear. In other words, neither state of the world is well defined. Finally, value can be either positive (benefits) or negative (costs or damages) depending on whether the change reflects an increase or a decrease in well-being.

People can capture value in three ways. There are two types of *use value:* direct and indirect. Direct use value is obtained from service streams that are captured immediately by the individual. Note that this includes both consumptive uses, such as eating food or cutting timber, and nonconsumptive uses, such as recreation and scenery. These firsthand effects are the simplest type of value to identify. Humans can also receive benefits indirectly. For example, pollination is a critical service in ecosystems, yet in itself it provides no direct benefit to humans. Rather, this supporting service stream is necessary in the production of streams of provisioning services such as honey, fruit, and flowers. Regulating service streams can also indirectly benefit humans. For example, plants transform carbon dioxide into oxygen.

Value can also be captured without use through a special category of values economists call *existence values, nonuse values,* or more recently *passive use values.* These are values that people place on goods or services that they do not actually use.[5] The argument is that an individual might benefit from the existence of a service stream without using it. For instance, people contribute money for the preservation of endangered species in faraway countries they will never see, give money to the Nature Conservancy for land they will never visit, and pay a premium to eat dolphin-safe tuna.

Including these three types of value (direct, indirect, and nonuse) in the analysis improves the range of economic valuation. Anthropocentric valuation includes all service streams that are connected to humans. While deep ecologists and others who attribute intrinsic value to the existence of non-human species may object, we find this to be the only feasible approach to making comparisons among states of the world that result from different policy choices.

Valuing an Ecosystem Service

Estimating the economic value of a change in an ecosystem service flow
that results from some anthropogenic change in an ecosystem involves
four steps:

· Identify the service stream of interest and its boundaries
· Determine the nature and size of the environmental change
· Predict changes in the service flow as a result of environmental change
· Use existing economic tools to assess change in human welfare

In order to predict the change in the service flow from the ecosystem, we
need to understand the link between the structure and function of the ecosystem and the service flow that it supports. As with scientific uncertainty
about ecosystems themselves, identifying this link will not always be easy.
But one approach is to think of the relevant components of the ecosystem
as being involved in a production process. Under this approach, the ecosystem is assumed to be an equilibrium system that can be subjected to comparative static analysis to determine changes in service flows in response to
changes in ecosystem conditions.[6]

One complication is that ecosystems are multiproduct systems in which
jointness in production is likely to be a dominant feature. For example, a
species of bird might be valued both for its pollination of a commercial fruit
species and for its control of insects that damage another commercially valuable plant. The value of the bird species is the sum of the values of all of its
services. But the jointness in production must be taken into account when
estimating the values of these individual service flows. Also, some species
can engage in both welfare-enhancing and welfare-decreasing activities.

Another complication is that the responses of ecosystems to perturba-
tions might display nonlinearities, discontinuities, multiple end points, and
even chaotic behavior, especially for changes in the populations of species
and fluxes of energy or nutrients (Levin and Pacala 2003). In fact, some
aspects of ecosystem behavior might be fundamentally unpredictable (Huisman and Weissing 2001). For these reasons, economists may have more success in estimating the values of changes in the spatial extent of an ecosystem
than changes in other characteristics of the system.

Once the change in the service flow has been predicted, we can deploy
the standard tools of welfare economics to assess the changes in well-being
that result. When an ecosystem service supports the production of a marketed commodity, the value of a change in that service is the sum of the

changes in consumers' and producers' surpluses in that market. For example, an increase in the population of a pollinating insect could increase the output of agricultural crops, resulting in lower prices to consumers and/or greater quasi-rents to producers. As another example, tidal wetlands are known to shelter the young of commercially valuable fish species. Changes in the area of wetlands have been related to changes in commercial harvest of blue crabs and fin fish (Lynne, Conroy, and Prochaska 1981; Bell 1989).

When ecosystem functions support nonmarket environmental services, we may be able to draw on the array of nonmarket valuation methods to determine the economic values of changes in these service flows. For example, if a physical change results in improved quality of outdoor recreational experiences, travel cost and related models of recreational demand can be used to estimate the change in value of the service flow. Stated preference methods might be used to value aesthetic services.

The following three examples demonstrate how service streams can be modeled and valued. Ricketts et al. (2004) examined the economic value to agriculture of the pollination services provided by tropical forest insects. In the area of Costa Rica that they examined, coffee is a major cash crop, yet managed honeybees are not used to ensure complete pollination. Instead, farmers rely on feral bees that reside in patches of remnant indigenous forest. The authors measured the variation in fruit set, seed mass, and peaberry frequency in areas adjacent, proximate, and distant from patches of forest. Each of these seed characteristics is attributable to pollination service and directly affects the value of the harvest.

The authors found that the value of pollination was substantial: "Pollination services from these patches therefore contributed an average of U.S. $62,000 per year (i.e., 7% of total farm income) in 2000–2003, years of depressed coffee prices" (page 12581). This number may seem rather modest; the study is limited to a single 1,065-hectare farm. By isolating the pollination services, the value is largely attributed to 191 hectares of indigenous forest in three nearby patches. This implies an approximate value per acre of forest of $144.

The authors go on to claim, "Because [the farm] does not own these forest patches, the additional income constitutes a subsidy to the farm, for which the forest is not valued and its owners not compensated" (page 12581). If the same agent owned both the forest and farm, the self-interested agent would provide the ecosystem service in the optimal quantity. Instead, the farm manages to free ride on the natural pollination service because the forest's owners (the patches are owned by different individuals, in one case a private individual and in another a timber company) are unable to capture the gains of the pollinators. Ecosystem valuation quantifies the magnitude of the positive externality that contributes to human (farmer) welfare. Market provision of pollination services is common in the United States as Cheung (1973) has demonstrated, although not yet in Costa Rica. Apparently, the farmers feel that the net benefits of incomplete pollination by natural bees are higher (since the cost of them is zero) than the net benefits of pollinating with domesticated bees.

A second example of valuing a single service stream comes from Barbier, Strand, and Sathirathai (2002). The coastline of Thailand is dominated by mangroves that support artisanal fisheries. However the mangroves are being cleared and replaced, largely by commercial shrimp farms. The rate of loss has been estimated at three thousand hectares per year (Barbier, Strand, and Sathirathai 2002, 346). The authors tried to place an economic value on this loss in the form of reduced market value of harvested fish.

The authors defined the ecosystem change as the loss of a single hectare of mangrove area. Once a figure was calculated for one hectare, a value of the annual loss of three thousand hectares per year was estimated. It seems likely that mangroves actually provide a bundle of service streams, but the authors focus only on the single service flow to be valued, that is, the support of the harvested species of fish. The authors make the simplifying assumption that on average, mangroves produce roughly equivalent service flows per acre to extrapolate to the value of the loss of three thousand hectares.

The connection between mangroves and fisheries relies on two assumptions. The first is that the system is in ex ante equilibrium. The second is, "The influence of mangrove area . . . is assumed to be positive . . . as an increase in mangrove area will mean more carrying capacity for the fishery and thus greater biological growth" (page 349). Thus changes in mangrove stocks will be reflected by changes in the fishery. The fish stock depends on mangrove area via a natural production function for fish. The fish stock is also affected by the harvest, which in turn depends on fishing effort and market price. Mangrove area does not affect fishing effort. Because the fishery is open access, it is assumed that all rents will be dissipated in the long run. The welfare loss will be in the form of higher prices to consumers of fish because of the reduced supply of fish.

Since the loss is in the form of a marketed good, the economic value of mangrove conversion depends in part on the properties of the demand for fish. The authors estimate the range of lost value between $135.44 and $3.98 per hectare, depending on the elasticity. Estimates of the aggregate annual loss are $408,000 to $11,900. The large range illustrates the sensitivity of ecosystem values to economic parameters such as preferences.

The third example is the maintenance of biodiversity. The resilience of an ecosystem depends in part on the number of species in it, but pinning down an economic value for biodiversity is more difficult.[7] One potential benefit of exploiting biodiversity in itself is in developing pharmaceuticals.[8] By this logic, if somewhere in the endangered tropical rain forest is a species containing the as-yet-undiscovered cure for cancer, the enormous potential human benefits justify preserving the forest (at least until the requisite species is found). Simpson, Sedjo, and Reid (1996) showed that this calculus is overly optimistic. "The upper bound on the value of the marginal species—and, by extension, of the 'marginal hectare' of threatened habitat—may be fairly small under even relatively favorable assumptions" (page 183). In this case, the value of ecosystem services is smaller than we might otherwise expect, or than some advocates might hope.

These examples show how ecosystem valuation can work in the simple case of single service streams, but they also demonstrate the need for ecological as well as economic information and the potential ranges of uncertainties in the estimates. Reliable valuations of ecosystem service streams are difficult to come by, in part because there are many sources of uncertainty. As mentioned above, it can be very difficult to isolate a particular service stream in order to analyze it. For example, if we want to examine the value of river flow in the Columbia River basin, we are soon sidetracked by irrigation technology, salmon biology, and an unparalleled amount of reinforced concrete. In this sort of case it is easier to examine a whole system rather than just a part.

Scientists routinely use results from small experiments to reach conclusions about broader environments. Scalability becomes increasingly problematic as we address larger and larger service streams.[9] If we assume that one hundred acres of wetlands provide one hundred times the benefits of one acre, we implicitly assume that nature has constant returns to scale. However, it is far more likely that different service streams offer decreasing, constant, or even (locally) increasing returns to scale. In fact, increasing returns to spatial scale is the rule, at least over some range, because of the well-established relationship between the viability of a population of a species and the size of its habitat.

Prevailing institutional structures are critical to determining ultimate welfare impacts. McConnell and Strand (1989) tried to evaluate the benefit of improved water quality on commercial fisheries. Since many commercial fisheries are open access, it is not surprising that they find potential welfare benefits to be squandered in these cases. "All methods of regulating which do not tax output or allocate property / harvest rights to a given quota will tend toward an equilibrium where the only net returns to society are potential improvements in consumers' surplus" (page 290). In such a case, although physical improvements in water quality have been made, in terms of economic value these benefits are smaller than otherwise expected because of the institutional structure.[10]

Since so many ecosystem services are open access or publicly owned goods, we should not be surprised to find rent dissipation playing a significant role in reducing the economic value of some service flows. Perfect competition or optimal regulation is a common assumption in economics, but we find this assumption to be too strong with respect to many ecosystem services. Rent dissipation in the open-access case or deadweight loss in a noncompetitive market affect the ultimate value of the resource. Where property rights do not exist or are expensive to enforce, we expect a similar divergence from the private, competitive equilibrium.

Ecology emphasizes the interconnectedness of organisms and their surroundings. Although discussing valuation of individual service streams is convenient theoretically, it is not practical. In the real world we see whole ecological systems providing concurrent service streams. We now turn our attention to these larger problems.

Estimating the Value of the Stock of Natural Capital

The process of estimating the value humans place on ecosystem services outlined above is laborious and information intensive. Given the broad array of ecosystem services, it might seem easier to simply value the entire stock of natural capital.

There are two ways to think about the value of the stock of natural capital. The first is borrowed from the way the Bureau of Economic Analysis in the U.S. Department of Commerce develops estimates of the tangible wealth of the U.S. economy (e.g., Katz and Herman 1997). These estimates are based in principle on counts of the numbers of each type of productive asset and a set of unit values or "prices" for each asset that are assumed to be constant. The measure of wealth is the summation of the price-times-quantity calculations for each asset type. It has long been understood that the result of the price-times-quantity calculation does not represent the total value of the stock of wealth any more than gross domestic product (also a price-times-quantity measure) represents the value that people place on the nation's output. Both calculations use marginal values or unit prices and have no way to capture the value of inframarginal units.

The second way to think of the value of the stock of natural capital is to see it as the discounted present value of the economic values of all of the streams of service flows from all of the ecosystems of the world. Using concepts of value central to welfare economics, we determine how much the society values the loss.

In a widely cited paper in the journal *Nature*, Robert Costanza and co-authors (Costanza, d'Arge et al. 1997) estimated that the annual flow of ecosystem services around the world was worth $33 trillion. They obtained this figure by estimating the annual per-hectare values of seventeen different ecosystem services from sixteen different types of biomes (ecosystems). On the basis of particular field studies, assuming that these unit values (dollars per hectare) were fixed and invariant around the world, and simply multiplying the unit values by the global areas of each type of biome, the authors pronounced the sum to be the "value of the world's natural capital." Aside from some technical and methodological flaws in their study (Freeman 2002), Bockstael et al. (2000) pointed out that Costanza et al. were implicitly asking one of the following questions:

· How much would the global population be willing to pay to prevent the loss of all of the earth's ecosystem services?
· How much would the global population require in compensation to accept the loss of all of these services?

Since the loss of all of the world's ecosystem services would undoubtedly make the planet uninhabitable, the answer to the first question is the total income of the global population, which was much less than $33 trillion; while the answer to the second question is that there is no finite compensation that we would agree to accept.

What we are suggesting here is that an estimate of the total value of the stock of natural capital is not an answer to a meaningful question. As we said above, economic valuation involves the comparison of two different states of the world, perhaps with the thing being valued versus without it, or between two different levels of provision of the thing being valued. Meaningful valuation questions involve differences between meaningful and policy-relevant states of the world, and a state of the world when the entire stock of natural capital is gone is neither meaningful nor policy relevant.

To estimate the value of a stock of natural capital, we must first establish the spatial boundaries of the natural system being valued. For example, we might be interested in a specific ecosystem or collection of ecosystems (e.g., the state of Maine). We must focus on a specific change in the structure and/or function of the ecological system being valued. This is because the value of the change will depend at least in part on the size of the change and also on the ecological conditions outside of the area being evaluated. For example, the value of a change in the function of a freshwater wetland will depend on whether similar wetlands nearby could substitute for the services provided by this wetland. Thus, valuation studies will produce estimates of the values of changes in the stock of natural capital, not estimates of the total value of the stock of natural capital, and these values will depend on the setting within which the change occurs.

Values are often expressed as unit values, such as dollars per hectare. These values are typically assumed to be fixed when values are aggregated over space or a range of services, but unit values will not be fixed for large changes in the state of the ecosystem or size of the service flow. Values depend on the spatial scale of the aggregation and the state of the surrounding ecosystems.

For specified changes in the size of a given stock of natural capital, its aggregate value can be estimated as the sum of the values of each of its constituent service flows if two conditions are met. The first concerns the proper sequencing of the value estimates for each service flow. For example, for an increase in the stock, the value of the increased service flow A is estimated conceptually holding the levels of all other service flows at their original levels and then estimating the values of the change in service flow B given the increase in A, but holding all the remaining service flows at their original levels, and so forth until all of the service flows are at their new levels.[11]

The second condition is that double counting of service values be avoided. The problem is analogous to estimating value added in national income accounting. For example, counting the value of harvested materials from an ecosystem and counting the pollination or insect control services provided by certain species is double counting, because the harvested value includes the contribution to that harvest from the pollination or insect control services. With market failures (e.g., large positive externalities associated with pollination) we may have to consider counting the service streams separately to avoid undercounting. But in general, double counting is a more prevalent concern because of the aforementioned jointness of production common to ecosystems.

Some Policy Implications

From an economic perspective, is maximizing the wealth of nature an appropriate goal for environmental and resource policy? A policy to alter the ways in which a given stock is utilized, that is, to alter the stream of ecosystem services it generates, should be evaluated by comparing the benefits (increases in some services) with the costs (decreases in other services). This perspective is broadly consistent with economists' arguments regarding the management of human impacts on the environment over the past thirty-five to forty years. Efficient utilization of a given stock of natural capital is a necessary condition for achieving an efficient allocation of resources overall.

This interpretation takes the stock of natural capital as exogenous. We have to recognize that we can augment the existing stock by devoting labor, human capital, and manufactured capital to activities such as restoration ecology or improving harvesting practices.[12] Regulatory responses banning certain activities in previously exploited natural systems (for example by establishing marine protected areas or limiting road construction in national forests) may have similar effects. By including policies to augment the stock of natural capital in the choice set, we can see that it is possible to overinvest in natural capital just as it is possible to overinvest in certain forms of manufactured capital or human capital. Critics of conventional economics have correctly pointed out that if the services of natural capital are undervalued, the result can be underinvestment in natural capital and the provision of ecosystem services. But it is also true that if the values of ecosystem services are exaggerated, the result can be overprovision of ecosystem services. And if some ecosystem services are overvalued while others are undervalued, the result can be an inappropriate mix of these services and a loss of economic well-being.

Today's policy problem is how to develop appropriate institutional frameworks to ensure that necessary ecosystem services will be provided at an appropriate level. Is the development of an improved property rights regime feasible?

Because many ecosystem services, especially regulating, support, and cultural services, are not bought and sold in markets, it is reasonable to expect that they are not provided in optimal quantities. Underprovision of these types of services is to be expected because property rights are not well defined or enforceable. This leads us to the question of appropriate policy interventions.

Ecosystem services can be local, regional, or global in scale. Addressing ozone depletion requires different tools than ensuring diverse soil biota. Creating appropriate property rights for ecosystem services preservation can be a challenge. Institutions for wildlife must be scaled corresponding to the problem (Lueck 1991). Consider summer insect control services provided by neotropical songbirds in the northeastern United States. Given that the services are being provided in a densely populated area with an affluent population, and that insect control has very real human benefit, we might expect the economic value of this service stream to be quite significant. However, the birds that provide the services are migratory. Reasonably narrow habitat requirements proscribe appropriate winter range, which is often in a different country. Additionally, during spring and fall migrations the birds must have suitable stopover points. Coordinating actions over thousands of miles for thousands of birds is no mean feat. We might expect contracting costs alone to dissipate any rents associated with preserving habitat for these birds.

Property rights can be used to solve problems that migratory species present. Ducks Unlimited and other groups have done great work providing habitat for North American ducks from Canada to the tropics. However, these efforts have been successful only because they have been augmented by both federal and state wildlife agencies that set, coordinate, and enforce game laws. While property rights regimes are an important part of the solution, it remains unclear whether the Ducks Unlimited model would be successful in the absence of the direct use value of ducks. Neotropical songbirds lend themselves to some limited direct use values, such as bird watching, but their benefits are largely indirect. Insect control is also a service stream that we are able to replace technically. However, carpet bombing the northeastern United States with insecticide is likely to impose costs that Americans are unwilling to bear. In fact, neotropical songbirds are likely to be part of a cost-effective strategy for seasonal insect control, even if there are nontrivial contracting costs. Quilting a suitable collection of property rights across thousands of miles at various times of year is a daunting task. While there is no indication that immediate action is needed, we are provided with an example of the problems associated with ecosystem services property rights.

Property rights can certainly be created for some ecosystem services. Perhaps the best recent example of institutional creation and adjustment has been the activity on in-stream water rights. These property rights have allowed the use of market forces to allocate bundles of ecosystem services associated with in-stream flow: resident and migratory fish, hydroelectric potential, and recreational opportunities (Landry 1998). Institutional creation and design are bound only by the self-imposed limits of human creativity.

Another option to improve efficiency is to more clearly define property rights to make it easier to engage in transactions involving ecosystem services. In the case of Costa Rican coffee plantations examined above (Ricketts et al. 2004), the native forest that supports the native pollinators is not owned by the plantation. If the forest owner had enforceable property rights in the insect pollinators, the farm's management could be required to pay for the pollination services of the forest-dwelling insects.

In those cases where establishing property rights is not feasible or where ecosystem services have the characteristics of public goods, valuable lessons can be learned from the economics of pollution control about the design of market-based incentives such as environmental fees and taxes and tradable permits to achieve the economically efficient level of provision of these services through private actions. The new carbon emissions program in Europe and the existing sulfur emission trading program in the United States both offer templates for tradable permits in resources hitherto considered public goods.

In addition to well-defined and enforceable property rights policy, the effective functioning of a system of markets requires well-informed market participants. If people do not understand the role of ecosystem services, especially those of the indirect form, in affecting their welfare, they cannot make good decisions about the purchase or sale of these services or the resources that provide them. Ecologists are currently attempting to identify the pertinent components of the natural "production function." Increasing scientific understanding of the natural world will allay the informational failure about what services are available and why they are important.

It is also the case that if people are ignorant about the contributions of ecosystem services to their well-being, analysts cannot infer valid economic values for these services from the choices that we observe people to be making or that they say they would make when asked stated preference questions. Thus another policy implication is that it will be important to increase the degree of ecological literacy of potential participants in any marketlike institutions that are created to deal with ecosystem services and natural capital. Nature is not exogenous; as consumers of nature, people need to become more discerning. Given better information about what is available, individuals must recognize that they may have to make hard choices about which service streams are most important to them.

Conclusions

The strength of the ecosystem valuation approach is that it recognizes that the wealth of nature depends on a wide array of service streams. Some of the literature gives insufficient attention to ecosystem services other than recreation and amenities.[13] Around the country land is being shifted from production of natural resource commodities, such as timber and livestock, to more intensive recreational and residential uses. One might say that these shifts in land use reflect the market moving resources (land) into their highest valued uses. But from our reading in ecology, we understand that these changes in the landscape can lead to fragmentation of habitat, increase in edge effects, changes in hydrology (runoff, etc.), and perhaps significant changes in the species compositions on affected lands. This can result in decreases in some of the ecosystem services that we have tried to highlight here, especially the indirect regulation and supporting services for which it would be hard to create markets. Thus, it is not clear that these changes are resulting in an increase in the wealth of nature.

That said, we must acknowledge that at this point in time there is very limited empirical evidence concerning the relative values of the recreational and amenity services being generated in comparison with the indirect ecosystem services that might be in decline.[14] Ecologists and economists are only beginning to try to estimate the values of these ecosystem services and how these values change with changes in human impacts on ecosystems. Without a better understanding of these impacts, it is not possible to say whether these land-use changes are increasing or decreasing the wealth of nature. Although we are optimistic for an increased role for markets in managing some ecosystem services, we see substantial barriers to greater reliance on markets for determining the optimal levels of many others. Much work remains to be done on integrating approaches to ecosystem valuation and institutional factors.

The concept of the wealth of nature that we have outlined here is thoroughly grounded in ecology and reflects the best-available understanding of how nature and institutions interact to provide service streams. Adopting a coarser view of natural processes that focuses only on a subset of ecosystem services may brighten prospects for implementing the valuation and management of those services. However, this comes only at the cost of ignoring what might turn out to be crucial service streams. A tradeoff exists between scientific accuracy and practical applicability in the identification and valuation of ecosystem service streams. Concentrating on only a small subset of service streams and ignoring other potential pathways to human welfare systematically miscounts the wealth of nature.

Notes

1. The wealth of nature is often referred to as *natural capital* in the ecological economics literature (Costanza, Cumberland et al., 1997).

2. For example, the Millennium Ecosystem Assessment (2003), National Research Council (2004), and U.S. Environmental Protection Agency (2004).

3. For more information on the objectives of the Science Advisory Board's project for Valuing the Protection of Ecological Systems and Services, see http://www .epa.gov/sab/03project/proj0306.htm.

4. For more extended discussions of some of these issues, see Bockstael et al. (2000), Freeman (2003), and the Millennium Ecosystem Assessment (2003), as well as references cited there.

5. The concept of nonuse values has a long history in environmental and resource economics, but it is not without controversy. See Freeman (2003), chapter 5, especially pages 137–143, for an overview and references. Measurement of nonuse values requires the use of stated preference methods, another area of controversy. See Freeman (2003), chapter 6, for an overview and cautiously optimistic assessment of stated preference methods of economic valuation.

6. For discussion of the production function approach, see Barbier (1994, 2000). For examples of empirical applications, see Finnoff and Tschirhart (2003a and 2003b).

7. Tilman (1997) sketches the intellectual history of biodiversity and how it affects ecosystem stability.

8. A market example of this is an agreement between the pharmaceutical company Merck and the Costa Rican biodiversity agency (INBio). Merck donated $1.35 million for forest preservation in exchange for bioprospecting rights, with an agreement for royalties should any new products be commercially successful. See Heal (2000, 102).

9. See Brown (1994) for a more complete discussion of the difficulties of scaling ecological research.

10. See also Freeman (1991).

11. See Hoehn and Randall (1989).

12. See, for example, Fitzgerald's description of the Lasater Ranch in Colorado (Fitzgerald 2005).

13. A prime example is the praise heaped on the St. Joe Company beach side resort development in northwest Florida (Yablonski 2005).

14. See the references in notes 2 and 3 above.

References

Allaby, Michael, ed. 1998. *A Dictionary of Ecology*. 2nd ed. New York: Oxford University Press.

Anderson, Terry L., and Donald R. Leal. 1997. *Enviro-Capitalists: Doing Good While Doing Well*. Lanham, MD: Rowman & Littlefield.

Barbier, Edward B. 1994. Valuing Environmental Functions: Tropical Wetlands. *Land Economics* 70(2): 155–173.

————. 2000. Valuing the Environment as Input: Review of Applications to Mangrove-fishery Linkages. *Ecological Economics* 35(1): 47–61.

Barbier, Edward B., Ivar Strand, and Suthawan Sathirathai. 2002. Do Open Access Conditions Affect the Valuation of an Externality? Estimating the Welfare Effects of Mangrove-Fishery Linkages in Thailand. *Environmental and Resource Economics* 21: 343–367.

Bell, Frederick W. 1989. *Application of Wetland Evaluation Theory to Florida Fisheries*. Tallahassee, FL: The Florida Sea Grant College.

Bockstael, Nancy E., A. Myrick Freeman III, Raymond J. Kopp, Paul R. Portney, and V. Kerry Smith. 2000. On Measuring Economic Values for Nature. *Environmental Science & Technology* 34: 1384–1389.

Boyd, James W., and H. Spencer Banzhaf. 2005. Ecosystem Services and Government Accountability: The Need for a New Way of Judging Nature's Value. *Resources* 158: 16–19.

Brown, James H. 1994. Grand Challenges in Scaling Up Environmental Research. In *Environmental Information Management and Analysis: Ecosystem to Global Scales*, ed. William K. Michener, James W. Brunt, and Susan G. Stafford. Bristol, PA: Taylor & Francis.

Cheung, Steven N. S. 1973. The Fable of the Bees: An Economic Investigation. *Journal of Law & Economics* 16(1): 11–33.

Christensen, Norman L., Jr., and Jerry F. Franklin. 1997. Ecosystem Function and Ecosystem Management. In *Ecosystem Function and Human Activities: Reconciling Economics and Ecology*, ed. R. David Simpson and Norman L. Christensen Jr. New York: Chapman and Hall.

Costanza, Robert, Ralph d'Arge, Rudolf de Groot, Stephen Farber, Monica Grasso, Bruce Hannon, Karin Limburg, Shalid Naeem, Robert V. O'Neill, Jose Paruelo, Robert G. Raskin, Paul Sutton, and Marjan van den Belt. 1997.

The Value of the World's Ecosystem Service and Natural Capital. *Nature* 387: 253–260.

Costanza, Robert, John Cumberland, Herman Daly, Robert Goodland, and Richard Norgaard. 1997. *An Introduction to Ecological Economics.* Boca Raton, FL: St. Lucie Press.

Daily, Gretchen C. 1997. What Are Ecosystem Services? In *Nature's Services: Societal Dependence on Natural Ecosystems,* ed. Gretchen C. Daily. Washington, DC: Island Press.

Daily, Gretchen C., and Katherine Ellison. 2002. *The New Economy of Nature: The Quest to Make Conservation Profitable.* Washington, DC: Island Press.

Finnoff, David, and John Tschirhart. 2003a. Harvesting in an Eight-Species Ecosystem. *Journal of Environmental Economics and Management* 45(3): 589–611.

———. 2003b. Protecting an Endangered Species While Harvesting Its Prey in a General Equilibrium Ecosystem Model. *Land Economics* 79(2): 160–180.

Fitzgerald, Timothy. 2005. The Lasater Ranch: Grass-fed Cattle Restore the Prairie. *PERC Reports* 23(1): 12–13.

Freeman, A. Myrick III. 1991. Valuing Environmental Resources Under Alternative Management Regimes. *Ecological Economics* 3(3): 247–256.

———. 2002. How Much Is Nature Really Worth? An Economic Perspective. In *Valuing Nature: A Set of Papers Resulting from the Shipman Workshop.* Brunswick, ME: Bowdoin College. Online at http://academic.Bowdoin.edu/environmental_studies/dissemination/valnat.pdf.

———. 2003. *The Measurement of Environmental and Resource Values: Theory and Methods.* 2nd ed. Washington, DC: Resources for the Future.

Heal, Geoffrey. 2000. *Nature and the Marketplace: Capturing the Value of Ecosystem Services.* Washington, DC: Island Press.

Hoehn, John P., and Alan Randall. 1989. Too Many Proposals Pass the Benefit Cost Test. *American Economic Review* 79(3): 544–551.

Huisman, Jef, and Franz J. Weissing. 2001. Fundamental Unpredictability in Multispecies Competition. *American Naturalist* 157(5): 488–494.

Katz, Arnold J., and Shelby W. Herman. 1997. Improved Estimates of Fixed Reproducible Tangible Wealth, 1929–95. *Survey of Current Business* (May 1997). Washington, DC: U.S. Department of Commerce, Bureau of Economic Analysis.

Landry, Clay J. 1998. *Saving Our Streams Through Water Markets: A Practical Guide.* Bozeman, MT: PERC.

Levin, Simon A., and Stephen W. Pacala. 2003. Ecosystem Dynamics. In *Handbook of Environmental Economics,* Vol. 1, ed. Karl-Goran Maler and Jeffery R. Vincent. Amsterdam, The Netherlands: Elsevier.

Lipton, Douglas W., Katherine Wellman, Isobel C. Sheifer, and Rodney F. Weiher. 1995. *Economic Valuation of Natural Resources—A Guidebook for Coastal Resources Policymakers.* NOAA Coastal Ocean Program Decision Analysis Series No. 5. Silver Spring, MD: NOAA. Online at http://www.mdsg.umd.edu/programs/extension/valuation/handbook.htm.

Lueck, Dean. 1991. Ownership and Regulation of Wildlife. *Economic Inquiry* 29(2): 249–260.

Lynne, Gary D., Patricia Conroy, and Frederick J. Prochaska. 1981. Economic Valuation of Marsh Areas for Marine Production Processes. *Journal of Environmental Economics and Management* 8(2): 175–186.

McConnell, Kenneth E., and Ivar E. Strand. 1989. Benefits for Commercial Fisheries When Demand and Supply Depend on Water Quality. *Journal of Environmental Economics and Management* 17(3): 284–292.

Millennium Ecosystem Assessment. 2003. *Ecosystems and Human Well-being: A Framework for Assessment.* Washington, DC: Island Press.

National Research Council. 2004. *Valuing Ecosystem Services: Toward Better Environmental Decision-Making.* Washington, DC: National Academy Press.

Ricketts, Taylor H., Gretchen C. Daily, Paul R. Ehrlich, and Charles D. Michener. 2004. Economic Value of Tropical Forest to Coffee Production. *Proceedings of the National Academy of Science* 101(34): 12579–12582.

Simpson, R. D., R. A. Sedjo, and J. W. Reid. 1996. Valuing Biodiversity for Use in Pharmaceutical Research. *Journal of Political Economy* 104(1): 163–185.

Tilman, David. 1997. Biodiversity and Ecosystem Functioning. In *Nature's Services: Societal Dependence on Natural Ecosystems*, ed. Gretchen C. Daily. Washington, DC: Island Press.

U.S. Environmental Protection Agency (EPA). 2004. *Ecological Benefits Assessment Strategic Plan, SAB Review Draft.* Washington, DC.

Yablonski, Brian. 2005. Marketing the Wealth of Nature: The St. Joe Company in Northwest Florida. *PERC Reports* 23(3): 12–15.

CHAPTER ELEVEN

Do Resource States Do Worse?

RONALD N. JOHNSON

In the early development of the United States, natural resource exploitation played a critical role in the historical development of many states (Irwin 2000). The evidence presented in this chapter, however, reveals that states with a relatively high share of their economies engaged in natural resource–intensive sectors, particularly extractive industries, grew at slower rates over the period 1977–2002. Contributing to the slow growth of natural resource–oriented states have been declines in resource commodity prices and outputs, although some commodity prices have experienced an upsurge in recent years. Although declines in the resource extractive sectors have contributed to relatively slow growth, the evidence also indicates that the nonresource sectors of these states' economies have failed to expand at a sufficiently rapid pace to overcome declines in the natural resource sectors.

These results present a challenge to those who advocate that the real wealth of nature is not in commodity extraction, but in preserving rural natural landscapes. Their fundamental argument is that protection of natural landscapes and the environment will contribute more to economic growth than allowing traditional natural resource–based industries to expand.[1] Supposedly, protection of natural landscapes and rural lifestyles underlies a quality of life that sufficiently contributes to economic growth in order to offset a decline in extractive resource–based industries. Although mining and oil and gas extraction often employ highly skilled and well-paid workers, the contention is that even these jobs can be replaced with higher wage skilled workers in the service sector who are attracted to the area by its rural lifestyle and natural amenities.[2] Contributing to this alleged shift are improvements in communications that have reduced the isolation and costs of living in rural areas. Concomitantly, it has been argued that public values have shifted toward protecting environmental quality. Indeed, some rural communities have rebounded from declines in natural resource extraction (Power 1996). But as the empirical results presented here indicate, the aggregate picture reveals that declines in natural resource–extraction sectors are not quickly followed by expansion in the other sectors of a state's economy.

To address the empirical question of whether resource states do worse economically than other states, this chapter draws on recent literature that examines cross-country evidence on the relationship between reliance on natural resource–oriented industries and economic growth. Some policy advocates believe that reliance on natural resources can have adverse consequences for economic growth (Auty 2001a). Over the past twenty or thirty years, economic growth across countries has varied inversely with a variety of measures of natural resource abundance (Auty 2001b; Gylfason 2001; Sachs and Warner 1997). This phenomenon, often referred to as *the curse of natural resources,* seems at odds with popular images of oil-rich nations and countries well endowed with nutrient-laden soils and abundant timber or fish stocks. Although few authors go so far as to claim that discoveries of natural resource wealth leave countries poorer in the long run, the mechanics of relatively slow growth over the long run seem to suggest that possibility.

In the following section, I consider the applicability of international evidence on the resource curse to the U.S. experience. Although simple correlation analysis indicates a negative relation between the relative size of the resource-based sector and economic growth, the more popular explanations for the resource curse do not apply to the U.S. experience. Instead, the rural geography of states with relatively high natural resource–intensive sectors appears to have hindered their potential for growth. As Rappaport and Sachs (2003) have shown, economic activity in the United States is overwhelmingly concentrated along its ocean and Great Lakes coasts. Relatively high population density along these coastal areas appears to contribute to productivity, while proximity to the coastal areas contributes to the quality of life.

International Evidence

The search for key determinants of economic growth has proved to be an elusive quest (Easterly 2001). Because the standard production function approach, with its physical capital and human capital components, lacks empirical robustness, the door has been open to a myriad of causal arguments. Indeed, there seems to be no limit to the number of hypotheses concerning the sources of economic growth, with each having its moment of fame.[3] Many of these arguments are supported, at least to some degree, by cross-country correlations. To this list can be added the notion that countries well endowed with natural resources have experienced relatively slow growth.

Casual observation supports the hypothesized curse of natural resources. Although there is no strong consensus on how to measure a country's stock and use of natural resources, few resource economists would consider Singapore, South Korea, and Hong Kong to be richly endowed with natural resources. In contrast, countries such as Saudi Arabia, Kuwait, and the United Arab Emirates are richly endowed, at least with oil. Yet, annual growth rates of real per capita gross domestic product (GDP) over the past thirty years are substantially greater for the former group of countries than the latter. Moreover, the few available cross-country measures of resources all seem to show a consistent and strong negative correlation between resources and economic growth. Gylfason (2001), for example, used 1994 World Bank estimates of the share of natural capital in total national wealth for eighty-six countries. The correlation between the World Bank's measure of resource abundance and annual growth of per capita gross national product over the period 1965–1998 was $\rho = -0.51$. Studies using such indicators as per capita land area and share of the labor force in the primary sector have also lent support to the hypothesized curse of natural resources.[4] But the most-cited studies are by Sachs and Warner (1997, 2001), who use the ratio of primary-product exports to GDP as their key indicator. Their results indicate their key variable had a negative impact on economic growth even after a host of controlling variables, such as the level of education and the degree of openness of the economy, had been accounted for.

Numerous studies have followed Sachs and Warner's lead. In particular, many authors have attempted to identify the mechanisms through which the resource curse operates. Explanations for the resource curse abound, but three channels of transmission from abundant natural resources to stunted economic development have received considerable attention: (1) countries rich in natural resources engage in frivolous consumption and neglect education; (2) the natural resource sector is especially prone to corruption and rent seeking, and many resource-oriented countries lack strong institutions that protect property rights; and (3) natural resource booms drive up factor prices, such as wages and the real exchange rate, thus harming the exports of other economic sectors that are major contributors to long-term growth (the so-called Dutch Disease).

A recent example of this literature is an article by Sala-i-Martin and Subramanian (2003). The authors examined GDP growth rates across seventy-one countries between 1970 and 1998. They used a number of different measures of natural resource intensity, including the share of exports of four types of natural resources—fuel, ores and metals, agricultural raw material, and food—in GDP and in total exports. Importantly, Sala-i-Martin and Subramanian attempt to control for variation in institutional quality by incorporating a rule-of-law measure. They also employ a two-stage estimation procedure that allows them to infer both the direct and indirect effect of natural resource intensity on economic growth. Their results indicate that the curse operates through a negative impact on the rule-of-law variable. Essentially, natural resource intensity does not lead to slow economic growth, but failed institutions do.

An underlying premise in the literature on the resource curse is that natural resources provide a bounty. In particular, natural resources are a source of economic rents, which purportedly set the stage for the numerous stories of how natural resource wealth is misspent on frivolous consumption and misguided governmental projects. Moreover, the natural resource economics literature is replete with examples of how the rental value of a resource can be dissipated if property rights are either nonexistent or ill defined (e.g., Anderson and Hill 1990; Brown 2000).

Consider, for example, the case of the fishery. Under open-access conditions the value of harvested fish could approximate the cost of boats and crew, leaving few rents that can be attributed to the fishery. Recall that the key variable in the Sachs and Warner (1997, 2001) model is the share of primary exports in GDP. A country that harvests large quantities of fish could, by their measure, be labeled as well endowed with natural resources. But if open-access conditions prevail, the export value of the fish may merely reflect the opportunity cost of the crew and boat.[5] Accordingly, frivolous consumption and misguided governmental projects are not the only mechanisms through which the resource curse can operate. The lack of property rights to the resource can result in the dissipation of rents and a failure to generate the very bounty that could lead to further investments and economic growth.

Like many of the statistical analyses of the determinants of economic growth, the correlations supporting the resource curse phenomenon appear fairly robust. Of course, the great disparity among countries in terms of their human capital, physical attributes, and institutions raises questions about whether this substantial variation can be adequately explained by a handful of right-hand-side variables. Supposedly, variation is less within a country. Moreover, the United States rates high on the rule-of-law scale, suggesting that factors other than failed institutions may contribute to the negative relationship between resource intensity and economic growth.

The U.S. Experience

The United States is generally considered to be well endowed with rich fertile land and extensive oil and mineral deposits. It has also experienced exceptional economic growth over the past two centuries, offering a counterexample to the resource curse phenomenon. As mentioned above, however, states with a relatively high share of their economies engaged in natural resource–intensive sectors (particularly extractive industries) grew at slower rates between 1977 and 2002. This section presents the results, based on standard growth models, supporting that conclusion and considers some of the common explanations for natural resource intensity and slow growth.

Comparisons of economic growth, both international comparisons and across U.S. states, commonly use measures of per capita income or product. The U.S. Department of Commerce Bureau of Economic Analysis estimates state personal income beginning in 1929; this is the longest series available. The Bureau of Economic Analysis also prepares estimates of gross state product (GSP) for sixty-three industries beginning in 1977.[6] For each industry, GSP has three components: employee compensation, indirect business tax and nontax liability, and property-type income. Importantly, GSP attributes capital income to the state in which the business activity occurs, whereas personal income attributes it to the state of residence of the asset holder. Since the net benefits of natural resources can accrue largely in the form of economic rents, GSP is the better choice for studying state economic growth.[7] However, the results reported in this chapter are largely invariant to the use of real per capita personal income or real per capita GSP in measuring economic growth.[8]

Table 11.1 provides annualized percentage rates of growth in GSP for the fifty U.S. states for the period 1977–2002. The data are listed in descending order. Casual observation of the table suggests a negative correlation between resource abundance and economic growth. Delaware, Massachusetts, and Connecticut were three of the fastest growing states, but it is difficult to consider these three eastern states as relatively well endowed with natural resources. On the other hand, Louisiana and Alaska were the two slowest growing states. Although one could argue that Alaska is unique, and it is, the exclusion of that state from the sample does not have any significant effect on the empirical results. Indeed, GSP in 1977 for states such as Wyoming were even more heavily weighted by oil and gas extraction than was Alaska.

I follow Sachs and Warner, and others, and measure natural resource

TABLE 11.1

Percent annual growth of real per capita state gross product, 1977–2002

State	Annual growth, %	State	Annual growth, %	State	Annual growth, %
Delaware	3.41	Florida	2.12	Kansas	1.66
Massachusetts	2.99	New York	2.06	Mississippi	1.63
Connecticut	2.88	Pennsylvania	2.05	Iowa	1.62
New Hampshire	2.84	Nebraska	1.94	Michigan	1.55
New Jersey	2.74	Alabama	1.93	Texas	1.51
Virginia	2.57	Washington	1.93	Oregon	1.48
North Carolina	2.55	Utah	1.91	Idaho	1.48
Vermont	2.53	Arizona	1.89	Hawaii	1.36
Georgia	2.47	Wisconsin	1.88	New Mexico	1.35
Rhode Island	2.45	Arkansas	1.86	Nevada	1.26
Maine	2.33	Missouri	1.78	West Virginia	1.13
South Dakota	2.32	North Dakota	1.77	Oklahoma	1.11
South Carolina	2.31	California	1.76	Montana	0.99
Maryland	2.31	Illinois	1.74	Wyoming	0.82
Minnesota	2.28	Indiana	1.69	Louisiana	0.76
Tennessee	2.22	Ohio	1.68	Alaska	–0.01
Colorado	2.21	Kentucky	1.67		

SOURCE: U.S. Department of Commerce, Bureau of Economic Analysis.

abundance at the beginning of the sample growth period.[9] In this case, the beginning period is 1977 and resource abundance is measured as the share of natural resource–related industries in GSP. The period 1970–1977 was one of rapid expansion in the energy sector, followed by a decline in the 1980s. Hence, 1977 is an excellent starting date for examining natural resource booms and subsequent effects on growth.

Because they are likely influenced by different political factors and circumstances, two different resource sector shares are utilized.[10] The first is the share of GSP accounted for by oil and gas extraction and coal, metal, and nonmetallic mining (SHAREMINING). The second is the share of GSP accounted for by agriculture, forestry, and fishing (SHAREAG). The latter variable is dominated by commercial farms, and the former is dominated by oil extraction and coal mining. Tables 11.2 and 11.3 show the share data for the two natural resource sectors. Although the mining and agricultural

TABLE 11.2

Share of gross state product accounted for by oil and gas extraction and coal, metal, and nonmetallic mining, 1977–2002

State	Share	State	Share	State	Share
Wyoming	0.339	Virginia	0.020	Oregon	0.003
Louisiana	0.240	Nevada	0.019	North Carolina	0.002
New Mexico	0.182	Pennsylvania	0.018	South Carolina	0.002
West Virginia	0.176	Idaho	0.014	Iowa	0.002
Oklahoma	0.130	Minnesota	0.014	Delaware	0.002
Texas	0.120	California	0.013	Wisconsin	0.002
Alaska	0.113	South Dakota	0.012	New York	0.002
Kentucky	0.081	Ohio	0.011	Washington	0.002
Montana	0.073	Illinois	0.010	Connecticut	0.001
Utah	0.056	Tennessee	0.009	New Hampshire	0.001
North Dakota	0.046	Florida	0.008	Maryland	0.001
Colorado	0.039	Michigan	0.008	New Jersey	0.001
Kansas	0.039	Missouri	0.007	Rhode Island	0.001
Arizona	0.031	Indiana	0.006	Massachusetts	0.000
Mississippi	0.025	Vermont	0.005	Maine	0.000
Alabama	0.025	Georgia	0.005	Hawaii	0.000
Arkansas	0.022	Nebraska	0.004		

SOURCE: U.S. Department of Commerce, Bureau of Economic Analysis.

sectors accounted for only 5.3 percent of total U.S. GDP in 1977, it is clear from the two tables that their importance varied substantially across the states.

Both SHAREMINING and SHAREAG experienced sharp general declines over the period 1977–2002, and in real dollars those two sectors were either essentially stagnant or declining (Figures 11.1–11.4), a status they held in common with only a few other sectors such as textiles. That time frame, especially after 1981, corresponds to a sharp decline in the real price of oil and coal, the two main components of SHAREMINING. Concomitantly, after a sharp jump in the 1970s, agricultural prices continued their long-term secular decline. For those states with relatively high shares of GSP in natural resource–based industries, achieving equivalent growth to more diversified states would require a relatively large expansion in the other

TABLE 11.3

Share of gross state product accounted for by agriculture, forestry, and fishing, 1977–2002

State	Share	State	Share	State	Share
South Dakota	0.164	Washington	0.033	Utah	0.017
North Dakota	0.131	Florida	0.032	Ohio	0.016
Iowa	0.109	North Carolina	0.031	Delaware	0.015
Nebraska	0.107	Oregon	0.031	Michigan	0.013
Idaho	0.087	Oklahoma	0.029	Alaska	0.013
Arkansas	0.072	Wyoming	0.029	Virginia	0.012
Minnesota	0.069	Colorado	0.028	Nevada	0.011
Montana	0.064	California	0.028	Pennsylvania	0.011
Kansas	0.063	New Mexico	0.028	Maryland	0.010
Mississippi	0.060	Illinois	0.027	New Hampshire	0.009
Wisconsin	0.047	Texas	0.024	Connecticut	0.006
Kentucky	0.039	Alabama	0.023	Rhode Island	0.006
Vermont	0.037	Hawaii	0.022	New York	0.006
Missouri	0.036	Tennessee	0.021	Massachusetts	0.006
Maine	0.034	South Carolina	0.020	New Jersey	0.005
Arizona	0.033	Georgia	0.020	West Virginia	0.005
Indiana	0.033	Louisiana	0.019		

SOURCE: U.S. Department of Commerce, Bureau of Economic Analysis.

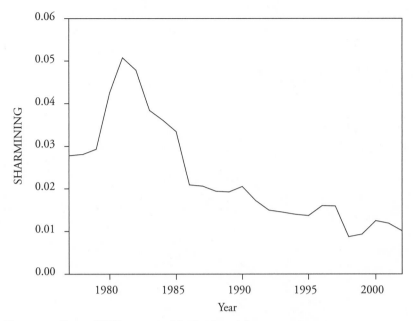

Figure 11.1. Share of GSP accounted for by the mining sector, 1977–2002

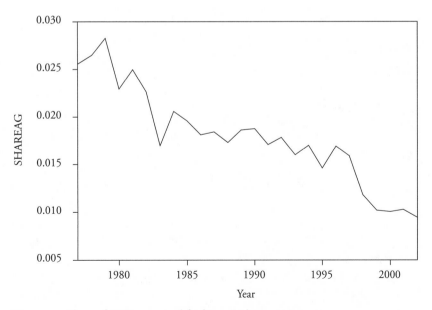

Figure 11.2. Share of GSP accounted for by agriculture, 1977–2002

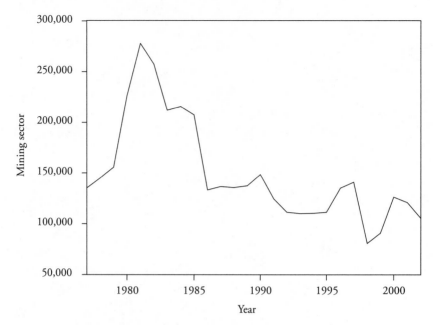

Figure 11.3. Mining sector in inflation-adjusted dollars, 1977–2002

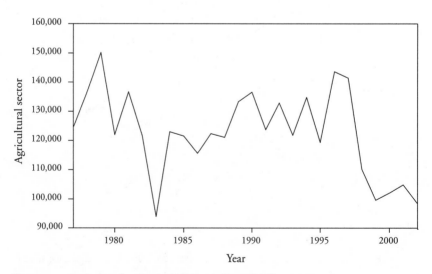

Figure 11.4. Agricultural sector in inflation-adjusted dollars, 1977–2002

sectors of those states' economies. Both simple correlation analysis and the regression results presented in Table 11.4, column 1, suggest that expansion did not occur.[11]

As reported in Table 11.4, column 1, the coefficients on both the SHARE-MINING and SHAREAG variables are negative and significant at the 5 percent level or better, implying that states with high shares of GSP in agriculture or resource-extraction sectors in 1977 grew at significantly lower rates than other states. To better gauge the impact on annual growth, consider the effect of a one standard deviation change in either of these two variables.[12] The coefficient on SHAREMINING is −4.73 and the standard deviation of this variable is 0.068. Multiplying these two numbers yields a negative growth effect of 0.32 percent per year. The coefficient on SHAREAG is −3.99 and its standard deviation is 0.034, implying a negative growth effect of 0.14 percent per year. These effects are smaller than

TABLE 11.4

Regressions of annual per capita GSP growth (1977–2002)
on natural resource intensity and other controlling variables

Variable	(1)	(2)	(3)	(4)	(5)
Log GSP per capita, 1977	−1.20 (−3.08)	−1.66 (−3.86)	−1.57 (−3.42)	−1.89 (−3.66)	−1.60 (−3.30)
SHAREMINING, 1977	−4.73 (−4.69)	−4.12 (−4.08)	−4.20 (−4.09)	−4.18 (−4.10)	−3.32 (−3.41)
SHAREAG, 1977	−3.99 (−2.04)	−3.20 (−1.67)	−2.96 (−1.49)	−2.67 (−1.35)	−0.06 (−0.03)
Education, 1977	— —	0.05 (2.18)	0.06 (2.20)	0.07 (2.55)	0.06 (2.24)
Tax rate, 1977	— —	— —	−0.03 (−0.57)	0.004 (0.07)	−0.037 (−0.62)
SHAREGOV, 1977	— —	— —	— —	−10.34 (−1.32)	−3.66 (−0.49)
Population density, 1977	— —	— —	— —	— —	0.97 (3.06)
Constant	5.90 (4.92)	6.39 (5.45)	6.33 (5.34)	7.65 (4.96)	6.49 (4.45)
Adjusted R-squared	0.48	0.52	0.51	0.52	0.60

NOTE: t-values in parentheses. GSP indicates gross state product; SHAREMINING, share of GSP accounted for by oil and gas extraction and coal, metal, and nonmetallic mining; SHAREAG, share of GSP accounted for by agriculture, forestry, and fishing; and SHAREGOV, see text.

the 0.93 percent negative impact for cross-country comparisons reported by Sachs and Warner (1997), but they imply significant negative effects. Of course, Sachs and Warner and others also included a number of controlling variables.

In most studies of the resource curse, additional controlling variables are introduced to see whether their inclusion negates the effect of the resource abundance variable on economic growth. Included in a number of studies is a rule-of-law variable to account for variations in underlying institutions. As North (1990) has so successfully argued, institutions—or the rules of the game—are likely the major determinants of economic performance. Moreover, there is growing evidence that institutional factors are important for understanding how some countries managed to misspend their natural wealth (e.g., Sala-i-Martin and Subramanian 2003). Across the United States, however, the rules appear to be relatively similar. Nevertheless, even with similar institutions, states can generate different outcomes by adopting different tax structures and expenditure programs.[13] These structures and programs may in turn be affected by natural resource abundance. We continue by examining how the inclusion of variables measuring educational levels of the population, tax rates, size of government, and population density affect the coefficients on SHAREMINING and SHAREAG.[14] In the process, we will attempt to assess whether the more prominent explanations for the resource curse apply to the U.S. experience.

Neglect of Education

Initial levels of human capital, usually measured in terms of years of schooling, are generally considered to have a positive effect on economic growth (Barro 1997). Gylfason (2001) argues that countries well endowed with natural resources have often neglected the education of their people. In support, he presents results showing that expenditures on education and school enrollment are negatively correlated with the World Bank's 1994 measure of share of natural capital in national wealth. There are, of course, exceptions to this pattern, such as Norway. But Gylfason (2001, 858) argues that more commonly, "resource-rich countries become overconfident and therefore tend to underrate or overlook the need for good economic policies as well as for good education." The question is whether this pattern extends to the United States.

Consider the result in Table 11.4, column 2. The regression reported there includes an educational attainment variable, measured as the percentage of the state's population having completed four or more years of college in 1977.[15] The coefficient on the education variable is positive and is both statistically and economically significant. The simple correlation coefficients between the education variable and SHAREAG and SHAREMINING are negative, and the inclusion of the education variable reduces the magnitude and significance of the coefficients on SHAREMINING and SHAREAG. Thus, controlling for the educational level of a state's populace appears to negate, at least partially, the resource curse argument, particularly as it applies to agriculture.

Nevertheless, the argument that an abundance of natural resources leads to neglect of education within the United States seems inconsistent with other evidence. Agricultural states, for example, have long been considered to be educational incubators, having a young mobile workforce that migrates to urban areas (Goldin and Katz 2000). Importantly, it is not at all evident that states with high shares of GSP in natural resource–related industries typically spend less on education.[16] Indeed, by controlling for the income base, the opposite appears to be the more likely scenario. Throughout the period 1977–2002, the ratio of public school expenditures divided by state personal income is positively correlated with both SHAREMINING and SHAREAG. Thus, the evidence for the United States does not support the notion that having a large sector of the economy based on natural resources leads to neglect of education. However, those same states do not appear to have attracted a more highly educated population, as both SHAREMINING and SHAREAG are negatively correlated with the educational attainment variable.

Corruption, Rent Seeking, and Government Size

There is little question that natural resource extraction and corruption have been frequent companions, especially in developing countries.[17] Abundance of natural resources does not, however, by itself create opportunities for corruption. Rather, corruption is symptomatic of the absence of well-defined property rights to those resources, a condition that seems to be present in many developing and transitional countries. In the absence of property rights, or where rights are somehow defective, resource rents can be dissipated and the growth rate of the economy slowed. Because the term "corruption" is often taken to imply illegal acts, such as bribery, a focus on corruption alone could deflect attention away from completely legal activities that have the same root cause and can have similar consequences. These activities, which are perhaps more germane to the U.S. political scene, involve rent seeking, the socially costly pursuit of wealth transfers. In particular, the focus here will be on rent-seeking activities that lead to the expansion of state and local governments.

State governments often tax a portion of the value of natural resources extracted within their jurisdictions. The expansion of the energy sector in the early 1970s substantially increased state severance tax receipts, and some states became highly dependent on energy-related taxes. For example, 1985 severance taxes on oil and gas accounted for almost 70 percent of Alaska's state tax receipts, and Wyoming obtained 15 percent of its total tax receipts from coal and almost an equal amount from oil.[18] The bonanza that befell states endowed with energy resources presented opportunities for expanding the state's infrastructure, but it also increased the amount of rent-seeking activities.

Consider first the impact of state taxes on economic growth. There is competition among states, and that limits the extent to which a state can increase taxes before people and businesses move to other states with more favorable tax bases (Benson and Johnson 1986). Nevertheless, states do get out of line with their competition, and the evidence favors the opinion that relatively high taxes have a negative effect on growth (Holcombe and Lacombe 2004; Wasylenko 1997). Much depends, however, on how governments spend the money and the type of taxes imposed. Although the type of taxes imposed matters, a commonly used single indicator of whether a state is a high- or low-tax state is the ratio of total state and local tax revenues to total income.[19] The results in Table 11.4, column 3, provide little evidence that a relatively high state comprehensive tax rate in 1977 lowered later economic growth. Moreover, the simple correlation between this tax rate variable and SHAREMINING, although statistically insignificant, is negative, suggesting that states with a large share of their GSP accounted for by extractive industries were not, in general, high-tax states.

Although the ratio of tax revenues to state income is a rather broad measure, as states have other sources of income besides direct taxes, how they use their funds likely matters for long-term growth. If, for example, rent-seeking activities result in an expanded and cumbersome bureaucracy, economic growth can be retarded. A relative measure of the size of state and local governments is that sector's share of GSP. A major component of the state and local government sector in GSP is employee compensation.

Accordingly, that sector's share of GSP provides a relative measure of the size of government across states.

The variable SHAREGOV in Table 11.4, column 4, is for 1977. The sign on its coefficient is negative, but it is not statistically significant at the 5 percent level. Moreover, the coefficient of SHAREMINING remains negative and highly significant, although the impact of the variable SHAREAG on growth has been largely negated. But even these limited effects may be overstated. It is generally recognized that the per capita cost of providing government services is lower in urban areas, and states with high shares of GSP in natural resource–related industries are mainly rural states. Thus, even the limited effect of SHAREGOV on the coefficients of the variables SHAREAG and SHAREMINING may be due to the rural nature of those states and not reflective of any particular proclivity toward rent-seeking activities that promote the size of government.

To further examine this possibility, state population density for 1977 is included in Table 11.4 as an explanatory variable. Population density appears to be a robust variable for explaining variations in growth rates across countries (Sala-i-Martin, Doppelhoffer, and Miller 2004). In addition, Rappaport and Sachs (2003) have shown that economic activity in the United States is positively related to population density. The results shown in Table 11.4, column 5, support these arguments. The coefficient on population density is positive and statistically significant at the 1 percent level. The negative effect of SHAREAG on growth has been completely negated and that of SHAREMINING substantially reduced.[20]

The story that emerges, thus far, is that the natural resource–extraction sectors themselves are not the culprit. Instead, the slow economic growth of states with relatively high SHAREMINING and SHAREAG values is largely explained by the low population density and relatively lower educational levels of the population of those states. But as mentioned previously, these states have not neglected education. Instead, rural states appear to have experienced difficulty in attracting and maintaining a highly educated workforce.[21]

The Crowding-out Effect (the Dutch Disease)

One of the more popular explanations for the resource curse uses a crowding-out logic, generated by an export boom in the primary commodity-exporting country. Supposedly, these booms create distortions that are not simply transitory effects. Rather, the boom affects the structure of the economy and alters the types of synergies that occur over the longer run. The mechanism involves a positive wealth shock from the natural resource sector that generates excess demand for nontraded goods. In particular, the excess demand increases the prices of nontraded input costs and wages. As a consequence of this increase in input costs, profits are squeezed in traded activities, such as manufacturing, that bid for the same inputs as the natural resource sector. The natural resource export boom also alters exchange rates, increasing the price of traded goods. This squeeze not only results in a decline of the other traded-good sectors, but it is argued that relative to activities in the natural resource sector, these other sectors are more prone to positive spillover effects generated by technological synergies and have higher returns to learning by doing. Thus, natural resource abundance renders the export of other traded goods less competitive, and resource-abundant countries fail to experience the same degree of export-led growth as countries with poor endowments of natural resources.

The above scenario, and variants of it, are referred to as the Dutch Disease (e.g., Neary and Wijnbergen 1986; Sachs and Warner 1997). Its origin is the discovery of huge quantities of natural gas in The Netherlands in the late 1950s. The first fifteen years brought a gas-fueled economy to The Netherlands and resulted in substantial growth and expansion of governmental services. But this initial phase was followed by a stagnation in overall production and accelerating unemployment. It has been amply noted that the Dutch Disease is not really a disease, and its characterization as such seems ungrateful in the sense that the Dutch did experience a substantial increase in wealth. Moreover, there is a lack of direct tests of the theory's general applicability. Sachs and Warner (2001), however, provide support by showing that countries with natural resource–intensive economies tend to have higher price levels.

Although the exchange rate is the same across U.S. states and inputs are likely more mobile than across countries, the Dutch Disease phenomenon remains applicable to the United States. It is the real exchange rate that matters, and frictions in labor and other input markets remain (e.g., booms can lead to increases in local land prices). The 1970s were a boom period for natural resource–extraction sectors of the economy and to a lesser extent for agriculture. Agricultural commodity prices, especially those for grains, spiked in 1973 (U.S. Department of Agriculture, Table 596, 1980). The energy boom continued through 1980, and growth in state per capita personal income over the period 1970–1977 is highly correlated with

SHAREMINING, ρ = 0.53, while the correlation between income and SHAREAG is low, ρ = 0.25. After 1981, agriculture and energy prices continued their long-term decline (see Figures 11.1–11.4). Thus, the stage for a Dutch Disease phenomenon was set.

Importantly, after a boom in the natural resource sector, the Dutch Disease phenomenon requires a crowding out of the other sectors of the economy. Supposedly, the boom retards growth of nonresource sectors. Accordingly, consider the results in Table 11.5. The dependent variable is the annual rate of growth in per capita GSP after subtracting the contribution from the agricultural and natural resource–extraction sectors. The coefficients on SHAREAG and SHAREMINING are not statistically significant, while the coefficients on the control variables are very close to those reported in Table 11.4, column 5. Thus, the evidence does not support the notion that resource abundance retards the growth of other sectors of a state's economy.

TABLE 11.5

*Regression of annual per capita growth of GSP
less the contribution of agriculture and resource
extraction sectors (1977–2002) on natural resource
intensity and other controlling variables*

Variable	(1)
Log GSP per capita, 1977	−2.00 (−3.85)
SHAREMINING, 1977	−0.61 (−0.58)
SHAREAG, 1977	3.03 (1.41)
Education, 1977	0.07 (2.26)
Tax rate, 1977	−0.05 (−0.91)
SHAREGOV, 1977	−5.19 (−0.64)
Population density, 1977	1.05 (3.08)
Constant	7.97 (5.06)
Adjusted R-squared	0.49

NOTE: t-values in parentheses. See Table 11.4 for definitions.

These results not only fail to support the Dutch Disease phenomenon for the United States, but there are parts of the theory that do not seem to fit the U.S. experience or experiences elsewhere. Why natural resource sectors would have fewer positive spillover effects than, say, manufacturing has not been established. Manufacturing has its rust bowls and old smokestacks, and it is difficult to imagine what positive spillover effects those activities might generate. In contrast, there is the high-tech sector, which did exceptionally well in the 1990s. But agriculture has also experienced a series of revolutions in biotechnology (Ruttan 2002), and the mining industry has seen numerous advances in exploration, drilling, and extraction (Wright and Czelusta 2004). It is difficult to imagine that these advances failed to generate significant spillovers of knowledge to other sectors of the economy.

Importantly, the results in Table 11.5 also indicate that the voids left by the two natural resource sectors were not quickly eclipsed by an expansion of those states' nonresource sectors. For the offset to have occurred, we would have expected the coefficient on SHAREAG or SHAREMINING to be both positive and statistically significant. Although declines in natural resource commodity extraction may provide the opportunity for the expansion of other economic activities that benefit from their proximity to rural landscapes, it is clear from the results in Tables 11.4 and 11.5 that increases in those activities were not sufficient to overcome the declines in the commodity-extraction sectors.

Discussion

The two natural resource sectors examined in this chapter were declining, in both real and relative terms, between 1977 and 2002. It could be argued that these declines are simply the continuation of a long-term decline in resource scarcity, as suggested by the results of Barnett and Morse (1963). But resource prices can fluctuate widely, and the time periods analyzed can profoundly affect the results. If growth in GSP is replaced with growth in per capita personal income, the time frame analyzed can be expanded. For example, using 1970 for the starting date instead of 1977 and estimating regressions similar to those reported in Table 11.4 yields the result that neither of the two resource-abundance measures is ever statistically significant. Furthermore, if the time frame used in this chapter is truncated at 2000 instead of 2002, the results suggest the resource curse phenomenon to be somewhat stronger (Johnson 2006). Recent increases in energy prices are likely to reduce the negative impact on growth even further. But a rebound based on increases in commodity prices hardly supports the argument that protection of natural landscapes and the environment will contribute more to economic growth than allowing traditional natural resource–based industries to expand.

This is not to say that protection of natural landscapes and the environment does not provide substantial benefits, as there are numerous examples of their vast intrinsic wealth. But the argument can be easily overdone and result in policy prescriptions that reduce rather than increase wealth. In particular, there are localities where natural resource extraction occurs that are unlikely to attract viable alternatives.

Mining has always been associated with discoveries, booms, and busts. The ghost towns of the western United States are testimony to this sequence. Many of these places were geographically isolated, and once the stocks were depleted, few opportunities remained. Depletion would eventually lead to declining payroll and rental flows. Labor would leave the area, and the natural resource bounty would be invested elsewhere, if at all. The story of boom and bust is evident in the data used in this chapter.[22] As mentioned previously, the SHAREMINING variable is positively correlated with state personal income growth in the 1970s and negatively thereafter. Moreover, SHAREMINING is positively correlated with state population growth between 1970 and 1980 (ρ = 0.31) and negatively between 1980 and 2000 (ρ = -0.11). These numbers suggest that declining prices and production, especially for oil, over the period 1977–2002 followed the standard boom-and-bust scenario.

A similar story pertains to agriculture, but for a different reason. Agricultural output per acre has been increasing since the beginning of the twentieth century (Ruttan 2002). Although advances in technology may increase the value of land, and that is by no means certain, the proportion of the population engaged in agriculture has been declining for the past century. The simple correlation between SHAREAG and population growth between 1980 and 2000 is negative (ρ = -0.24). States with relative high GSP shares in either of the two resource sectors tend to be rural states. In general, these states do not appear to have attracted sufficient investment and population to compensate for the decline in those two sectors.

An understanding of the underlying causes behind the boom-and-bust scenario is essential when remedies are being proposed. In particular, the isolated communities often associated with commodity-extraction activities are unlikely to be future areas of growth, and investing vast sums of public funds in their infrastructure is a mistaken policy. Again, this is not to say that some of these communities will not be able to prosper. But determining which communities are best positioned to take advantage of the wealth of nature will depend on individual perceptions and, thus, is best left to the marketplace.

Notes

1. This contention underlies some of the key points found in policy statements of the Western Governors' Association (2002).

2. See, for example, Power (1996, 240). However, in a later book Power and Barrett (2001) provide data indicating that many of the new jobs in the American West are lower paying.

3. An attempt to identify the variables with the most explanatory power is offered by Sala-i-Martin, Doppelhoffer, and Miller (2004). However, since their criteria are purely statistical, it is unlikely that their list of the most robust variables will be considered definitive. Nevertheless, a number of the determinants these authors identify as being robust are used in this study.

4. See the volume edited by Auty (2001a) for a recent survey of these studies as well as the contributions contained therein. Those articles offer a variety of explanations for and extensions to the literature on resource abundance and economic development. But, also see Mikesell (1997), who argues that there is no single or even dominant explanation for the resource curse.

5. In addition to natural resource rents, rents or quasi-rents can also accrue to other factors of production engaged in extraction or cultivating practices. See Johnson and Libecap (1982).

6. Although data on GSP exist back to 1963 (see Barro and Sala-i-Martin 1992), the Bureau of Economic Analysis does not make these data readily available, claiming they are not consistent with their post-1977 data. The GSP data were recently updated to conform with new industry classifications.

7. Unfortunately, GSP does not account for depreciation of natural and other capital. However, it is not clear that doing so would alter the basic conclusions offered in this chapter. See Neumayer (2004) for an attempt to measure "genuine income" and its limited effect on the resource curse argument.

8. Real GSP was derived using the GDP deflator. The consumer price index was used to obtain measures of real personal income.

9. Since shares of GSP and the growth rates of GSP are potentially endogenous, the use of initial values largely negates the problem of endogeneity.

10. These two sectors have often been treated very differently in the U.S. political arena. In terms of taxation, the mining and extraction sectors are often subject to high severance taxes, while the agricultural sector has generally been a beneficiary of tax revenues.

11. The basic growth model that has become the standard for investigating the determinants of growth across countries (see, e.g., Barro 1997) is

$$(LogGDP_T^i - LogGDP_0^i) / T = \alpha + \beta_1 LogGNP_0^i + \beta' X^i + e^i.$$

The dependent variable is the annualized growth rate for country I, and X represents controlling variables. Here, we replace GDP with GSP, and country with state. Note that the coefficient on the log of initial GSP is interpreted as a conditional rate of convergence. In Table 11.4, column 1, the estimated coefficient of –1.20 (t-statistic –3.08) is statistically significant at the 1 percent level and implies a convergence rate of about 1.2 percent per year. Although the implied rate of convergence is slow, it is consistent with estimates obtained by Barro and Sala-i-Martin (1992) using data on state personal income since 1840.

12. This is a static measure, as it does not account for the offsetting effect implied by the negative coefficient on the log GSP per capita 1977 variable.

13. Huang, McCormick, and McQuillian (2004) have constructed a U.S. Economic Freedom Index for the fifty U.S. states. They include a variety of measures of regulatory burden, judicial makeup, tax rates, size of government, and other factors in constructing their indexes. Unfortunately, their indexes apply to the years 1999 and 2004, the final periods of the time frame used in this study. Moreover, the simple correlations between their indexes and historic GSP growth rates, SHARE-MINING, and SHAREAG are not statistically significant.

14. Sachs and Warner 2001 also include a measure of investment. Unfortunately, the Bureau of Economic Analysis does not have comparable state-level data on investment. The more recent data series on state-level investment has been largely developed by researchers and generally involve extrapolation. See, for example, Garofalo and Yamarik (2002).

15. Initial period values are commonly used to avoid potential problems of endogenous variables. But, see the discussion in the appendix. The data on educational levels and expenditures utilized in this section are from the U.S. Census and U.S. Department of Commerce, *Statistical Abstract of the United States*, various issues.

16. States like Alaska and Wyoming have for years ranked near the top in terms of per pupil expenditures.

17. See, for example, Leite and Weidmann (1999), who present evidence showing a rather strong statistical relationship between various indexes of corruption and natural resource abundance. Also see Deacon (1999) on the role of various institutional factors and deforestation.

18. Source: U.S. Department of Energy, Energy Information Agency.

19. Source: Tax Foundation, Tax Burden by State, Washington, D.C. (http://www.taxfoundation.org/statelocal02.html), visited January 15, 2005.

20. To better examine both the direct and indirect effects of the natural resource sectors on economic growth, we also followed Sala-i-Martin and Subramanian (2003) and used an instrumental variables approach. See the appendix, Table 11.6.

21. Consider changes in the educational attainment variable over the entire sample period (Education 1977 to Education 2002). The simple correlation between this variable and SHAREMINING is $\rho = -0.42$. In contrast, the correlation between that variable and population density is $\rho = 0.37$.

22. It is also evident in the county data examined by Rasker et al. (2004). Their

results indicate that many counties in the western states that were once highly dependent on natural resource extraction have experienced relatively slow growth.

References

Anderson, Terry L., and Peter J. Hill. 1990. The Race for Property Rights. *Journal of Law & Economics* 33(1): 177–197.

Auty, Richard M., ed. 2001a. *Resource Abundance and Economic Development.* Oxford, UK: Oxford University Press.

Auty, Richard M. 2001b. The Political Economy of Resource-Driven Growth. *European Economic Review* 45(4–6): 839–846.

Barnett, Harold J., and Chandler Morse. 1963. *Scarcity and Growth: The Economics of Natural Resource Availability.* Baltimore, MD: John Hopkins University Press for Resources for the Future.

Barro, Robert J. 1997. *Determinants of Economic Growth: A Cross-Country Empirical Study.* Cambridge, MA: MIT Press.

Barro, Robert J., and Xavier Sala-i-Martin. 1992. Convergence. *Journal of Political Economy* 100(2): 223–251.

Benson, Bruce, and Ronald N. Johnson. 1986. The Lagged Impact of State and Local Taxes on Economic Activity. *Economic Inquiry* 24(3): 389–401.

Brown, Gardner M. 2000. Renewable Natural Resource Management and Use Without Markets. *Journal of Economic Literature* 38(4): 875–914.

Deacon, Robert T. 1999. Deforestation and Ownership: Evidence from Historical Accounts and Contemporary Data. *Land Economics* 75(3): 341–359.

Easterly, William. 2001. *The Elusive Quest for Growth: Economists' Adventures and Misadventures in the Tropics.* Cambridge, MA, and London, UK: MIT Press.

Garofalo, Gasper A., and Steven Yamarik. 2002. Regional Convergence: Evidence from a New State-by-State Capital Stock Series. *Review of Economics and Statistics* 84(2): 316–323.

Goldin, Claudia, and Lawrence F. Katz. 2000. Education and Income in the Early Twentieth Century: Evidence from the Prairies. *Journal of Economic History* 60(3): 782–818.

Gylfason, Thorvaldur. 2001. Natural Resources, Education, and Economic Development. *European Economic Review* 45(4–6): 847–859.

Holcombe, Randall G., and Donald J. Lacombe. 2004. The Effect of State Income Taxation on Per Capita Income Growth. *Public Finance Review* 32(3): 292–312.

Huang, Ying, Robert E. McCormick, and Lawrence J. McQuillian. 2004. *U.S. Economic Freedom Index: 2004 Report.* San Francisco: Pacific Research Institute.

Irwin, Douglas A. 2000. How Did the United States Become a Net Exporter of Manufactured Goods? Working Paper 7638. Cambridge, MA: National Bureau of Economic Research.

Johnson, Ronald N. 2006. Economic Growth and Natural Resources: Does the Curse of Natural Resources Extend to the Fifty US States? In *Explorations in Environmental and Natural Resource Economics: Essays in Honor of Gardner M.*

Brown Jr., ed. Robert Halvorsen and David F. Layton. Northampton, MA: Edward Elgar Publishing.

Johnson, Ronald N., and Gary D. Libecap. 1982. Contracting Problems and Regulations: The Case of the Fishery. *American Economic Review* 72(5): 1005–1022.

Leite, Carlos, and Jens Weidmann. 1999. Does Mother Nature Corrupt? Natural Resources, Corruption, and Economic Growth. Working Paper No. 99/85. Washington, DC: International Monetary Fund.

Mikesell, Raymond F. 1997. Explaining the Resource Curse with Special Reference to Mineral-Exporting Countries. *Resources Policy* 23(4): 191–199.

Neary, Peter J., and Sweder Van Wijnbergen. 1986. *Natural Resources and the Macroeconomy.* Cambridge, MA: MIT Press.

Neumayer, Eric. 2004. Does the "Resource Curse" Hold for Growth in Genuine Income as Well? *World Development* 32(10): 1627–1640.

North, Douglas C. 1990. *Institutions, Institutional Change, and Economic Performance.* New York: Cambridge University Press.

Power, Thomas Michael. 1996. *Lost Landscapes and Failed Economies: The Search for a Value of Place.* Washington, DC: Island Press.

Power, Thomas Michael, and Richard N. Barrett. 2001. *Post-Cowboy Economics: Pay and Prosperity in the New American West.* Washington, DC: Island Press.

Rappaport, Jordan, and Jeffrey D. Sachs. 2003. The United States as a Coastal Nation. *Journal of Economic Growth* 8(1): 5–46.

Rasker, Ray, Ben Alexander, Jeff van den Noort, and Rebecca Carter. 2004. *Public Lands Conservation and Economic Well-Being.* Tucson, AZ: Sonoran Institute.

Ruttan, Vernon W. 2002. Productivity Growth in World Agriculture: Sources and Constraints. *Journal of Economic Perspectives* 16(4): 161–184.

Sachs, Jeffrey D., and Andrew M. Warner. 1997. Natural Resource Abundance and Economic Growth. Working Paper No. 5398. Cambridge, MA: National Bureau of Economic Research.

———. 2001. The Curse of Natural Resources. *European Economic Review* 45(4–6): 827–838.

Sala-i-Martin, Xavier, Gernot Doppelhofer, and Ronald I. Miller. 2004. Determinants of Long-Term Growth: A Bayesian Averaging of Classical Estimates (BACE) Approach. *American Economic Review* 94(4): 813–835.

Sala-i-Martin, Xavier, and Arvind Subramanian. 2003. Addressing the Natural Resource Curse: An Illustration from Nigeria. Working Paper No. 9804. Cambridge, MA: National Bureau of Economic Research.

U.S. Department of Agriculture. Various years. *Agricultural Statistics.* Washington, DC: GPO.

U.S. Department of Commerce, Bureau of Economic Analysis. 1977–2002. *Regional Accounts Data, 1977–2002.* Washington, DC: GPO.

U.S. Department of Commerce. Various years. *Statistical Abstract of the United States.* Washington, DC: GPO.

Wasylenko, Michael. 1997. Taxation and Economic Development: The State of the Economic Literature. *New England Economic Review* 2: 37–52.

Western Governors' Association. 2002. *Principles for Environmental Management in the West.* Online at http://www.westgov.org/wga/policy/02/enlibra_07.pdf. Visited December 1, 2004.

Wright, Gavin, and Jesse Czelusta. 2004. The Myth of the Resource Curse. *Challenge* 47(2): 6–38.

Appendix

To better examine both the direct and indirect effects of the natural resource sectors on economic growth, we follow Sala-i-Martin and Subramanian (2003) and use an instrumental variables approach. Here, the education, tax rates, and government size variables measured over the entire time frame of the study are utilized, not just the initial period values. After instrumenting for these variables in the first-stage regressions, we then include their predicted values in the growth equation. Since population density is expected to lead to a more highly educated population and lower costs of governmental services, it is utilized as one of the instruments in the first-stage regressions.

The results in Table 11.6, panel A, indicate that SHAREMINING has a negative effect on the educational attainment of the population and a positive effect on the size of government, even after controlling for population density. In contrast, the effect of SHAREAG on education, tax rates, or size of government is essentially nonexistent. The results in Table 11.6, panel B, indicate that the initial direct effect of SHAREAG (Table 11.4, column 1) on growth has been largely negated by controlling variables.

Since the educational attainment variable in Table 11.6, panel B, is positive and statistically significant, and SHAREMINING has a negative effect on educational attainment (panel A), there is evidence of an indirect effect on growth. But as mentioned previously, states with relatively high shares of GSP in oil, gas, and coal production have not neglected education. Instead, those states appear to have experienced difficulty in attracting and maintaining a highly educated workforce. While the results also indicate that SHAREMINING has a positive effect on the size of government (panel A), the coefficient on SHAREGOV in panel B is statistically significant only at the 7 percent level. Thus, the rent-seeking argument receives only very weak support. In general, the results in Table 11.4 and Table 11.5 tell similar stories. Both sets of regressions indicate the presence of a direct effect of SHAREMINING on economic growth that remains negative and statistically significant even after a host of controlling variables are included.

TABLE 11.6

Direct and indirect impacts of natural resources on per capita GSP growth

Variable	Panel A: First-stage regressions, dependent variables			Panel B: Second-stage regression, dependent variable
	(1) Education, average 1978–2002	(2) Tax rates, average 1978–2002	(3) SHAREGOV, average 1978–2002	(1) Real per capita GSP growth, 1977–2002
Log GSP per capita, 1977	−1.33 (−0.92)	−2.77 (−2.88)	−0.005 (−0.74)	−1.91 (−5.09)
SHAREMINING, 1977	−6.08 (−2.08)	0.98 (0.51)	0.04 (2.92)	−2.99 (−3.12)
SHAREAG, 1977	6.84 (1.14)	−0.76 (−0.19)	0.006 (0.24)	−2.25 (−1.32)
Education, 1977	1.12 (13.83)	0.02 (0.37)	−0.0007 (−1.96)	— —
Tax rate, 1977	0.02 (0.12)	0.63 (5.36)	0.0006 (0.74)	— —
SHAREGOV, 1977	−33.59 (−1.50)	−17.92 (−1.20)	0.64 (6.30)	— —
Population density, 1977	1.66 (1.76)	0.14 (0.22)	−0.006 (−1.36)	— —
Education, 1978–2002	— —	— —	— —	0.06 (3.01)
Tax rate, 1978–2002	— —	— —	— —	0.02 (0.19)
SHAREGOV, 197–2002	— —	— —	— —	−15.51 (−1.82)
Constant	9.04 (2.07)	13.44 (4.63)	0.05 (2.55)	7.88 (5.34)
Adjusted R-squared	0.88	0.40	0.62	0.65

NOTE: t-values in parentheses. See Table 11.4 for definitions.

Also considered was a simultaneous system that took into account how economic growth affected education, tax rates, and size of government as well as the impact those variables have on economic growth. Identification required the use of an additional exogenous variable. Mean temperature of the major city in the state was used. This approach produced results similar to those reported in Table 11.6, panel B.

CHAPTER TWELVE

Why Individuals Provide Public Goods

DAVID D. HADDOCK

> A fanatic is one who can't change his mind and won't
> change the subject.
>
> WINSTON CHURCHILL

Two people are rivals if each wants to wear the same pair of shoes, so economists call items such as shoes rivalrous goods. In contrast, an economist calls something a public good if consumption is nonrivalrous and non-excludable. In other words, one person's consumption of a public good is completely consistent with its consumption by another person, and neither can interfere with the choices of the other. You can either look at a beautiful vista or not as you prefer. Typically, however, you will neither know nor care whether I am looking, but you could not prevent me from enjoying the vista even if you wanted to. The view is a public good. Improving a view confers a positive externality on any bystander who appreciates the change but played no role in obtaining it.

Smog is a public bad because the suffering that it inflicts on you is unrelated to whether I am suffering. An increase in smog inflicts a negative externality on sufferers who have no influence over an actor's smog-producing decision. Negative externalities also affect rivalrous goods, as when a cigarette thrown from a passing automobile sets a wheat field afire, and that sort is much discussed as a general category. Economists rarely discuss public bads per se.

Public bads such as smog obviously exist and often are important, but a public bad implies symmetrical public goods. Since smog is a public bad, anything that mitigates smog is a public good; the benefit that you experience from a reduction of smog is unrelated to any benefit that I receive. Therefore, one can ask how to arrange for the proper amount of smog—the public bad—or how to arrange for the proper amount of mitigation—the public good; they are the same question. Following from the recognition that each public bad implies public goods, for each public good there are obverse public bads. Building a fence that hides a beautiful vista creates a public bad, for example. Failing to appreciate the symmetry between public goods and public bads, inexperienced observers imagine that the two require separate theories. Such thinking is erroneous, and the confusion encourages incoherent policy.

A straight line provides a useful analogue of public goods and public bads. A public good can be visualized as a movement in a positive direction from the status quo and a public bad as a movement in a negative direction. Because a movement in either direction entails costs as well as benefits, the optimal amount of a public good is rarely the most that is feasible; nor, speaking in the converse, would the optimal amount of a public bad ordinarily be zero. The ideal would be to create a public good whenever the benefit of doing so exceeds the cost, and to forego that movement from the status quo otherwise. More subtly, the ideal would be to create a public bad when more cost can be avoided than the benefit that is lost by that movement from the status quo. The last statement will seem an outrageous oxymoron until one recalls that a public bad does not translate as bad for everyone, merely as a nonrivalrous bad—bad for at least one person whose suffering will be unaltered if others suffer as well.

Those who appreciate beautiful vistas or abhor smog face a potentially crippling obstacle. Optimizing the number of beautiful vistas or amount of smog often requires widespread participation to finance a movement away from the status quo. If nonpayers cannot be excluded from the benefits, however, many potential beneficiaries will refuse to participate—the dilemma of free riding. In consequence, a desirable public good may not materialize, or the amount may be inadequate. That is to say, we may fail to move from an undesirable status quo, or fail to move far enough.

Scrutiny of the definition of public goods shows that the theory concerns consumption, not ownership or production. It is based on the meaning of *public* that is incorporated in phrases such as the general public—the public as a collectivity of individuals. Such a meaning is distinct from *public* as sometimes used to indicate government ownership, as in a public stadium. The owner of a stadium that is filled to capacity may be a government, but the stadium is no more a public good than are shoes; the seat you occupy is unavailable to me, and thus is rivalrous. Additional teams cannot be admitted to the playing field until the present contest concludes. Many other things that governments own or produce are rivalrous rather than public goods.

Many public goods—nonrivalrous in consumption—existed before governments formed to produce or own anything, and they exist today in the farthest reaches of the Amazon and Congo basins, where for practical purposes no formal government functions. There are vistas to see and birdcalls to hear all along the Amazon, as well as widespread benefits or detriments when one person burns a grove of trees to increase a ground-dwelling prey animal's food supply. American Indian nomads volunteered for substantial work and danger to participate in war parties that faced threats against the entire band, though individually they often had the option of simply leaving the group instead. Among anarchistic medieval Icelanders, elderly Njál's life was lost along with his wife's because he voluntarily (though unsuccessfully) tried to mediate a dispute that until then had scarcely involved him at all (*Njál's Saga* 2001).

Nonetheless, careless people often mistake the public in public goods as though the word were being used in a public stadium rather than in the general public. One need not resort to the scribbling of peripheral scholars to discover examples of that non sequitur, as shown in a book recently published by a group of senior Harvard economists and law professors:

> Goods (or services) that are nonexcludable and nonrival are called *public goods* by economists. . . . It is apparent that public goods will not be adequately supplied by the private sector. The reason is plain: because people can't be excluded from using public goods, they can't be charged money for using them, so a private supplier can't make money from providing them. . . . Because public goods are generally not adequately supplied by the private sector, they have to be supplied by the public sector. (Jackson et al. 2003, 361–363)

The quotation begins with a definition but ends with a fallacy. Every day Americans listen to radio and pass beautiful gardens on their way to the office, then they admire attractive colleagues after arriving. Radio broadcasts, gardens, and personal appearance provide collectively consumed but privately produced goods that are nonrivalrous in consumption and typically nonexcludable, hence are public goods. For many public goods it is not even obvious what "zero" would mean in terms of an amount; nearly anyone could look either worse or better, for instance, so some level of public good (or bad) issues automatically from a person's personal appearance. That explains why the status quo, not zero, was the starting point above in the straight-line representation of public goods and public bads.

Certainly, a danger that "public goods will not be adequately supplied by the private sector" is an issue worth pondering, but an ill-developed assertion that "they have to be supplied by the public sector" is unhelpful; there are several additional sources.

A few observers have been less fanatical about the government / public-goods nexus; incompatible evidence has changed their minds. That is hardly to say that they believe that private provision will inevitably result in the ideal amount of every public good, merely that a great many public goods are provided by private groups.

That private associations sometimes provide public goods has followed three distinct but mutually compatible paths. First, individual consumers sometimes volunteer contributions over and above the minimum required. Ticket prices, for instance, may be inadequate to keep a museum operating, and philanthropic contributions provide funds to make up the difference (Spiegel 1995).

Second, Olson (1965) argued that the incentive to free ride might be alleviated when an organization also provides other benefits that are excludable and supplied only to those who help provide the public good. A simple example illustrates: if only those who participate in collecting roadside trash are invited to a party at the completion of the project, many of the beneficiaries may prefer to contribute to the effort rather than miss the celebration.

The third path employs evolutionary models (North 1990; Ostrom 2000; Rubin 2003) that focus on social norms, cultural beliefs, and ideologies. The theory of bounded rationality holds that people are not entirely calculative. In other words, individuals do not and cannot carefully think through everything they do. Suppose that through some accident of fate a community begins to provide public goods for itself, while the free-rider problem prevents other communities from doing the same. The cooperative community would be more likely to have members survive hard times. Before they were old enough to appreciate free-rider opportunities, children in that more successful community would learn a mode of behavior that facilitated voluntary contribution to the provision of public goods. Though potentially costly to impose, overt or subtle penalties that the rest of the community threatened could more than deplete any advantage to a free rider. Free riding would be rare if that threat were widely understood, and the costly sanction would seldom be needed. The community would have an advantage over alternative communities, and public goods providers within it would do better than free riders.

This chapter admits that strict reliance on voluntary participation may lead to less than ideal provision of a subset of public goods, though government involvement sometimes exacerbates rather than mitigates the shortfall. Public goods may issue from acts of pure charity. An organization may successfully tie participation in the provision of a public good to an excludable benefit. A community may evolve norms, cultural beliefs, and ideology.

The chapter will focus elsewhere, however. First, a redefinition of property rights may facilitate the provision of public goods that appear superficially to be obtainable only with government intervention. Second, utilizing an unfortunately neglected idea of Buchanan and Stubblebine (1962), the chapter will show that a public good may be provided by an individual who acts unilaterally solely from self-interest. The reason is that people are far from identical, a fact that is both obvious and often neglected in scholarly work. Even if everyone else could overcome their free-rider problem and obtain the proper amount of a public good for their purposes, anyone with an abnormally strong preference for the good would remain dissatisfied. Such people cannot satisfy their supernormal preferences for the public good without privately arranging at least for the excess. But there is more: if the free-rider problem foils contribution from the rest of the community, a person with an abnormal preference may shoulder the entire burden. Once the public good is created, however, everyone can enjoy it, provider and free rider alike.

Through careful theoretical and institutional investigation, a government / public-goods nexus may plausibly be urged in certain instances, but that nexus can never be derived as a matter of pure theory. Sound theory is indispensable, but a proper understanding of public goods requires careful scrutiny of the nature and environment of the particular one at issue.

Sand Dunes

Contemplate the following public bad and the appropriate mitigation strategies. The world's largest concentration of freshwater sand dunes are scattered around Lake Michigan's perimeter. Like the Great Lakes themselves, the dunes are an ancient legacy of the most recent ice age, which began retreating from the region some twelve thousand years ago. The longest continuous swath of duneland threads through government and private property from the lake's southern extremity well up its eastern shore into Michigan.

About a quarter of a century ago, my friends purchased a vacation property there, the dunes shielding their cottage from the lakeshore. My first visit revealed an unbroken vista to the west. The highest dunes seemed to rise a hundred feet above the lake. Tall, coarse dune grass covered open sand, but in many places copses of trees cascaded down the slopes. Several narrow foot trails permitted traverse across the dunes and hikes along the crest.

Today, little dune grass grows there. Wind and gravity readily move the sand. A nearby cottage is situated somewhat closer to the dunes. Attempting to keep the sand at bay, the owners of the cottage have erected a concrete wall on the duneward side. The dunes farther south are little changed, a reference showing that their neighboring dunes have been reduced by perhaps ten or fifteen feet, or roughly a half-foot per year.

At some point after my first visit, that sector of lakeshore was discovered by dune buggy enthusiasts. First a few, then more, and by today quite a number of people have decided that speeding up and down, and back and forth across that stretch of sand is great fun. Unfortunately, buggy wheels quickly destroyed the dune grass that had been holding the sand in place over the millennia. The buggies often create their own traffic jams up top. In consequence, drivers spread farther afield. The damage is creeping northward.

Occasionally, people blaze new routes through the woods, and gullies eventually supplant their trails. If their roots become exposed, adjacent trees fall in. On cool evenings people break up these dried tree carcasses to feed small campfires. Some trees that do not topple become engulfed and smothered by sand. Today, it is necessary to hike some distance from the cottage to find living trees on the dunes.

An incessant beelike drone often infuses my friends' cottage from first light until well past dark—a few buggies have headlights. The passing roar of a poorly muffled engine heralds a new entrant rushing into the fray or an exhausted driver leaving it. Rather than anticipating sojourns at their cottage, today my friends often remain in their Chicago home during holiday weekends.

Figure 12.1. Tree line marks boundary between vegetated private land and degraded public land. Photo by David D. Haddock.

Ultimately, the dunes may become so degraded that the buggy drivers will abandon them for more exciting terrain. Preserving the dunes would appear to be a public good. Does the free-rider problem prevent private preservation?

Categorical Imperatives

I would conjecture that at least one hundred cottages are in my friends' immediate neighborhood, though there must be tens of thousands of similar ones in the four states that surround Lake Michigan. The cottage owners nearest the dunes regard buggy drivers with contempt. Those whose cottages are removed from the noise and dust are less disdainful. By now, however, a number of cottages house buggy drivers. Still others who lack any local landholding bring their vehicles in for day use.

Because of congestion and the readily apparent degradation of the dunes, even some of the buggy owners favor restrictions on dune use. The drivers who own a cottage think that keeping "outsiders" away would be the place to begin, though half-hearted extralegal attempts to do so have proved unavailing. Those whose buggies lack headlights would ban night-time driving. The old guard would prefer to be rid of the vehicles altogether. How is one to sort out the conflict of interest?

Those who oppose such dune use often answer with a categorical imperative.

> [T]hough sand dunes cannot be re-created once they are gone, Lake Michigan's . . . continue to be lost, acre by acre. The dunes are valuable, spectacular, and biologically diverse landforms . . . within the extraordinary Great Lakes ecosystem. . . . [According to] The Lake Michigan Federation's report, *Vanishing Lake Michigan Sand Dunes* . . . Michigan must enact legislation that [would add] 12,000 acres . . . to the Critical Dune Atlas and regulate activities in them as required by the Act, [removing] the loophole . . . that allows expansion into critical dunes from existing . . . operations. (Alliance for the Great Lakes 2004, Chapter 1)

A glaring weakness of the statement is the implication that a political solution is the only solution; Michigan, it says, *must* enact legislation, not that Michigan should consider legislation as one plausible approach to be compared with alternatives. Political solutions characteristically deprive one interest group of a use (without compensation) in order to provide (at a zero price) a different interest group with an incompatible use. The statement makes no attempt to compare the losses to be suffered by the first group with the benefits to be expected by the second.

Other people adhere to a different categorical imperative: a yearning for limited government. The opposing groups can agree that the dispute pits moral necessity against selfish irresponsibility, but they disagree about which side is being irresponsible. By the nature of the confrontation, one side inevitably will feel wounded but nonetheless will be taxed to impose on itself the will of their opponents.

Groups with greater political clout win political battles, and, contrary to the wishes of the Alliance for the Great Lakes, to this moment the winners have been their dune-exploiting opponents. It is of little avail for the Alliance simply to work harder to acquaint people with the degradation; that is general knowledge among those who visit the dunes. The problem is not ignorance or stupidity, but different priorities. I expect that everyone who visits or lives in the area would love to preserve the dunes in their entirety if that were costless. The real issue is different: how much to achieve in the face of a cost that is both positive and increasing with the magnitude of preservation. Obtaining dune preservation—something of value—requires the sacrifice of something else of value—a place to drive dune buggies, along with potential home sites and industrial sand uses at other locations.

A compromise might lead to results rather than acrimony. Weak desires of one group in an area would give way to strong desires by the other group, while the give-and-take would reverse elsewhere. Neither side would get everything it desired, but because the plots the competitors most intensely covet are unlikely to be identical, each side might get those things it most desired. To facilitate that compromise, the competing interest groups should spend more time searching for a mechanism to gauge the strength of competing individual desires and less time trying to shout down the opposition.[1]

Why not just vote? One-person-one-vote democracy does an admirable job of comparing positive with negative desires and thus is quite useful for advancing broadly congruent interests such as national defense, rescue operations following natural disasters, or suppression of epidemics. Democracy is poor at gauging the strength of conflicting desires, however. Anyone familiar with faculty meetings knows that an impatient and ill-informed group with weakly felt predilections can frustrate a slightly smaller though well-informed group with strongly felt preferences.

What is needed is not a way for one group to impose its preferences on another, but a mechanism that permits a group with intense preferences to persuade those with trifling ones to voluntarily step aside. This chapter turns next to an age-old mechanism that in appropriate circumstances facilitates just such an outcome, and then asks whether the circumstances are appropriate vis-à-vis the Lake Michigan dunelands.

Property Rights

Consider still a third categorical imperative: whenever the benefits exceed the costs, recognize and enforce property rights. In the case at hand, property rights were implicated, but the rights as structured proved unenforceable; they were rights in theory more than in reality. My friends own the final cottage along a private road that they share with ten other families. Since cottage owners often entertain visitors and occasionally let out their cottages for a week or two, it was never easy to determine whether a passing driver was entitled to be on that road. At the time my friends purchased their property, however, a sign that read Private Road was adequate, informing the few who had made an erroneous turn.

That changed with the coming of the buggies. There is alternative legal route onto the beach along the side of the dunes facing the lake, but it is quite a distance to the north. Despite the sign, a handful of aggressive buggy drivers began taking a shortcut along the private road and onto the dunes. That being inconsistent with the intended use, the cottagers erected a barrier of dead trees, branches, and the like to make it plain that the road ended thirty feet or so short of the foot of the nearest dune. The buggies detoured around the barrier, in the process driving through some shrubbery and destroying it. Trying to stop the road at its proper terminus imposed substantially more inconvenience on the cottagers than on the drivers.

The county sheriff was asked to issue citations. The sheriff judged that (1) more pressing problems demanded his meager budget; (2) given a legal, albeit less convenient, route, citations could do little to halt the neighborhood's true grievances—noise and dune degradation; and (3) the cottagers were entitled to sue the perpetrators for trespass.

Suits against perpetrators presented a difficult evidentiary matter; trespass along the private road could be completed in less than a minute. Once a buggy entered the duneland, it was on state property. Most of the cottages are vacation residences, and the owners usually are hours away tending to their jobs. Even when present, nobody was willing to spend vacation time lurking by a window merely to identify passing buggy drivers. Moreover, as Ellickson (1991) discovered in Shasta County, California, even when one knows a perpetrator, people who live in small communities rarely sue a neighbor; quite apart from the expense of legal action, too many unrelated matters would be tainted.

The neighborhood eventually dropped the matter. No longer serving its purpose, the Private Road sign was allowed to deteriorate. An informal spur off the state highway system, begun by a few aggressive buggy drivers with knowledge that they were violating private property, is now used at will by people who assume it is a county road. The moral of the story is that encroachment does not halt merely because it violates legal standards. The nearby dunes are already under the auspices of the state of Michigan. If the legislation that the Alliance for the Great Lakes demands is to preserve dunes, someone must be given the ability and incentive to enforce it.

That the dune degradation near my friends' cottage can be gauged against those farther south is informative. Recognized property rights extend to the lake's waterline there, and those dunes are fenced along both sides. Aggressive buggy drivers might wish they could invade that property, but they

Figure 12.2. Buggy tracks show clear violations; unenforced public rights are no rights at all. Photo by Marti DeBoer.

could not complete their trespass in a moment. Instead, they would be trespassing for as long as they were enjoying (and damaging) the dunes, substantially facilitating apprehension.

Rightly or wrongly, many people are resentful if a wealthy individual purchases a large area and in that way monopolizes the enjoyment of a landscape, whether or not that means the land is better preserved. The rights to the south, however, are communal rather than private. The dunes there are not owned by a wealthy individual but jointly by a community of cottagers whose individual properties are otherwise similar to those in my friends' neighborhood. That community is entitled by their more complete rights to exclude buggies. The southern dunes remain covered with grass and trees, much as when I first saw them. The dunes adjacent to my friends' cottage, on the other hand, are government property—some would say nobody's property—and no cottager has a legal right to order anyone off.

Though it forms no part of their intention, the communal dune owners to the south provide a public good for anyone who places existence value on Lake Michigan's dunes. Buggy owners in that neighborhood, however, have little incentive to give similar consideration to the dunes near my friends' cottage. The difference does not arise from a change in charitable attitudes as they exit their property, but from a difference in the extent of the property rights.

Transaction Cost

From a property rights perspective, it is insufficient to note that dunes are being degraded. It is impossible to live while altering nothing. The proper question is whether in some other way degradation increases the well-being of society more or less than would preservation. The task is not to rigidify the world or to return to some imagined Nirvana, but to decide which things to preserve and which to use for alternative purposes that are even more valuable. Where people value pristine dunes relative to the value derivable from driving buggies there rather than elsewhere, pristine dunes are the better use. Where people place a low value on maintaining a given stretch of pristine dunes relative to the value of driving buggies, dune buggies are appropriate. Similarly, that the highest and best use of some duneland is as a source of industrial sand is quite plausible. The task is to find a mechanism to weigh the relative values. A market would suffice if transaction cost were low.

Economists use the term *transaction cost* to mean the cost to mutually incompatible users of an asset of discovering each other and negotiating. Incurring a transaction cost does not mean that a transaction will necessarily occur, only that the parties can establish which one values the right more highly and can complete a transaction if that is necessary to transfer the right to the higher valued use. If property rights are well defined, eventually those who value them most will hold them, providing that the transaction cost is modest (Coase 1960; 1988).

The problem in this instance is that the transaction cost is substantial, so it is not obvious which value is greater. Indeed, the proper choice will likely vary according to the density of cottages along the lakeshore. Recognition of high transaction costs inevitably induces calls for government intervention, but such intervention is premature before it has been determined why the transaction cost is so high. Even if government intervention is appropriate, its proper form depends on the source of the high transaction cost.

There are a number of reasons that transaction cost might be substantial. That an insufficiently defined property right can lead to an insuperable transaction cost is often overlooked. In such instances, government intervention to better define rights will likely be preferable to more encompassing government directives.

To see the link between weak property rights and high transaction cost, imagine that the owners of the first rank of cottages place the higher value on the right to the dunes. Assume away the free-rider problem for the moment and imagine that the owners contributed sufficient funds to buy off the buggy drivers who have been using the local dunes. Thus, the parties are not relying on a property right but instead are attempting to sort out incompatible preferences contractually. Contractual rights bind only the contracting parties and thus are weaker than property rights, which are characterized as being good against the world (Merrill and Smith 2001). Those dunes, now devoid of traffic, would become more attractive to a completely different set of buggy drivers who had heretofore been dealing with congestion elsewhere. Indeed, those who had been paid to leave would likely increase congestion elsewhere rather than forego buggy driving, thus augmenting the relative attractiveness of the dunes near my friends' cottage. In consequence, a new set of drivers would arrive. Such strangers to the contract cannot legally be bound by it, so they too must be bought off in a separate transaction. In extreme cases, people who have hardly any interest in dune buggies might acquire one if that enables them to collect a part of the largess.

Reversing the hypothesized relative values will not eliminate the difficulty. If buggy driving is the more highly valued use, and in order to decrease the hazardous congestion the more avid drivers paid the less avid ones to leave, the less congested dunes would again attract strangers to the contract. When nobody holds recognized property rights to duneland, those who place the higher value on the right to use it will be unable to afford a contractual alternative if the population of potential entrants is large.

One might speculate in this instance that the cottagers would place the higher value on the dunes, given that the cottages existed before dune buggies arrived. Considering the age of most of the cottages, they must have been there well before the first dune buggy had even been built. Buggies are highly mobile by their nature, and there are other locales where they could be used. The drivers in my friends' vicinity must prefer those dunes to the alternatives, but how strong is the preference? The payment that would persuade them to go elsewhere might well be modest. In contrast, the cottages cannot be relocated economically. Even if the transaction cost were zero, buggy drivers might be unwilling to pay enough to obtain or retain the right. Without well-defined property rights, however, this is speculative, hardly an adequate basis for legal fiat.

Inadequate definition or enforcement of property rights may cause people to turn instead to a contractual substitute, which can augment transaction cost (possibly to prohibitive levels) if the number of people who are required to participate is large. People may even be induced to resort to other costly alternatives such as force (Haddock 2003). Other sources of high transaction cost are more obvious to the casual observer. Many commentators focus on the masses enjoying public goods while despairing of the prospect of taking a careful census, much less gauging individual preferences.[2] Comprehensive negotiations would prove insuperable even if individuals had no incentive to misrepresent interest, but people often do have that incentive. If everyone else accurately reported and paid according to private interest, one's own trivial addition would cause barely a ripple, whereas if each of the others, thinking along a similar line, conceals personal preference, one's forlorn bit would finance next to nothing.

So the best strategy seems to be concealing one's individual preference, the foundation of the free-rider problem that threatens to defeat adequate voluntary funding of public goods. For instance, my friends and their neighbors have not, to this time, collected enough funds to buy off the buggy drivers. Perhaps each of them is trying to free ride, hoping to receive the benefit while the others bear the cost.

To draw an illustration from a different part of the country, consider the market for timber. Absent a jointly produced forest amenity, an unfettered timber market would seem to provide lumber efficiently. But the amenity registers in formal markets much less comprehensively. Perhaps Dakotan bricklayers value Oregon's forests—as ecosystems, not as lumber—and if necessary would willingly pay a bit to preserve them, but high transaction cost prevents those who are interested from overcoming their mutual free-rider problem.

It seems that there will be enough shoes in the Dakotas but too few trees in Oregon unless a government intervenes—presumably the U.S. government because interested parties are more numerous outside than inside Oregon. But wait, some Quebecois and Paraguayans also value Oregon's forests. Even the U.S. government seems too constricted, so some would urge the United Nations to assume responsibility. Scoffers may point to Oregon's incentive to maintain woodland for tourists; but is that adequate, given the large number of people who never visit Oregon but nonetheless value knowing that great forests survive there?

Surprisingly, as the next section discusses, there may be no public goods shortfall with respect to Oregon's forests despite substantial existence value to those who never visit them.

Illusory Transaction Cost

People are not plants or sponges that must live or die wherever their embryos happen to lodge. Not everyone who lives in Oregon is there to enjoy the evergreens, but someone who deeply loves forestland will more likely end up in Oregon than an otherwise identical person who does not care for trees. People move to locations that afford more of those public goods that they value and try to avoid locations that impose the public bads that they find odious. A forest provides nonpecuniary income to anyone who enjoys it. Holding pecuniary returns constant, a forest lover would fare better in Oregon than would other people. One who loves forests will enjoy Oregon more than someone who only likes forest; unlike a political outcome, it is not merely positive versus negative preference but the strength of preference that counts.

Thus, anyone who likes Oregon's forests will be more likely to accept a job there if it is offered, while someone who loves forests will be quite likely to accept that job, or even to become self-employed in order to move to the state if no offer is forthcoming. People who are enthralled by Oregon's forests predictably would be especially common in Oregon, and those who most intensely love badlands would be concentrated in the Dakotas. Thus some (not all) Oregonians want more forest in their state than do most non-Oregonians.

Few evergreens are Christmas trees, but each household wants its own Christmas tree so the children can place baubles on it. In contrast—and here is the beauty of it—tree-loving Oregonians enjoy the amenity that their state's forests exude as a sense of solitude, the sights and sounds and smells of the flora and fauna, just knowing the forest is there. These joys in no way interfere with simultaneous enjoyment by people from the Dakotas, most of whom are not even in Oregon right now and some who never will be. Oregon's forests, in other words, provide public goods, including that particular form of public good called existence value.

Of course, several million people live in Oregon, so perhaps the governmental task of determining the appropriate amount of forest amenity has merely been localized rather than eradicated. Even so, a federal system with states handling state-sized problems and the national government limited to nation-sized problems would have distinct advantages. The government in Salem, the state capital, rather than the one in the District of Columbia could better govern any high-transaction-cost / free-rider problem relating to Oregon's forest amenities.[3] Though people from elsewhere enjoy those forests, most of them have less intense preferences than do many Oregonians.

Point taken, but in many instances even the localized-not-eradicated viewpoint fails. Far out in the distribution's tail a few Oregonians will have atypically intense preferences for the forest in their neighborhood relative even to the majority of their fellows. It is clear that most other state residents also enjoy Oregon's evergreens, just not nearly as much as those who are way out in the tail of the statistical distribution. If those in the tail achieve an amount of forest adequate for their preferences, taking into account the cost, other Oregonians might well be satiated. The tail dwellers may satisfy themselves through county or local government, but even locally some will have more intense preferences than others. If they achieve enough forest to satiate themselves, other people in the locale may be satiated, and if everyone in the county is satiated, everyone in the state may be satiated, and so on. Indeed, a nonpolitical solution does not depend on where people with intense preferences live, only that they be few.

Economists are skeptical of the existence of some "bliss point" where people become satiated with good things in general; however, people do demonstrably become satiated with particular good things. Indeed, goods can become bads if they become too abundant. Perhaps you enjoy tomatoes (a rivalrous good), but if generous neighbors leave too many of them on your doorstep, they become a garbage disposal problem. Similarly, suppose your neighbor is a pianist who performs with the best symphonies in the world. You may enjoy listening to her practice for the performance next month (a public good since your listening does not interfere with your neighbors' ability to listen). But as she repeats the piece over and over, trying to get it down perfectly, you gradually lose interest. When it dawns on you that the repetition is likely to be a three-hour-per-day prospect until the performance, a willingness to expend resources to shield yourself materializes. You have moved so far past satiation with a public good that it has become a public bad.

Thus, matters of special concern to a fringe present no inevitable high-transaction-cost / free-rider problem—certainly none more daunting than those attending political alternatives—and thus would be irrelevant even if millions of others benefit from the efforts of those few. Private parties will often deal with such problems more effectively than any diligent bureaucracy could even be imagined doing.

In some instances, as the following section shows, even when numerous people enjoy a public good, the relevant transaction cost may be minimal or nonexistent.

Free Range Bison

Wealthy media mogul Ted Turner loves the West. When the Flying D cattle ranch, which spans a narrow valley in southwestern Montana, came on the market some years back, Turner purchased it. Mountains wall the ranch, so all of the land that Turner can see from the Flying D ranch house belongs to him.

It is well known that Turner likes wildlife. He would have noticed that bison, antelope, grizzly bears, and other wildlife occasionally came onto the Flying D. If Turner was satisfied with the amount of wildlife that he observed, he could enjoy it without reducing the pecuniary returns he derived from his ranch. Turner, however, was dissatisfied, and in consequence substituted bison for the cattle that had previously been raised on the ranch. Meat from the bison is marketed much as had been the beef before the substitution. Bison are large, short-tempered, and therefore dangerous animals—more difficult to manage than cattle. Consequently, bison are more costly to raise, and the ranch's profitability would have been reduced, as Turner's accountant must have pointed out.

Assuming no amenity value was attributable to the cattle that were on the Flying D, their value and the cost of raising them could be observed objectively from market prices. The same would be true of the bison meat marketed after they were substituted for the cattle. Because Turner does not market the amenity attributable to the bison, however, but in a manner of speaking consumes it, its value has no objective measure to contrast with the reduced ranch profits. Thus, an observer such as Turner's accountant would be unable to ascertain the ranch's optimal use pattern; only Turner could do that. If a man of Turner's acute business sense is prepared to sacrifice some profits from the Flying D in order to see bison rather than cattle outside his ranch house, the bison's amenity value to him must be greater than the lost profits.

Other costly wildlife-friendly alterations were available. Herbivores such as antelope had competed with the cattle for the limited grass on the Flying D pastures, and now competed with the bison. Rather than shooting them or driving them away, Turner might permit the antelope to mix with the bison on the pastures. Because the antelope are not marketed, they would yield no pecuniary benefit to Turner, but would impose a cost to the extent that the productivity of the bison herd fell. Turner would willingly bear that cost if the value to him of seeing antelope nearby was greater. Predators such as the grizzlies had threatened the cattle, and now threatened the bison. Again, rather than shooting them or driving them away, Turner would tolerate those animals if the amenity value to him exceeded the losses from the animals that the bears killed. Turner pursued each of those options to the extent it pleased him personally. Because of its rich population of wildlife, the Flying D ranch now puts some national parkland to shame.

Note that in the somewhat peculiar jargon of economics, the wildlife would be a public good even under the present assumption that only Turner visits the Flying D; his act of viewing the wildlife would have no impact on the ability of anyone else to view it. Under the assumption, it just happens that nobody else would be present to view it. That public—Turner alone—faces no free-rider problem and therefore will be able to see that the optimal amount of wildlife—the amount that satiates Turner, given the cost—lives in the valley. The wildlife amenity is a public good with no free-rider problem. The assumption, however, has trivialized the policy issue that ordinarily arises, but that can be corrected.

A small state road traverses the valley, wending its way between a highway in the Gallatin Valley and a state-owned campsite. Drivers passing along the road can see and photograph the animals living on the Flying D. Legally, Turner cannot charge for the excellent views because the drivers are on a state road. This complication does not necessarily alter the conclusion that there is no relevant free-rider problem in the valley. In the terminology of Buchanan and Stubblebine (1962), the wildlife may provide an irrelevant positive externality. The amenity may be a public good that raises no policy issues of relevance to the general public.

It has been seen that Turner has satiated himself with wildlife, given the cost that wildlife imposes on his ranch. Because Turner is on the ranch more often and for more extended periods than those who drive through, and visits parts of the ranch that cannot be seen from the highway, the drivers might well be satiated with fewer animals than Turner has selected solely to satisfy his personal preference. Assume for the moment that this is true. Then, to rephrase a point made with respect to Oregon's forests, the joy that Turner experiences by having wildlife on the Flying D does not interfere with simultaneous enjoyment by other people, including some who never will drive through the valley but are gratified to know of the wildlife habitat there. Because observation does not consume the animals, we can all enjoy the exact same ones at the exact same moment, but by the present assumption we are satiated before Turner is. Public goods may create a lot of positive externalities, but a lot of those externalities are irrelevant to optimal public policy.

The additional animals that are required to satiate Turner comprise a public good in the economist's nonrivalrous sense, but the public interest can hardly be implicated. Though taken in its entirety Turner's investment confers a positive externality on those driving by, their free ride is inconsequential if only Turner is able to notice the last few animals that have been added, and is willing to add them at his own expense. People driving along the highway cannot be excluded from enjoying the view though they pay no part of the expense, but the animal population on the Flying D would be optimal nonetheless.

The free riding would actually increase the value of the wildlife. If Turner could demand a fee from passing drivers, some would be unwilling to pay. Those drivers would be denied the ability to see the wildlife, which is of positive value to them though insufficient to justify the price Turner asked. No countervailing increase in enjoyment by other people would ensue, however, because observation of wildlife is nonrivalrous.

As to the Flying D, no public involvement will be necessary to achieve the optimal amount of the public good. Turner has selected it of his own volition and at his own expense. A public good certainly exists because people enjoy viewing the animals while driving through the ranch but depreciate nobody else's enjoyment in the process. There is free riding because the passersby bear none of the cost, but that is irrelevant.

The intuition that more users inevitably require more of a good betrays careless thinking. Given a willingness to pay at least incremental cost, it is indeed appropriate that all demands for a rivalrous good such as shoes affect output. But relatively weak preferences have no effect on the optimal amount of a public good. People with weak demands may value the public good, but they are satiated before their preferences affect optimal provision. Paradoxically, the irrelevant demanders are the lucky demanders—they are able to enjoy the public good while paying none of its cost.

Even if, given the drivers passing by, the ideal wildlife population is larger than Turner selects to satisfy his personal preference, an appropriate adjustment might be accomplished through voluntary negotiation. But with a potentially large group of drivers passing by, how likely is a transaction cost low enough to permit that outcome? Surprisingly, low transaction cost is plausible precisely because the amenity is a public good and consequently is not denied to less avid consumers merely because more avid ones rush to enjoy it. Various drivers undoubtedly have varying interests in viewing wildlife. As a result, even though (under this new assumption) Turner has failed to satiate the drivers passing by, a private arrangement whereby the most avid passerby pays Turner to expand the wildlife population might potentially satiate all the other drivers. It hardly matters how many drivers pass by, two or two million; only the most avid of their preferences is relevant, only that one need negotiate with Turner, and all the others can free ride.

Perhaps two million people might eventually drive through the Flying D or derive benefit from the existence value of the ranch's wildlife. The cost if all two million of them attempted to negotiate with Turner would certainly be prohibitive, but just as certainly pointless. Imagine what would be discovered if new technology reduced transaction cost to zero?—that after Turner had satisfied himself and possibly one or a few passersby, nobody else would pay one iota to expand the wildlife population even further. Thus, the level of a many-party transaction cost is irrelevant if either (1) because of a greater number and duration of his visits, Turner inadvertently satiates all the passing drivers, or (2) transaction cost between Turner and a relevant few passersby is modest.

Turner is attuned to the market for bison meat, to local transport, to the prices of hay and all the other inputs he uses, and thus can cheaply judge the opportunity cost of additional wildlife on his ranch. Bureaucrats can find objective information for some of such variables, though collecting the information is costly. Suppose that the bureaucracy manages to hit the nail on the head. Market prices of meat, timber, hay, and the like are unlikely to be static. Thus, even a perfect bureaucratic judgment is unlikely to remain perfect. Of course, if one believes that a tolerable bureaucratic estimate yesterday was plausible, a tolerable bureaucratic estimate tomorrow is plausible. But formulating a new estimate after the relevant variables have changed requires canvassing those affected—in other words, once again obtaining costly information that the participants already possess. Partly because of that greater information cost, bureaucratic policy tends toward inflexibility and episodic but large changes. This has actually understated the bureaucrat's problem. The few most avid passersby are the only reliable judges of the subjective value to them of the amenity, just as Turner is the only reliable judge of the amenity value to him. No bureaucrat, regardless of motivation, can measure the subjective values of anyone but himself or herself.

Transaction cost for public goods—even those demonstrably enjoyed by millions—are chronically overestimated in policy discussions. Only one or a few avid parties often determine both actual and ideal provision, and even two million free riders can be irrelevant.

Nonoptimal Government Provision of Public Goods

Erroneous though it is, a belief that "public goods are generally not adequately supplied by the private sector, [so] they have to be supplied by the public sector" does not logically imply that "public goods are generally adequately supplied by the public sector." Nevertheless, the government / public-goods nexus forms a focal point that distracts attention from demonstrable government failures. Even if shown examples of adequate private provision, nexus fanatics often believe that designating the government as the default provider is wise. Private arrangements are imperfect, but so are government arrangements (Demsetz 1969).

This section explores two failures to optimize government-provided public goods. The first concerns the national park system, where a separate and inconsistent policy reduces public goods to rivalrous goods. The second analyzes the effort to protect endangered species, which concentrates so large a share of the cost of the public good on particular individuals that potential allies become saboteurs.

National parks in the United States are often referred to as a national treasure. Surely there are enough people with an avid preference for, say, Yellowstone National Park to frustrate optimal private provision. Perhaps. Speaking counterfactually, present congestion in Yellowstone *might* have arisen because high transaction cost frustrated private efforts; speaking factually, it *did* materialize despite a century and a third of government preemption of private efforts.[4] We have little evidence regarding private amenity provision in Yellowstone, though initially people were able to enjoy it solely through the efforts of three private railroad companies, the Union Pacific, the Burlington, and the Milwaukee (Anderson and Hill 1994; 1996). Motivated by company, not public, benefit, the railroads then lobbied for national government (and national treasury) involvement.[5]

All that is beside the point. Though Yellowstone's amenities are nonrivalrous during low season, so many members of the public try to enjoy the park during high season that the amenity becomes rivalrous.[6] One cannot visit Yellowstone during summer without diminishing others' enjoyment because government policy prevents the admission fee from clearing all manner of queues. Transaction cost for dealing with the queues is the cost of one ranger at the entrance collecting a fee from one automobile at a time, which is borne already. It is a fraction of the transaction cost one bears to purchase a pair of shoes. Thus the good is nonrivalrous but excludable. The low-fee policy is justified as making it possible for anyone to visit the part regardless of income, but anyone who could not afford even a tenfold increase in the admission fee at national parks cannot afford the much greater expense of getting there. A tenfold increase in the fee would divert some of those who can afford the trip to alternative attractions. The main beneficiaries of present policy are middle-class and wealthy individuals who can afford the trip but are spared the higher fees that would maintain the public goods nature of our national treasures. Thus, despite self-serving claims to the contrary, the policy is regressive.

The second illustration of a discrepancy between the ideal and a government-provided public good concerns the Endangered Species Act. Superficially, the legislation is straightforward: when a rare species is discovered at a site, development of the site that would alter the habitat is severely restricted. This provides a public good; the joy that I experience by knowing the rare species exists over a previously unexpected range does not interfere with your joy. You and I pay nothing in exchange—unless one of us owns the land upon which the species has been found. One person, the landowner, is forced to bear the entire cost of a public good that benefits the whole world. Most of us are prepared to bear such a cost to maintain particular goods for which our individual preference is especially avid. Some people, such as Ted Turner, are prepared to bear substantial cost in such a cause. If they are the first to detect on their land a rare species for which they feel no such avidity, however, some landowners resort to what is known colloquially as the Three S Policy—shoot, shovel, and shut up. In other words, kill the animal or plant, dispose of it quietly, and speak of it to nobody. Some landowners who fear they are at risk do not wait to discover the endangered species but alter the likely site to render it an incompatible habitat (Lueck and Michael 2003).

Fanatics of the government/public-goods nexus often treat examples such as these two as aberrations. The solution, they believe, is merely to root out the system's occasional miscarriage. Given enough space, however, I could relate dozens of substantial deviations between the policy the government pursues with regard to a public good and the policy the government should pursue with regard to it. I have little doubt that the readers could come up with thousands of additional examples.

Conclusion

The point of this chapter certainly should not be taken as a claim that private action inevitably produces an ideal amount of any particular public good. Rather, the point is that though government provision might potentially be an improvement in particular instances, there exists no inexorable nexus. Moreover, private and government actions can both be imperfect. Government sometimes provides excessive amounts of a public good or moves in the wrong direction altogether (Haddock 2006). The task, then, is not to identify perfection as a theoretical matter but to select the avenue that comes closest. Discovering that a good possesses public goods attributes should not end careful analysis so much as set it in motion.

We are awash in externalities, including those conferred by many public goods (and inflicted by many public bads). Many people believe that properly managing such impacts requires government intervention. This chapter is a rebuttal of that view, challenging several of its tenets. First, it disputes the notion that the optimal amounts of public goods can be inferred from a theory that was derived to understand rivalrous goods. Because a public good is not used up as an individual enjoys it, the appropriate amount cannot be determined from the population of users, but instead depends on the preferences of a subset of users—the most avid one(s). Similarly, the optimal amount of a public good has no logical connection with the sum that a typical user would pay to enjoy the good if forced to do so. Thus, many surveys intended to establish that amount are beside the point, quite apart from the difficulties that they have in eliciting accurate responses. Second, the chapter contradicts the notion that free-rider problems inevitably become more severe as the number of parties consuming a public good grows. Third, it argues that private parties can readily arrange for an appropriate amount of many public goods.

A public good, even one enjoyed by a very large public, creates no policy issue if other people are satiated by the most avidly interested person's own voluntary decisions. Even if others are not satiated in that way, no policy issue arises unless transaction cost seriously burdens negotiations between that person and the other relevant people, in Buchanan and Stubblebine's meaning of relevant. Given enough interpersonal variance among preferences, the other relevant parties may consist of only a few people, and little transaction cost would be incurred to negotiate the proper amount.

That scholars would fail to notice voluntary provision of a public good by an individual is especially peculiar given that the provision of public goods is an important component of our own output. Many scholars are employed by universities such as Harvard (founded in 1636), Yale (1701), Dartmouth (1769), and Northwestern (1851) that existed before government became involved in higher education. The entire academic salary bill is not provided by the government even today.

To be sure, some research yields private benefits such as salary increments and prestige—just as Turner's bison yield private benefits to him. Although the private benefits explain why scholars pursue ideas so avidly, once developed, an idea's use by one person rarely destroys its usefulness to another. Some ideas would have been anticipated to yield the provider little private reward apart from personal satisfaction; a price theory text placed on its author's Web site after the book is out of print is an easily examined example (Friedman 1990). Similarly, Einstein was driven to his paradigm-shifting view of the universe by a long-standing yearning to understand the nature of light, an obsession that most contemporary physicists thought so inane that Einstein could obtain no university position for years.

Hiking trails in Great Britain often traverse farmland. The farmers maintain their land for private purposes but do not resist anonymous hikers who enjoy seeing it and "take nothing but memories; leave nothing but footsteps"—the same motto that is urged on hikers in our national parks. Some parts of the Appalachian Trail cross private land. Guest ranches in the West seek out especially beautiful locales and then purchase and preserve them in order to maintain high occupancy. Enjoyment of the views is definitely nonrivalrous, so the views are public goods, often nonexcludable, and they provide existence value.

Even if some government involvement might prove beneficial, production itself would often be better done privately. In most nations, government ownership and operation of radio and television are the norm, but opportunistic censoring of news is a problem in a majority of those nations. In the United States noncommercial set-asides are a long-standing government policy, but with very few exceptions, ownership and operation of the individual stations has been placed in the hands of privately organized nonprofit organizations. Such organizations often receive government subsidies, but the proportion of operating expense that is drawn from private sources has risen dramatically in recent years.

In a similar way, rather than being government-operated parks, sites such as Yellowstone that provide exceptional environmental amenities could be designated geographic noncommercial set-asides, with their operation endowed to privately organized nonprofit organizations, with intrusive forms of development barred. Supervision would be near at hand and would be concerned with an individual site rather than being thousands of miles away in the District of Columbia and intermingled with issues peculiar to any of hundreds of other parks.

The government / public-goods nexus should be seen as a special case, not a general rule. One may ask how to determine whether government provision of a public good or one of the private alternatives is to be preferred. The answer is that the policy maker must leave the ivory tower from time to time. Theory can tell us what a screwdriver is capable of and what a saw can do. One can never know whether to use the saw or the screwdriver without first determining whether the task requires cutting the wood or fastening it together. Theory exists on a pedestal in universities, often to the exclusion of serious institutional and empirical analysis. Theory is a tool, however; it can never put aside the necessity of observation.

Much mischief arises from a misapprehension that a large number of public good beneficiaries creates prohibitive transaction cost. This will be true only if comprehensive negotiation among them is necessary, but comprehensive negotiation will be unnecessary with a large variance across beneficiaries in the strength of their interest in the good. Nor does widespread, even rampant, free riding necessarily recommend a headlong charge up the capitol steps. For public goods, there can be such a thing as a free lunch.

Notes

1. Such a possibility is no academic pipe dream. Acting on suggestions put forward by Meiners and Kosnik (2003), parties holding mutually inconsistent demands for water use in southern Oregon have initiated negotiations that aim to convert what had seemed to be an intractable conflict into an orderly mechanism for channeling the water where its use is most critical during any given period. See Chapter 5.

2. Boudreaux, Meiners, and Zywicki (1999) review the literature and critique frequent overreaching.

3. Or the problem might best be delegated to specialized agencies with borders not coincident with any other political unit's, being either larger than a state—perhaps Washington and northern California (even British Columbia) in addition to Oregon—or smaller—Oregon's Willamette Valley might encompass a complete unit. More external effects would no doubt spill across the borders of a smaller unit, but it would simultaneously provide information and offset agency costs while mitigating the monopoly potential of geographically large sovereigns. The matter involves cost versus benefit rather than good versus bad (Haddock 1997).

4. In 1872 Congress removed the Yellowstone area from the domain that could be claimed by private individuals, though technically it became a national park only when the National Park Service was created in 1916. Until then such reserves were administered directly by the Department of the Interior.

5. Similarly, a recent Public Broadcasting System series revealed that railroad companies were instrumental in opening both the south (Santa Fe) and north (Union Pacific) rims of the Grand Canyon, as well as the areas that became Zion and Bryce Canyon national parks (Union Pacific again).

6. Having less of a public (during low season) makes the Yellowstone amenities public goods; having more of a public (during high season) means that they are not!

References

Alliance for the Great Lakes. 2004. *An Advocate's Field Guide to Protecting Lake Michigan.* Chicago: Alliance for the Great Lakes. Online at http://www .lakemichigan.org/field_guide/habitat_sand.asp. Visited December 8, 2005.

Anderson, Terry L., and Peter J. Hill. 1994. Rents from Amenity Resources: A Case Study of Yellowstone National Park. In *The Political Economy of the American West,* ed. Terry L. Anderson and Peter J. Hill. Lanham, MD: Rowman & Littlefield, 113–127.

———. 1996. Appropriable Rents from Yellowstone Park: A Case of Incomplete Contracting. *Economic Inquiry* 34: 506–518.

Boudreaux, Donald, Roger Meiners, and Todd Zywicki. 1999. Talk Is Cheap: The Existence Value Fallacy. *Environmental Law* 29(4): 765–809.

Buchanan, James M., and William Craig Stubblebine. 1962. Externality. *Economica* 29: 371–384.

Coase, Ronald H. 1960. The Problem of Social Cost. *Journal of Law and Economics* 3(1): 1–44.

———. 1988. *The Firm, the Law, and the Market*. Chicago: University of Chicago Press.

Demsetz, Harold. 1969. Information and Efficiency: Another Viewpoint. *Journal of Law and Economics* 12(1): 1–22.

Ellickson, Robert C. 1991. *Order Without Law: How Neighbors Settle Disputes*. Cambridge, MA: Harvard University Press.

Friedman, David D. 1990. *Price Theory: An Intermediate Text*. Cincinnati, OH: South-Western Publishing. Online at http://www.daviddfriedman.com/Academic/Price_Theory/PThy_ToC.html. Visited December 8, 2005.

Haddock, David D. 1997. Must Hydrological Regulation Be Centralized? In *Water Marketing—The Next Generation*, ed. Terry L. Anderson and Peter J. Hill. Lanham, MD: Rowman & Littlefield, 43–61.

———. 2003. Force, Threat, Negotiation: The Private Enforcement of Rights. In *Property Rights: Cooperation, Conflict, and Law*, ed. Terry L. Anderson and Fred S. McChesney. Princeton, NJ: Princeton University Press, 168–194.

———. 2006. *A Bad Public Good: Cutting Off a Cutoff*. PERC Working Paper, Bozeman, MT.

Jackson, Howell E., Louis Kaplow, Steven M. Shavell, W. Kip Viscusi, and David Cope. 2003. *Analytical Methods for Lawyers*. St. Paul, MN: Thomson-West Foundation Press.

Lueck, Dean, and Jeffrey A. Michael. 2003. Preemptive Habitat Destruction Under the Endangered Species Act. *Journal of Law and Economics* 46(1): 27–60.

Meiners, Roger E., and Lea-Rachel Kosnik. 2003. *Restoring Harmony in the Klamath Basin*. PERC Policy Series, No. PS-27, Bozeman, MT.

Merrill, Thomas W., and Henry E. Smith. 2001. What Happened to Property in Law and Economics? *Yale Law Journal* 111(2): 357–398.

Njál's Saga. 2001. Translation by Robert Cook. New York: Penguin Group.

North, Douglass. 1990. *Institutions, Institutional Change, and Economic Performance*. New York: Cambridge University Press.

Olson, Mancur. 1965. *The Logic of Collective Action*. Cambridge, MA: Harvard University Press.

Ostrom, Elinor. 2000. Collective Action and the Evolution of Social Norms. *Journal of Economic Perspectives* 14(1): 137–158.

Rubin, Paul. 2003. Folk Economics. *Southern Economic Journal* 70(1): 157–171.

Spiegel, Menahem. 1995. Charity Without Altruism. *Economic Inquiry* 33(3): 625–639.

Conclusion

Can the vision of the carefree cowboy of the western frontier blend with the more modern "river runs through it" vision that many people are seeking today? Up to this point, acting out these competing visions has been acrimonious. This volume has addressed why these conflicts occur and how they might be minimized. To avoid conflicts over alternative resource uses, new institutional arrangements and related incentive systems must be created to manage access to and use of the West's natural wealth. The authors of this book have only begun to explore innovative combinations of private and public, local and national, contractual and trust arrangements.

Part One laid out both the conceptual strengths and weaknesses of a property rights approach to better managing both the commodity and amenity aspects of the West's natural wealth. In the "Old West," as Anderson explained in Chapter 2, people bore the costs and reaped the benefits of developing institutions that encouraged good stewardship and discouraged fighting over Mother Nature's bounty. On the basis of their on-the-ground experiences, pioneers hammered out customary grazing rights, mining laws, and the prior appropriation water doctrine. These institutions served well for allocating natural resources among alternative uses, especially for commodity production, and could be a useful management tool for natural resource use in the West today.

The character, however, of some important environmental services as well as cultural and political constraints limit the acceptability of market mechanisms in some settings. Power explained in Chapter 1 that natural processes such as waste assimilation and the production of naturally clean water are examples of ecosystem services that are largely gifts of nature, not the product of human agency. Because most beneficiaries of these natural services do not understand how they are produced, it is not clear to beneficiaries how they could act to protect such natural assets by using market tools. Furthermore, in some political circumstances legislative bodies have prevented land managers from charging fees for services. In Montana, for instance, the legislature designated all of the state's largest parks as primitive and forbade both the levying of fees for access and the construction of amenities that would justify such fees. The motivation behind this decision was not a desire to create wilderness parks, but rather to keep fees from being charged for mere access to public lands. Power argued that this mentality stems from a cultural belief that citizens are entitled to public land and that paying admission fees undermines the value of interacting with nature.

When market mechanisms are difficult to establish, more decentralized local government management or private nonprofit management constrained by contractual arrangements may be better equipped to address local issues. Specifically, decentralization or devolution of control and management of public lands—the focus of Part Two—could improve the incentive to find cooperative solutions to conflicting resource use. Kemmis and Fretwell, in Chapters 3 and 4, respectively, largely accepted the continued governmental ownership of significant parts of the natural landscape and asked how the management of those lands could be improved to better match the shifting demands for natural resources.

The practical potential of property rights and markets was explored in more detail in Part Three where it was applied to the water-use conflicts in the Klamath Basin (Chapter 5), coastal fisheries (Chapter 6), and the use of land trusts to protect amenities (Chapter 8). In these three case studies, the central resources at issue—water, fish, and land—have familiar private good aspects to them even though they also are the basis for significant amenity and ecosystem values. In settings like these, we know that the extension of property rights and the use of markets can make significant contributions to more effectively protecting natural values. Also in Part Three, Meiners and

Morriss (Chapter 7) boldly advocated a return to the nineteenth-century regime of allowing private individuals to claim public lands for the pursuit of whatever values they perceive are associated with those lands, just as the 1872 Mining Law allows those lands to be claimed for mineral production. Clearly, there are cultural and philosophic problems yet to be resolved in this area as well as practical questions as to what the likely outcome of such a privatization policy would be for the natural amenities on which this book has focused.

This book has used such theoretical and empirical phrases as the *wealth of nature, natural landscape values, natural amenities,* and the *value of ecosystem services*. Though all of these phrases suggest that there can be substantial value beyond market values, they beg the question of how we can critically measure economic values that markets, thus far, have not directly valued. Given the absence of market prices, how can we distinguish between unsupportable speculation and economic reality?

This is the substance of environmental economics and regional economics that Part Four explored. Fitzgerald and Freeman (Chapter 10) discussed in detail the ways in which economists have tried to quantify nonmarket environmental values. Hanssen (Chapter 9) and Johnson (Chapter 11) critically investigated some of the literature dealing with the role of both natural resource commodity development and the pursuit of natural amenities in driving local economic development. And Haddock (Chapter 12) presented a conceptual analysis concluding that a few private individuals acting to protect natural amenities that they value are likely to produce an adequate supply of those amenities for the general public. All of the authors in Part Four, while recognizing the reality and importance of nonmarket environmental values, also pointed out some significant exaggerations that have crept into the public dialogue over the role of environmental values in determining our economic well-being. As concern over the economic role of the wealth of nature increases, careful and critical quantitative analysis is necessary in support of new public policy proposals.

At the risk of unnecessary redundancy, the conclusions we draw from the essays in this book can be briefly restated:

· Property rights and markets can be powerful tools in protecting and wisely using the wealth of nature. We have only begun to deploy those tools.
· It is not yet evident in some aspects of the wealth of nature how property rights and markets can be productively brought to bear either because of

the very nature of the natural values at issue or because of cultural objections to the extension of property rights and markets to new areas.

· Where property rights and markets cannot be deployed, institutional innovation aimed at improving governmental and nonprofit organizational decision making is important if "win-win" agreements are going to be found. These include experiments with clearer specification of rights and obligations, decentralized decision making, carefully crafted incentives, and cooperative negotiations, to name a few. This is the realm in which we face our greatest challenges to improving our collective management of the wealth of nature.

· Finally, because quantitative market information often is not available on the benefits and costs associated with protecting or using the wealth of nature in particular ways, speculation, wishful thinking, and ideological commitment can substitute for accurate information to the detriment of public policy. Innovation is necessary to improve the quality of the environmental economic analysis that can support informed public policy.

Current institutional arrangements dissipate the wealth of nature by pitting potential winners against potential losers in a zero-sum game. Instead, we need institutions that encourage a more meaningful tradeoff between competing uses. A key theme emerging from this book is that we can do a better job promoting institutions that give people the ability and incentive to reallocate natural resources when values change.

The commodity-based visions of the Old West and the amenity visions of the New West can intermix if institutions that govern who controls how resources are used are determined by people who have a direct incentive to find win-win solutions to competing uses. As this book suggests, the range of possibilities for managing nature's bounty is much broader than the public debates indicate. Only our imaginations limit the innovative institutional arrangements we can craft.

Contributors

Terry L. Anderson is the executive director of the Property and Environment Research Center (PERC), Bozeman, Montana; senior fellow at the Hoover Institution, Stanford University; and professor emeritus at Montana State University. His work helped launch the idea of "free market environmentalism" with the publication of his book, coauthored with Donald R. Leal, by that title. Anderson is the author or editor of thirty books, including the most recent, *Self-Determination: The Other Path for Native Americans*, coedited with Bruce L. Benson and Thomas E. Flanagan. He has published widely in both professional journals and the popular press, including the *Wall Street Journal*, the *Christian Science Monitor*, and *Fly Fisherman*.

Timothy Fitzgerald graduated in 1997 from Bowdoin College with a bachelor's degree in economics and is now a graduate student at the University of Maryland. His research spans wildlife, energy, and institutional topics. Fitzgerald formerly ran an outfitting business in western Colorado, guiding anglers and hunters and also running cattle for local ranchers on federal lands. Fitzgerald was a Research Associate with PERC, and his article "The Quincy Library Affair" was featured in the March 1998 issue of *PERC Reports*.

A. Myrick Freeman III is the William D. Shipman Professor of Economics Emeritus at Bowdoin College where he taught for thirty-five years before retiring in 2000. He has also held appointments as a senior fellow at Resources for the Future, a visiting college professor at the University of Washington, and the Robert M. La Follette Visiting Distinguished Professor at the University of Wisconsin–Madison. He is the author of many journal articles and several books, including *The Benefits of Environmental Improvement: Theory and Practice* (1979) and *The Measurement of Environmental and Resource Values: Theory and Methods* (1993), which were cited by the Association of Environmental and Resource Economists as Publications of Enduring Value in 2003. Freeman has also served on the Science Advisory Board of the U.S. Environmental Protection Agency.

Holly Lippke Fretwell is a PERC research fellow and an adjunct professor at Montana State University, where she earned a bachelor's degree in political science and master's degree in resource economics. She is author and coauthor of numerous articles on natural resource issues; her current emphasis is on public lands management. She has presented papers promoting the use of markets in public land management and has provided expert testimony on the state of our national parks and the future of the U.S. Forest Service.

David D. Haddock is an economist who has been a member of the Northwestern University faculty since 1988 and a senior fellow of PERC since 1997. Haddock is a specialist in law and economics as well as several related fields and holds the rank of professor in both the economics department and the law school. He has contributed chapters to a number of PERC books. Haddock sees his present mission as helping to correct the widespread and costly misunderstandings regarding the meaning and implications of the economic concept of public goods.

F. Andrew Hanssen is associate professor of economics at Montana State University. Hanssen has published articles in a number of refereed journals, including the *American Economic Review*; the *Journal of Law and Economics*; the *Journal of Law, Economics, and Organization*; and the *Journal of Legal Studies*. Several of his articles have been republished in books. Hanssen received a B.A. and M.A. from Johns Hopkins University, and an M.B.A. and Ph.D. from the University of Chicago. Before getting his Ph.D., he was a management consultant, working in Europe, Latin America, and the Far East.

Laura E. Huggins is a research fellow and director of development at PERC as well as a research fellow at the Hoover Institution, Stanford University. Huggins is the author, along with Terry L. Anderson, of *Property Rights: A Practical Guide to Freedom and Prosperity* (2003). She also edited *Population Puzzle: Boom or Bust?* (2004) and *Drug War Deadlock: The Policy Battle Continues* (2005). Huggins has published several articles and papers, including "A Property Rights Path to Sustainable Development," which appeared in *The Legacy of Milton and Rose Friedman's Free to Choose: Economic Liberalism at the Turn of the 21st Century* (2004). Huggins holds a master's degree in public policy from Utah State University.

Ronald N. Johnson received his Ph.D. in economics from the University of Washington in 1977 and joined the faculty at the University of New Mexico as an assistant professor. He moved to Montana State University in 1981 and retired as full professor in 2001. Since, he has been a visiting professor at the Economics Education and Research Consortium, National University of Ukraine, and the University of California, San Diego. Johnson's research has focused on natural resource issues, industrial organization, and political economy. His articles have appeared in the *American Economic Review, Journal of Political Economy, Review of Economics and Statistics, Journal of Law and Economics, Economic Inquiry*, and numerous other journals.

Daniel Kemmis is a senior fellow at the University of Montana's Center for the Rocky Mountain West. A past director of the center, Kemmis was formerly mayor of Missoula, Montana, and a former speaker and minority leader of the Montana House of Representatives. Kemmis is the author of three books: *Community and the*

Politics of Place; The Good City and the Good Life; and *This Sovereign Land: A New Vision for Governing the West.*

Donald R. Leal is a senior fellow at PERC, where he has been carrying out research in natural resource and environmental issues since 1985. Leal has written numerous articles on such topics as privatizing ocean fisheries, water marketing for fish and wildlife, creating self-sustaining parks, and applying the trust concept to public lands. His pieces have appeared in the *Wall Street Journal, New York Times,* and *Chicago Tribune,* as well as specialized journals. His current projects include assessing the impact of individual transferable quota programs in fishery management throughout the world. He received his B.S. in mathematics and M.S. in statistics from California State University at Hayward.

Roger E. Meiners is the Goolsby Distinguished Professor of law and economics at the University of Texas at Arlington and a senior fellow of PERC. His research focuses on common law and market solutions to environmental issues and on the economics of higher education. Meiners serves on the board of the Institute for Policy Innovation and has published numerous books, including *Taking the Environment Seriously* (with Bruce Yandle), *Government v. the Environment* (with Donald Leal), *Agricultural Policy and the Environment* (with Yandle). He has also published in various popular and scholarly journals.

Andrew P. Morriss is the H. Ross and Helen Workman Professor of Law and a professor of business at the University of Illinois and senior fellow at PERC. He is coauthor of *Regulation by Litigation* (with Bruce Yandle and Andrew Dorohok) (2008).

Dominic P. Parker is a senior research fellow with PERC and is also a National Science Foundation fellow and Ph.D. student in economics and environmental science at the University of California, Santa Barbara. His research to date has focused on private land conservation, economic development on American Indian reservations, and the economics of public bureaucracies. He holds an M.S. degree in applied economics from Montana State University where his research on wildlife agencies was awarded Best Thesis by the American Agricultural Economics Association.

Thomas Michael Power is a professor of economics and chair of the economics department at the University of Montana. He specializes in natural resource and environmental economics and their relationship to local and regional development. He is author of five books, including *Lost Landscapes and Failed Economies: The Search for Value of Place* (1996) and *Post-Cowboy Economics: Pay and Prosperity in the New American West* (2001).

Index